J. HUDSON TAYLOR

A MAN IN CHRIST

J. HUDSON TAYLOR
A MAN IN CHRIST

ROGER STEER

FOREWORD BY BILLY GRAHAM

An OMF Book
Harold Shaw Publishers
Wheaton, Illinois

This edition has been published by special arrangement with Overseas
Missionary Fellowship, U.S. OMF BOOKS is an imprint of Harold Shaw
Publishers.

ISBN 0-87788-377-7

Library of Congress Cataloging-in-Publication Data

Steer, Roger, 1945-
    J. Hudson Taylor : a man in Christ / Roger Steer ; foreword by
Billy Graham.
        p.   cm. — (An OMF book)
    Includes bibliographical references.
    ISBN 0-87788-377-7 (pbk.)
    1. Taylor, James Hudson, 1832-1905. 2. Missionaries—China—
Biography. 3. China Inland Mission—History. 4. Missionaries—
England—Biography. 5. China—Church history—19th century.
I. Title. II. Series.
BV3427.T3S44   1993
266'.0092—dc20
    [B]   93-21508
                                                           CIP

---

99   98   97   96   95   94   93

10   9   8   7   6   5   4   3   2   1

FOREWORD

Few men have been used to touch China for God as Hudson Taylor was. He willingly broke with tradition and adopted Chinese dress. Eagerly he built teams across denominational lines. His vision was always to penetrate new frontiers with the gospel. His motivation was neither reckless adventure nor self-fulfilment, but a deep concern for those without Christ. His life was impelled by a growing confidence in the faithfulness of God.

Millions of Chinese Christians now echo that same spirit of confidence, proving God's faithfulness in their own adventure of commitment. With all today's interest in China and deep concern for her leadership as well as for the believers there, this is a timely book. Stripped of so many freedoms and conveniences taken for granted by an affluent church, Chinese Christians both then and now shame us with their peace and stability, which comes from simply acting on the belief that "there is a living God, He has spoken in His Word, He means what He has said and will do all that He has promised."

The principles of simple lifestyle, well-reasoned obedience, confident prayer and patient endurance so clearly described in this story compel us to examine afresh what it means to be a man in Christ. I am delighted that this book is being published. May God use it for our encouragement and for His glory.

Billy Graham

CONTENTS

ABOVE THE SHOP 1

"Dear God, if you should give us a son, grant that he may work for you in China."

On a raw Yorkshire evening, James and Amelia Taylor prayed in the parlour behind Barnsley's busiest chemist shop. An enormous bookcase dominated the room, its shelves creaking under the weight of a growing collection of books. James was intrigued by all things Chinese. It fascinated him that once-famous empires like Persia, Greece and Rome had risen and fallen — but the Chinese Empire remained, the world's greatest monument to ancient times. He was concerned that the nineteenth century had opened without a single Protestant missionary ever setting foot in China.

The days lengthened. Amelia's waistline expanded. Winter gave way to spring and on May 21, 1832, when she was 24, her child was born. They called him James Hudson Taylor — Hudson was his mother's maiden name.

Both sides of the family were Methodists, and some of Hudson's earliest memories were of being taken to the small chapel on Pinfold Hill, Barnsley, built by his stonemason great grandfather, James Taylor. The boy loved to hear stories of the day when his great grandfather had entertained the family's most distinguished visitor. In June 1786, John Wesley himself, then aged 82, had visited Barnsley and stayed at James Taylor's cottage. He had preached to a large congregation near the market place and noticed that they seemed to drink in every word.

The house where Hudson spent his childhood and teenage years, 21 Cheapside, Barnsley, was not far from the spot where Wesley had preached. It looked on to the market place on May Day Green, and on this prime site Hudson's father was building a successful business as an apothecary — part chemist, part doctor. He had soon established a reputation for integrity, hard work and concern for his customers.

Business in the shop on the ground floor was always brisk, and James Taylor sometimes used the parlour behind the shop as a consulting room. Though his clients trusted his diagnoses, they found him rather shy and at times withdrawn. He practised hypnotism to give sleep to insomniacs, and is said to have mesmerized a neighbour's dog so successfully that it abandoned its annoying bark!

James was most at ease with close friends, to whom the house was always open. They would talk about the progress of Yorkshire Methodism, or the prospects for missionary work abroad. Years later, Hudson's sister Amelia remembered how the children loved to hear their father and his friends talk. "Theology, sermons, politics, the Lord's work at home and abroad, all were discussed with earnestness and intelligence. It made a great impression on us as children."

Hudson himself would sometimes say, "When I am a man, I mean to be a missionary and go to China." His parents would remember their special prayer, exchange glances, but say nothing.

Hudson grew up with two sisters: Amelia, born when he was three, and Louisa, born when he was eight. Brother William, who came between him and Amelia, died at the age of seven. Once every day, James Taylor would take the children into his bedroom, kneel at the four-poster bed and, with his arms around them, pray for each of them. After that, Hudson and his sisters would go to their own rooms to read their Bibles for a while.

"Learn to love your Bible," their father said. "God cannot lie. He cannot mislead you. He cannot fail."

In the afternoons, Amelia and Louisa would join Hudson for lessons in the parlour behind the shop. Their mother would sew while the children read aloud to her or wrote while she dictated. She would never tolerate slovenly use of words, grammatical errors or bad pronunciation.

※ ※ ※ ※ ※

James Taylor was stern and sometimes quick tempered. No one was allowed to be late for meals. But there was another side to his character. When he knew that a customer couldn't afford the cost of medical treatment he often returned part of the fee. Or he would say, "It's all right, we'll send the account to heaven and settle it there."

It was their father who taught the children French, Latin and arithmetic. When they had had enough of this, he would turn to his favourite subject.

"What Empire is over one hundred times the size of England and occupies one-tenth of that area of the earth's surface where people can live?"

"China."

"Correct. If all the Chinese were ordered to stand in single file, with a yard between each of them, they would circle the globe seven times at the equator. And who invented gunpowder, the compass, paper, and discovered the art of printing?"

"The Chinese."

"Correct. Gunpowder and paper were invented in China at the beginning of the Christian era. They learned how to print during the reign of our Saxon King Athelstan."

James Taylor didn't insist that life for his children should be all work and no play. He took them on long Saturday afternoon walks down the Cudforth Road to Lunn Woods and the Yorkshire countryside. Hudson and Amelia would take their hoops, and their father would forget China for a while and tell them all he knew about butterflies, birds and flowers.

Hudson began to love nature, and learned to grow ferns and flowers he had collected in the woods. His father encouraged this by subscribing to a natural history magazine, and supplying him with pillboxes from the shop for his collection of insects and butterflies.

Autumn 1843, six years into Queen Victoria's reign: Hudson Taylor, now eleven, was off to school for the first time. But this experience lasted for little more than two years. When a less satisfactory headmaster took over the school, Hudson returned to be taught at home and help his father in the chemist shop. The curly-headed boy in the white apron enjoyed learning to mix, pound and wrap medicines.

Soon after Hudson's fifteenth birthday, a vacancy occurred for a junior clerk in a Barnsley bank. James Taylor was anxious that his son should learn how to keep accounts and write business letters, and Hudson was accepted for the post.

The new job certainly broadened his experience of life, as he came into contact with a sceptical and materialistic world beyond 21 Cheapside. His colleagues at the bank began to poke fun at what they called his old-fashioned notions about God. They tied him in knots with their arguments, and introduced him to language he'd no idea existed.

"Christians are hypocrites," they said. "They claim to believe their Bibles, but they live just as they would if they never read them!"

Hudson didn't know how to answer this, and a time of intense inner turmoil followed. He spent hours brooding on his upbringing. From his earliest years he had seen the value of prayer and reading the Bible. Every morning after breakfast his father read from the Scriptures. That was fine, but then he would pray for twenty minutes in magnificent biblical language which had begun to irritate Hudson. All at once his father seemed tiresomely pompous.

And yet, Hudson thought, *if there is such a Person as God, then to trust Him, to obey Him, and to be fully given up to His service must surely be the best and wisest course.* And so he tried somehow to *make* himself a Christian. This didn't succeed. He began to feel a failure. *For some reason or other I cannot be saved,* he concluded. *The best thing I can do is to enjoy the pleasures of this world, for there's no hope for me beyond the grave.*

He listened to his colleagues describing goings-on quite unknown to the child of an upright Methodist family. He gave up praying and found going to church a bore. He came to think like his sceptical colleagues. If what they believed was right, there was no need to worry about the doom which his parents thought awaited the ungodly.

As winter drew on, he developed an infection in his eyes which forced him to give up being a banker after just nine months. He returned to working in his father's shop, more aware of the world around but less sure of himself or what he believed. His father couldn't understand his unhappiness and was irritated by his brooding. His mother understood him better and decided not to probe, but to rely on tenderness and prayer.

✳ ✳ ✳ ✳ ✳

A month after his seventeenth birthday, in June 1849, Hudson was enjoying an afternoon off work. He wandered into the parlour, looked through the massive bookcase to find something to pass the time, and picked up a gospel tract.

There'll be a story at the beginning, he thought, *with a moral at the end. I'll read the story and skip the sermon.*

He didn't know that fifty miles away his mother, who was staying with her sister in Barton-upon-Humber, also found herself that afternoon with several hours to spare. After lunch she went to her room, locked the door, and made up her mind not only to pray for Hudson's conversion but to stay in the room until she felt sure her prayers were answered.

Meanwhile, back at Barnsley, Hudson had taken the tract across the yard at the back of their house to an old warehouse, where he often went to read without interruption. The tract was about a coalman in Somerset who was seriously ill with tuberculosis. Before he died some Christians visited him and talked to him about passages from the Bible. The coalman was particularly struck by the verse which says that Jesus bore our sins in His own body on the cross. When the visiting Christians spoke of Jesus' cry from the cross, "It is finished", the coalman understood its meaning and became a Christian.

It was a simple tale and yet it made sense. It rang true. It made all the clever talk of his former banking colleagues seem cheap and trivial.

As Hudson reflected on the tract, he became intensely aware of his own sin and the danger of doing nothing about it. He was also intrigued by the words "It is finished". What was finished? From sermons he had heard but not fully grasped, and from his own knowledge of the Bible, he soon answered his own question: "A full and perfect atonement and satisfaction for sin: the debt was paid by the substitute. Christ died for my sins."

What is there left for me to do? he thought. *What was the point of all my efforts to make myself a Christian?*

Then it seemed to him, as he put it, "that light was flashed into my soul by the Holy Spirit, that there was nothing in the world to be done but to fall down on one's knees, and accepting this Saviour and His salvation, to praise Him for evermore."

And so Hudson Taylor knelt on the floor of a Barnsley warehouse and became a Christian. And in her room in Barton-upon-Humber, Hudson's mother felt she need pray no longer. Instead, she began to praise God for the firm conviction — she was sure it came from the Holy Spirit — that Hudson had been converted.

Several days later, Hudson told his sister Amelia what had happened and made her promise that for the time being she would keep the news to herself. A fortnight later their mother returned, and Hudson was the first to meet her at the door.

"Mother, I've such good news for you!"

Mrs Taylor flung her arms around his neck.

"I know, my boy. I've been rejoicing in your news for a fortnight!"

"Why, has Amelia broken her promise? She said she'd tell no one."

"Amelia kept her promise. It wasn't from any human source that I learned this. I know when you were converted, and it was in answer to my prayers."

Some time later, Hudson picked up a notebook which was exactly like his own. Before he realized it was his sister's, he caught sight of a short entry she had written some weeks earlier: "I will pray every day for Hudson's conversion." Amelia's prayers had been answered within a month of her resolution.

✳ ✳ ✳ ✳ ✳

The summer of 1849 was a happy one for the Taylors. The sparkle returned to Hudson's eyes and the tensions between father and son all but disappeared. Mother and elder daughter were delighted that their prayers had been answered.

Hudson and his sister grew closer. They decided to stop going to Sunday evening services for a while and went instead to the poorer parts of Barnsley, calling from door to door, handing out tracts, and sometimes speaking about their faith in Christ.

But September brought a blow. Amelia was sent away to a boarding school at Barton-upon-Humber run by her mother's sister, Mrs Hodson. In exchange, Aunt Hodson's eldest son John was apprenticed to his uncle James in Barnsley and shared Hudson's room. John's cheerful flippancy didn't suit Hudson's mood following his conversion — he badly wanted peace and quiet to read his Bible and to pray.

Despite John's interruptions, Hudson began to soak up Scripture. But then he went through a bad patch when he found it an effort to pray, and the Bible seemed dull and boring. Three things helped to bring this difficult time to an end. First, an article in the *Wesleyan Magazine* on "The Beauty of Holiness" made goodness seem once again irresistibly attractive.

Then he was given a church membership card with a text from Ezekiel 36:26: "I will give you a new heart and put a new spirit in you; I will remove from you your heart of stone and give you a heart of flesh."

"Dear Lord," Hudson prayed, "please take away my heart of stone and give me a heart of flesh! Help me to believe the promises of your Word! My heart longs for this perfect holiness."

The third thing was a mission at the Pitt Street Chapel. Hudson was asked to help with counselling and more than a hundred became Christians at the mission.

On the Sunday, a cold kept Hudson at home. He decided to send a letter off to Barton-upon-Humber. "Thank God," he told his sister, "I feel very happy in His love, but I am so unworthy of all His blessings. I so often give way to temptation. I am apt to be frothy and giddy, and sometimes yield to my teasing disposition. Pray for me, dear Amelia, pray for me. I am seeking entire sanctification."

That evening, he went to his room and spent his time talking to God and trying to listen to Him. He experienced a sense of the presence of God and a feeling of joy quite unlike anything he had known before. He repeatedly thanked Jesus for what He had done for him.

"Dear God," he prayed, "please give me some work to do for you, as an outlet for my love and gratitude."

After the assurance of God's presence came an unmistakable awareness that he knew just how God wanted him to spend the rest of his life. "I felt that I was entering into a covenant with the Almighty. I felt as though I wished to withdraw my promise but could not. Something seemed to say: 'Your prayer is answered'. And from that time the conviction has never left me that I was called to China."

FROM A-LO-PEN TO GUTZLAFF 2

The history of Christian advance into China begins with a remarkable adventure. In AD 431 a man named Nestorius was condemned as a heretic, but by late in the fifth century the Persian church had become officially Nestorian, and the Nestorian church continued to reach out eastwards. In AD 635, Nestorian Christian A-lo-pen arrived in China, in the capital of the Tang Empire. The Emperor received him well, studied Christianity, approved of it, and ordered that it should be propagated.

Nestorian Christianity lasted more than two centuries in China. Its brand of the faith was mainly monastic — a familiar way of life in a land used to Buddhism[1] — and the influence of the monks probably did not extend far beyond their monastery walls.

Trouble hit the Nestorians in 845 when another Tang Emperor, in a move against monasticism in general, issued a decree prohibiting Buddhism, dissolving the monasteries, and ordering all monks to return to private life. The Christian

[1]For details of Chinese religion see Chapter 8

Map of China and surrounding countries, showing modern boundaries

church in China dwindled for several centuries after that; in 987 a monk returned to Europe with the news that he could find no trace of Christians in the whole Chinese Empire.

In the thirteenth century, the Mongol Genghis Khan conquered northern China. He understood the importance of religion and laid it down that all religions were to be respected. As a result the Nestorian church was re-established throughout Central Asia and in 1275 an archbishopric was set up in Beijing (Peking), the new capital of Genghis's grandson, Kublai Khan.

In this same period, the explorer Marco Polo visited China several times. On return from their first journey to China, Marco Polo's uncles brought a message to the Pope from Kublai Khan asking for a hundred men of learning, devoted to the Christian faith. Their job would be to prove "to the learned of [Kublai Khan's] dominions, by just and fair argument, that the faith professed by Christians is superior to and founded on more evident truth than any other."

Twenty years passed before much attention was paid to this request, and then the Pope sent John of Monte Corvino to China. John arrived in Beijing in about 1294 and was warmly received by Timur, Kublai Khan's successor. He didn't manage to convert the Emperor, who had "grown too old in idolatry". But he built a church and claimed to have baptized six thousand people by 1305. Pope Clement V made John an archbishop, but following John's death in 1328 the Christian church in China went into two hundred years of decline.

In 1557 the Portuguese managed to install themselves in the tiny settlement of Macao not far from Hong Kong. The colony became a jumping-off point for many missionary enterprises including those of Jesuit Matthew Ricci, one of the most famous Roman Catholic missionaries in the East. In 1600, Ricci entered Beijing and won the Emperor's admiration through his ability as a clock repairer and map maker. Ricci remained in the capital for ten years, gradually bringing into being a church of about two thousand people which included some members of notable families and distinguished intellectuals. He also produced a Chinese liturgy and other Christian literature.

Like many missionaries after him, Ricci had to grapple with the problem of finding Chinese equivalents for Christian terms, and of deciding how far ancient Chinese customs could be reconciled with the Christian faith. If Christianity were to be acceptable to the Chinese, its foreign aspects would need to be minimized — but this was easier said than done. After much study and thought, he decided that Chinese rites in honour of Confucius and the family only had civil significance, and that new converts to Christianity could continue to engage in them. He would trust Chinese Christians to decide eventually what they could and couldn't do.

Ricci was succeeded by a German Jesuit, Johann Adam Schall von Bell, who arrived in Beijing in 1622. Schall was a clever astronomer who prophesied eclipses and earned himself a place on the board which regulated the calendar. Baptisms into the Christian church increased, including one of the Emperor's wives and her child. Schall survived the fall of the Ming dynasty by convincing the Manchu conquerors that he was indispensable.

During the course of the seventeenth century other orders, mainly Franciscans and Dominicans, joined the Jesuits and worked with some success in China. In 1674 the Pope appointed the first Chinese bishop.

Controversy continued, however, over which Chinese terms to use for God in the liturgy and the extent to which Chinese Christians could practise ancient customs. As a result relations between the Vatican and the Chinese church became sour. Persecution of Christians in China increased during the eighteenth century; congregations declined and churches were ruined. By the end of the century the work of Roman Catholic missionaries in the Chinese Empire had very nearly collapsed, although a few valiantly held on in secret, often in danger of their lives.

Hudson Taylor's father must often have told him about

the first Protestant missionary to China, Robert Morrison, who arrived in Guangzhou (Canton) in an American ship in September 1807. For a while he was forced to live virtually in hiding; but by 1809 he was appointed translator to the East India Company. This gave him protection, a measure of security, and an income to live on. He became an expert in Chinese literature and wisdom, describing this as "one of the greatest gifts ever bestowed by God on any race."

For more than 25 years Morrison stayed in Guangzhou, the only foothold Europeans had been able to secure in mainland China. He believed that what the Chinese needed above all was Christ, and he worked long and hard to extend his knowledge of Chinese culture and language so that he might communicate the gospel more effectively. Morrison's first convert was baptized in 1814, and by 1819 he had translated the whole Bible into Chinese; he then completed a great Chinese dictionary. More Chinese converts were baptized, one of whom was ordained to be an evangelist to his fellow-countrymen.

But when Morrison died in 1834, two years after Hudson Taylor was born, prospects for the evangelization of China were almost as bleak as when he had arrived. Up to that time only three more Protestant Christians had gone to serve God in China. Walter Medhurst, a printer who had arrived in China in 1817, travelled inland in disguise to distribute Christian literature in Chinese. Dr Wells Williams arrived in 1833, wrote a well-known book *The Middle Kingdom*, and worked in China for many years. And an American surgeon, Peter Parker, opened an eye hospital in Guangzhou and began to reduce prejudice against missionaries.

During Hudson's youth the name of the Honourable Dr Charles Gutzlaff, a member of the Netherlands Missionary Society and later interpreter to the British Government in Hong Kong, had been well known in England. His books had stirred the hearts of Christians, and his exploits on the Chinese coast were familiar among merchants, naval officers and politicians. He had imaginative ideas for the Chinese themselves to take the gospel to all eighteen provinces of their country, and he established an organization called the Chinese Christian Union to distribute and teach the Scriptures in mainland China.

Unfortunately Gutzlaff was badly hoaxed by Chinese evangelist members of his organization. Almost all of them turned out to be frauds and opium addicts, writing journals of travels they had never made and producing lists of converts they had never baptized. Gutzlaff, who seems to have been genuinely unaware of what had been going on, was overcome with grief when the scandals were exposed. He set out to reorganize his work but died before his new projects had got anywhere.

Chinese hostility to foreigners meant that, away from Guangzhou, the Empire was virtually inaccessible. For half a century English Christians had prayed that missionaries would be allowed to work more freely in China. This eventually came about primarily because of commercial and political pressures on China from the western nations. The first "opium war" between England and China broke out in 1839, partly because the British insisted on importing Indian opium into China against the wishes of the Chinese government. Other factors were at work too, particularly general Chinese restrictions on foreign trade, their contempt for treaty obligations, and their hostility to foreigners.

The war ended in the signing of the Treaty of Nanjing in 1842, which secured a number of advantages for westerners in China. Hong Kong became a British colony; five "treaty ports" — Guangzhou, Xiamen (Amoy), Fuzhou, Ningbo and Shanghai — were opened so that foreigners could live there; foreigners were guaranteed the right of trial under their own laws and by officials of their own country. Consuls were to take up residence in each treaty port, with equality of rank and access to the senior Chinese officials, the mandarins. British citizens were to be guaranteed freedom (at least on paper) from "molestation and restraints". The treaty actually said little about religion, but it was clear that missionaries no less than merchants would take advantage of these privileges.

Of course missionaries deplored the war, but they believed that God had overruled what was deplorable in itself to open up China to the gospel. However, the fact that Christianity seemed to enter China in the wake of gunboats was often a handicap to it later.

News of the treaty alerted British Christians to the new era of opportunity. The way was open for missionaries to study Chinese on Chinese soil, and even to build houses, schools, hospitals and churches in the British and international settlements in the treaty ports.

Impressed by these opportunities and also by Gutzlaff's energy and vision, British businessmen launched a magazine, *The Gleaner in the Missionary Field*, to promote overseas missions — and the Taylor family took the publication from its beginnings in March 1850. Hudson also discovered that an interdenominational society called the Chinese Association had been organized in London. It planned to employ Chinese evangelists to cooperate with existing missions in taking the gospel to the unreached interior of China.

Hudson wrote to the secretary of the Association, George Pearse, asking him to send circulars, collecting cards and anything which could help him introduce the work of the Association to his friends.

He also heard that Barnsley's Congregational minister had a copy of printer Medhurst's *China: Its State and Prospects* and decided to try to borrow it.

"You may certainly borrow the book," the minister told him. "And what, may I ask, is your interest in it?"

"God has called me to spend my life in missionary service in China," Hudson replied.

"And how do you propose to go there?"

"I don't know. But I think it likely that I shall need to go as the twelve and the seventy disciples did in Judea, without stick, or bag, or food, or money — relying on Him who had sent them to supply all their needs."

The minister gently placed his hand on Hudson's shoulder.

"Ah, my boy, as you grow older you will become wiser than that. Such an idea would do very well in the days when Christ Himself was on earth, but not now."

Many years later, Taylor recalled the incident and wrote: "I have grown older since then, but not wiser. I am more and more convinced that if we were to take the directions of our Master and the assurance He gave to His first disciples more fully as our guide, we should find them just as suited to our times as to those in which they were originally given."

Medhurst's book stressed the value of medical missions, and Taylor decided to concentrate on medical studies as a preparation for work in China. He also began to take more open air exercise, and got rid of his feather bed and other comforts in order to prepare for a rougher life.

He embarked on the study of the Chinese language with enormous enthusiasm. This was a task which an earlier missionary had said required "bodies of iron, lungs of brass, heads of oak, hands of spring-steel, eyes of eagles, hearts of apostles, memories of angels and lives of Methuselah."

Hudson had neither a Chinese grammar nor a dictionary, but he had been given a copy of the gospel of Luke in the Chinese Mandarin dialect. He and cousin John set about learning together. They would select a short verse in the English version of Luke, and then pick out a dozen or more verses, also in English, which had one word in common with the first verse. Then they would turn up the first verse in Chinese, and search through all the other verses for some character in common that seemed to represent the English word. They would write these down on a slip of paper as probable equivalents; then they would look through the Chinese for this same character in different connections. If, in every case, they found the same word in the English version, they copied the character in ink in their dictionary, adding the meaning in pencil. If later study confirmed this to be the true meaning, they inked it in.

After a while they grew familiar with most of the common

Chinese characters.

Hudson began to get up at five in the morning. "I must study," he wrote to Amelia, "if I mean to go to China. I am fully decided to go, and am making every preparation I can. I intend to rub up my Latin, to learn Greek and the rudiments of Hebrew, and to get as much general information as possible. I need all your prayers."

✳ ✳ ✳ ✳ ✳

Christmas, 1849: Amelia came home for the holidays. But she didn't come alone. With her was a vivacious young lady, Marianne Vaughan, one of the teachers in Aunt Hodson's school. Hudson was delighted. Most of the Taylor family were musical and played the piano: but Marianne! To hear her play and sing was — for Hudson — close to being in heaven. She was decidedly attractive and seemed to show some interest in the son of the houshold. Hudson, Amelia and Marianne went horse riding in the Peak District and, before the holidays were over, Hudson had fallen head over heels in love. For the time being, he wouldn't dwell on the fact that Marianne seemed only politely interested in China.

1850 turned out to be a year of turmoil for Hudson. He was sure God had called him to China, but how could he be sure it was right to take Marianne with him? And yet he couldn't bear the thought of going to China without her. Amelia suggested he could best provide for Marianne by being sent out by a recognized missionary society.

"Very true," replied Hudson, "but what society?"

The Wesleyans had no station in China. The Church of England had one or two, but he was not a churchman and wouldn't, he thought, do for them. The Baptists and independent churches had stations there, but he didn't share their views. The Chinese Association was very poor. "So God and God alone is my hope, and I need no other ..."

"Do you suppose she thinks or knows that I love her?"

he asked Amelia in a letter, with Marianne still on his mind. "Or does she, think you, care about me? Do answer these questions plainly."

His sister's reply (it has been lost) perplexed him. "I wonder how many times I have read and reread your letters, especially the last. As I do my mind is filled with conflicting hopes and fears. But I am determined to trust in God."

※ ※ ※ ※ ※

Five years in his father's business had made Hudson expert in dispensing medicines. But he needed to earn his own living, and felt that as assistant to a doctor he would make more progress with his medical studies.

He was writing regularly to George Pearse of the Chinese Association, and the Association for its part was taking Hudson seriously as a possible missionary to China. Pearse said that they might be able to help in paying for his medical education by providing for a course in a London hospital.

Taylor couldn't take up this offer because he had no means of supporting himself in London. But a vacancy occurred with one of the busiest doctors in Hull. Aunt Hannah's brother-in-law Robert Hardey needed an assistant, and Hudson accepted his invitation to join him.

TWO GERMANS 3

Hull in the 1850s was a mainly fishing town, straddling the River Hull where it joined the Humber. Hudson Taylor travelled there by train, and on Monday May 21, 1851, his nineteenth birthday, he reported for work. Robert Hardey lived and worked at 13 Charlotte Street, the Harley Street of Hull where most of the town's doctors had their consulting rooms. Besides his private practice, Hardey was a hospital surgeon, a lecturer at the medical school and a surgeon to several factories.

No 13 was on the sunny side of the street, and a Virginia creeper covered most of the front wall. Dr Hardey himself opened the door to greet his new assistant. Hudson liked him at once. He was tall and vigorous looking with an infectious sense of humour which, Hudson soon discovered, made him a popular figure in Hull. Hardey led Hudson to the dining room which overlooked a narrow strip of garden with a dispensary at the far end. He introduced Hudson to his wife who seemed as cold and severe as her husband was warm and hearty. With the minimum of pleasantries, she showed Hudson to his bedroom. And then it was down to a busy day's work. At eleven that night he wrote to Amelia: "From what I have seen of my new situation I think I shall like it exceedingly."

Hudson Taylor settled into his new job, dispensing medicines, keeping accounts, dressing wounds, going with Dr Hardey to midwifery cases, and attending lectures at the medical school. Hardey guided his reading of medical books and taught him in the course of their work. Hardey was an active Methodist, a class teacher, and the two men quickly became firm friends, praying together in the surgery.

On Sundays, Hudson Taylor began to worship at an assembly run by Andrew Jukes on lines similar to early Plymouth Brethren congregations. Jukes had been educated at Harrow, one of England's famous schools, and had previously been a deacon in the Church of England; he was a gifted teacher who thought deeply and made others think. Members of the fellowship became Hudson Taylor's companions when he began evangelistic work in Hull's dockland.

At Jukes' assembly Hudson heard of a remarkable man who was to have a profound effect on his thinking and development — George Muller of Bristol. Muller had been converted to Christ from a life of heavy drinking and deception while a student at the University of Halle in Germany. As pastor of a growing church in Bristol he had become concerned that few people, including members of his own congregation, believed in practice that God answers prayer. He longed for an opportunity to demonstrate that, as he put it, there is "reality in the things of God."

At that time Charles Dickens in *Oliver Twist* was drawing the British public's attention to the miserable plight of orphans. Muller decided that if he could establish and run an orphan home simply by prayer and faith, that would strengthen the faith of Christians and also show non-Christians that God was real.

Muller founded his first children's home in 1836 in rented premises in Bristol. In 1849 he opened a brand new purpose-built home high up on Ashley Down on the outskirts of

Bristol. By 1851 he was caring for three hundred children and planning a huge expansion of his work, besides sending large sums of money to missionaries in many countries. He never issued an appeal for funds or asked any individual to support him, preferring to rely on prayer and faith in a rich God. Hudson Taylor often heard letters from Muller read out at the Hull meetings.

✳ ✳ ✳ ✳ ✳

The Gleaner magazine was now being published by the Chinese Society (formerly the Chinese Association). In it Hudson Taylor often read of and admired the exploits of another great German, Wilhelm Lobscheid. Lobscheid had been a colleague of Charles Gutzlaff, and was one of the very few who could speak from experience about the possibilities for missionary work in China away from the treaty ports.

In September, 1851, The Gleaner announced that Lobscheid had arrived in England. The magazine appealed for men to go to China, especially evangelists with a knowledge of medicine.

Hudson Taylor decided to go to London to meet Lobscheid. The famous Great Exhibition, an attempt to show the world Britain's technological achievements, was about to open in Hyde Park. The new Crystal Palace housed hundreds of exhibits, and cheap excursion trains from every part of Britain tempted passengers to visit the spectacle.

Amelia's sixteenth birthday was on September 20. Robert Hardey gave Hudson a week off and an uncle, Benjamin Hudson, booked rooms for the two young people in his lodgings in Soho.

As they approached the glittering palace from Piccadilly, the sun shone on its glass dome amid the trees of Hyde Park. Brother and sister spent hours wandering around the exhibits; then, as a birthday treat for Amelia, they lunched in style at a restaurant, finishing off with a rare luxury for those days —a juicy pineapple.

They crossed the crowded city to the Bank of England, where a rendezvous had been arranged with George Pearse. As well as being secretary of the Chinese Society he was also a member of the Stock Exchange. Pearse arranged for them to go with him the following Sunday to another growing Brethren assembly, Brook Street Chapel, Tottenham, where they were finally introduced to Mr Lobscheid.

The German missionary looked hard at the short, fair lad from Barnsley with the blue-grey eyes.

"They call me a 'red-haired barbarian devil' and you see how dark I am. They would run from you in terror! You could never get them to listen at all."

"And yet," replied Hudson Taylor quietly, "it is God who has called me, and He knows the colour of my hair and eyes."

Before long Lobscheid revised his opinion of Taylor's suitability as a misssionary to China.

✳ ✳ ✳ ✳ ✳

Hudson's room at Robert Hardey's was now needed by a member of the family, so he moved to his Aunt Hannah's in Kingston Square, close to the surgery and opposite the medical school where he was attending lectures.

Richard, a photographer, and Hannah, a portrait artist, were not well off but they were generous and warmhearted and, with no children of their own, glad to entertain Amelia's son. They had a large circle of friends in Hull and Hudson enjoyed the friendly atmosphere at the home, especially when his sister came from Barton to spend Sundays with them.

But he was uneasy. After studying the relevant Bible passages, he had decided to earmark a minimum of a tenth of his income for God's work. But his salary included the amount he paid Aunt Hannah for his board and comfortable room in her home. Shouldn't he also tithe this? However, he calculated that if he deducted a tenth from the total this wouldn't leave him enough to live on.

After praying, he decided to find somewhere cheaper to lodge: a place where he could live in a way which would allow him to tithe the whole of his income.

He chose a ground-floor room in a terrace of newly built workmen's cottages a few minutes out of town. The terrace stood on the banks of a stream known as the Cottingham Drain. No 30, Cottingham Terrace, was owned by a ship's captain named Finch, whose visits home were few and far between. His Christian wife let the room to Taylor for three shillings a week. It was less than twelve feet square, furnished with a plain deal table, chair and bed, and boasted a fireplace opposite the window which Mrs Finch polished regularly with loving care.

From his room, Taylor could watch kingfishers and herons fishing, and water fowl nesting in the reeds. His neighbours left their milk churns up to their rims in the water to cool. On cold winter evenings, he could enjoy the warmth of the Finch's company or, if he chose to afford it, light a fire in the sparkling grate.

✳ ✳ ✳ ✳ ✳

On March 22, 1852, Hudson told his mother that he had made up his mind: his friends at Andrew Jukes' assembly now believed, as he did, that God was calling him to go to China as soon as possible.

In preparation for his great adventure, Hudson now had two objectives: learning to endure hardships and to live cheaply. He found that he could survive on very much less than he had thought possible. He discovered a brand of brown biscuits which were as cheap as bread and, he told his mother, much nicer. So for breakfast he ate brown biscuits and herring, which was cheaper than butter, washed down with coffee. Lunch might be roast potatoes and tongue followed by prune-and-apple pie; or rice pudding, peas instead of potatoes, and now and then some fish. He found a little place where he could buy cheese at four to six pence a pound

— and he fancied it tasted better than some he had had at home for eightpence. He pickled a penny red cabbage with three-halfpence-worth of vinegar, and made a large jarful.

Living cheaply but imaginatively meant that he was able to give away up to sixty percent of his earnings, and he discovered that the more he gave away the happier he became. He recorded: "Unspeakable joy all the day long, and every day, was my happy experience. God, even my God, was a living, bright reality; and all I had to do was joyful service."

But still he felt that his "spiritual muscles" needed strengthening. *When I get to China*, he thought, *I shall have no claim on anyone for anything; my only claim will be on God. How important, therefore, to learn before leaving England to move man, through God, by prayer alone.*

And so he embarked on a series of experiments with God.

A GOOD INVESTMENT 4

"Remind me whenever your salary is due," Robert Hardey had told Taylor breezily. This was his cue. He made up his mind never to speak to his employer about his pay, but ask God to do the reminding.

For a while there was no difficulty. But then the time came when a quarter's salary was due, and Hardey had apparently forgotten. On totting up his weekly accounts one Saturday night, Taylor found he had only a single coin left — one half-crown piece. He prayed hard.

Next day, after the Sunday morning service, he made his way along a familiar rutted farm track to the dockland area of Hull where hundreds of Irish labourers lived crowded together in slums and lodging houses. The area was notorious for violence and crime, and the police seldom visited it in groups of less than six. Perhaps because he worked for the well-loved Dr Hardey, Taylor found he could go into much of the area alone visiting patients, handing out tracts and even preaching to small groups. "At such times," he recorded, "it almost seemed to me as if Heaven were begun below, and that all that could be looked for was an enlargement of one's capacity for joy."

At about ten o'clock in the evening, he was addressed in a strong Irish accent.

"My wife is dying. Will you please come and pray with her?"

Taylor agreed, but asked: "Why haven't you sent for the priest?"

"I did. But he refused to come without a payment of eighteen pence. I don't have enough — my family is starving."

Taylor thought of his solitary half-crown. It was all he had, and it was in one coin. Back at his room, he had enough food for tomorrow's breakfast but nothing for lunch.

"It's very wrong of you to have allowed matters to get to this state. Why haven't you applied to the relieving officer?"

"I have, and am to meet him tomorrow. But I'm afraid she won't last the night."

If only, thought Taylor, *I had two shilling coins and a sixpence instead of this half-crown, how gladly I would give these poor people a shilling!*

Taylor followed the man into a courtyard where, on his last visit, they had torn his tracts to pieces and promised far worse treatment if he ventured there again. Anxiously he followed the man up a narrow flight of stairs into a dirty room.

Five children with hollow cheeks and eyes stood looking at him. Their mother lay exhausted, holding a newly born baby.

If only I had two shillings and a sixpence. Taylor thought again.

"Don't despair," he found himself saying. "There's a kind and loving Father in Heaven."

But something inside him said, *You hypocrite! Telling these people about a loving God, and not prepared yourself to trust Him without half-a-crown!*

He turned to the man. "You asked me to come and pray with your wife."

He knelt down. "Our Father, who art in Heaven," he began.

But his conscience spoke too. *Dare you kneel down and call Him Father with that half-crown in your pocket?* He could hardly get through the prayer.

"You see what a terrible state we're in, Sir," said the man. "If you can help us, for God's sake do!"

Taylor looked at him, and then at his wife and children. He remembered the words in Matthew 5: 42, "Give to the one who asks you."

He put his hand in his pocket, and took out the half-crown.

"You may think it a small thing for me to give you this," he said as he handed over the coin. "But it's all the money I have. What I have been trying to tell you is true. God really is a Father, and may be trusted."

As he walked through now-deserted streets and along the dark and muddy farm track to his cottage, his heart was "as light as his pocket". Back at No 30 he ate a bowl of thin porridge, and decided that he wouldn't have exchanged it for a prince's feast.

"Dear God," he prayed as he knelt beside his bed, "your Word says that he who gives to the poor lends to the Lord. Don't let the loan be a long one, or I shall have no lunch tomorrow!"

The woman lived, and the child's life was saved. Taylor reflected that his own spiritual life might have been wrecked had he not had the courage to trust God at that time.

Next morning, as he was eating his breakfast, Hudson Taylor heard the postman knock at the door. Mrs Finch handed him a letter. The handwriting was unfamiliar and his landlady's wet hand had smudged the postmark. Opening it, he discovered a pair of kid gloves inside a blank sheet of paper. As he held them, a gold half-sovereign fell to the floor.

"Praise the Lord!" he exclaimed. "Four hundred percent for twelve hours' investment; that is good interest. How glad the merchants of Hull would be if they could lend their money at such a rate!"

He resolved that "the bank which could not break" —

it was a phrase George Muller loved — should have all his money. "If we are faithful in little things," he concluded, "we shall gain experience and strength that will be helpful to us in the more serious trials of life."

This experience boosted Taylor's faith. But ten shillings, even then, didn't last for ever and he had to keep praying for the larger sum he needed.

But now none of his prayers seemed to be answered. Ten days after receiving the half-sovereign he was in almost the same scrape as before.

"Dear God, please remind Dr Hardey that my salary is overdue," he prayed urgently. It was not only a question of money: if his power with God in prayer proved inadequate, he would feel unable, in good conscience, to go to China.

On the Saturday a payment would be due to Mrs Finch. Shouldn't he, for her sake, speak to Hardey about his salary? But this would amount to admitting that he wasn't fit to be a missionary. He devoted nearly all his spare time on the Thursday and Friday to wrestling with God in prayer. On the Saturday he prayed, "Dear Father, please show me whether I should speak to Dr Hardey about my salary." It seemed to him that the answer came, "Wait. My time is best." He felt sure that God would act in some way on his behalf, and was quite relaxed.

At about five o'clock on the Saturday afternoon, Taylor and Hardey were together in the surgery. The doctor had finished his visiting rounds and had written all his prescriptions. He threw himself back in his armchair in his usual way and began talking about this and that.

Taylor was standing with his back to the doctor, watching a pan in which he was heating some medicine. Suddenly, Hardey said: "By the way, Taylor, isn't your salary due again?"

Hudson swallowed three times before he answered. Without lifting his eyes from the pan he replied, as unemotionally as he could, "It has been overdue for some time."

"Oh, I'm sorry you didn't remind me. You know how busy I am. I wish I'd thought of it sooner, because only this afternoon

I sent all the money I had to the bank. Otherwise I would pay you at once."

Taylor felt sick. Fortunately the pan boiled at that moment, and he had good reason to rush with it out of the room, where the doctor wouldn't see how upset he was.

As soon as Hardey had left the surgery, Taylor poured out his heart in prayer to God. After a while, he regained his composure, and felt sure that God would not fail him.

He spent the Saturday evening in the surgery reading his Bible and preparing some talks. At about ten o'clock he put on his overcoat and prepared to leave for Cottingham Terrace, glad that he would be able to let himself in with his own key. Mrs Finch would have gone to bed, and perhaps he would be able to pay her early the following week.

Just as he was about to turn out the gaslight in the surgery, he heard Hardey's footsteps in the garden. He was laughing heartily.

"Let me have the ledger, Taylor. An extraordinary thing has happened. One of my richest patients has just come to pay his bill — in cash!"

Taylor too thought it odd that a man rolling in money should come late in the evening to pay a doctor's bill, and paying in cash rather than by cheque made it even odder. He joined in Hardey's laughter.

Hardey entered the amount in the ledger and was about to leave. Then he turned to Hudson and handed him the wad of bank notes.

"By the way, Taylor, you might as well take these notes. I haven't any change, but we can settle the balance next week."

Taylor returned to Drainside praising God: he might, after all, go to China!

✳ ✳ ✳ ✳ ✳

In May, 1852, *The Gleaner* announced that the Chinese Society had become the Chinese Evangelization Society with expanded aims. It would no longer be content simply to aid missionary work in China: now it would send missionaries there and Wilhelm Lobscheid would be its first "agent". If the good news was to be successfully proclaimed, however, missionaries should go inland among the people and not settle in the five treaty ports. "China is ripe for the gospel," said *The Gleaner*. "We trust it may please God to raise up another European medical missionary."

One young medical student at least was able to move to London to advance his training. James Taylor happily agreed to release John Hodson to follow Hudson at Dr Hardey's. As to his financial support while in London, he still felt that he couldn't go to China without further developing and testing his ability to trust God — and a good opportunity to conduct such a test arose.

Hudson's father offered to meet all the expense of his stay in London (a considerable sacrifice). The Committee of the Chinese Evangelization Society (CES) also offered to bear his expenses. Hudson wrote to his father and to the CES asking for a few days to pray about it, and telling each about the other's offer.

After praying, he decided that he could without embarrassment decline both offers. The Society wouldn't know that he had decided to trust wholly in God for supplies, and his father would conclude that he had accepted the Society's offer.

Hudson made a booking to sail from Hull to London. Amelia came to see him off and spent her seventeenth birthday and her brother's last few days in Hull with him at Cottingham Terrace. At four o'clock on Friday September 24, 1852, the old paddle-driven coaster *London* steamed away from the pier at Hull harbour, with Hudson aboard waving furiously to Amelia in her bonnet and crinoline, tears rolling down her cheeks.

FROM BREAD AND WATER TO STEAK AND PORT 5

Hudson Taylor woke at daybreak in the Thames estuary and went up on to the deck of the *London* to enjoy a brightening sky and millpond sea. At noon they tied up in the Pool of London. Hudson walked to Mr Ruffles' Boarding House in Church Street, Soho, close to Shaftesbury Avenue. This was where his Uncle Benjamin lived. Hudson's mother's brother was well loved in the family but considered rather "worldly". He was good company, clever, witty and an excellent *raconteur*.

Uncle Benjamin was there to welcome his nephew and see him settle into rooms next to his own. He didn't have much time for Hudson's talk of "praying for the Lord to guide him", but was looking forward to introducing him to the surgeons among his own circle of friends, hoping they would offer him an apprenticeship.

Round the corner in Dean Street, but in and out of Ruffles, lived cousin Tom, brother of John who had succeeded Hudson at Dr Hardey's. Tom offered to share his room with Hudson to reduce his living expenses. Hudson gladly took him up on this and Tom, who was not a Christian, was intrigued to hear his cousin talk about his faith and see him reading his Bible and kneeling by his bed to pray.

As soon as possible, Hudson Taylor set off from Soho to find the CES office; there he was asked to invite his mother and Dr Hardey to write to the Society on his behalf.

"You can just state your opinion," he told his mother, "as to whether you think me converted or not, if you think me seriously intending to go to China, and anything you may know in me which would make me either suitable or unsuitable for missionary work. I don't want you to write as *my mother*, but as you would if your candid opinion were asked, in so momentous a matter, on any other person."

Mrs Taylor and Dr Hardey wrote their letters. A fortnight later, CES secretary Charles Bird told Taylor that he could start at the London Hospital in Whitechapel on the following Monday. The Society would pay his fees.

✳ ✳ ✳ ✳ ✳

Hudson Taylor had to walk the four miles from Soho to Whitechapel through Holborn, past drovers delivering their herds of bullocks to Smithfield market, up Ludgate Hill under the shadow of the massive dome of St Paul's Cathedral, along Cheapside, through Aldgate and along Whitechapel Road. All around him he saw the sights, and experienced the sounds and smells of mid-nineteenth century London: hand-carts rattling over cobbled stones, shouted traffic warnings, breakfasts doled out by hot-baked-potato men, bearded Jewish old-clothes sellers and street girls in poppy-red Garibaldi blouses.

His morning march ended as he walked up the ramp and under the arch into The London, as the hospital was known. It had room for about three hundred patients. Times were hard if you were ill. The only anaesthetic in regular use was alcohol, and Hudson heard screaming patients undergoing operations held down by attendants or strapped to the table. He heard the great bell "loud and harsh enough to make

Whitechapel shudder" ring out whenever more help was needed. "I like to hear a good honest scream," said one of the older surgeons — a horrifying nightmare for the patient, but an indication to the doctors that the patient was still alive.

Hudson Taylor lived frugally. On his evening walk home, he would buy a large loaf of brown bread and ask the baker to divide it for him, half for his evening meal and half for breakfast. He would set off each morning without breakfast and eat his half a loaf somewhere en route for a rest. Lunch usually consisted of a few apples. Despite this meagre diet, Hudson told his mother that his health was good and some even said he was getting fat! Though this, he believed, could "only be perceived by a rather brilliant imagination."

Not many weeks after his arrival, Taylor's ex-landlady, Mrs Finch, asked for his help. Her sailor husband had previously asked Hudson to collect and send part of his salary monthly to Mrs Finch in Hull. Now she wanted him to send the next amount as quickly as possible. Taylor was working long hours at The London, and studying for exams late into the evenings. So he sent his own money to Hull, intending to refund himself when he had time. But when he eventually called at the shipping office the clerk gave him bad news.

"Captain Finch has abandoned his ship. We believe he has gone to the gold diggings."

"Well, that's very inconvenient for me, as I've already advanced the money, and I know his wife will have no means of repaying it."

"I'm sorry," said the clerk, "but I'm acting under instructions and there is nothing I can do to help." Taylor reminded himself that he was depending on God for everything, and tried to trust and not worry.

That same evening he was sewing together some sheets of paper on which to take notes of his lectures. In the process he pricked a finger, but quickly forgot about it.

Next day, at the hospital, he continued dissecting the corpse of a man who had died of fever. Everyone worked on it with special care, knowing that if they scratched themselves even slightly this could be fatal.

About mid-morning, Taylor began to feel very tired. Going through one of the wards he felt suddenly sick and was forced to rush out of the ward. He felt faint for a while, though a glass of water revived him and he was able to rejoin the other students. But he began to feel more and more unwell, and during an afternoon lecture he found it impossible to hold his pencil. During the next lecture his arm and right side began to hurt intensely.

He went to the dissecting room, bound up the portion of the corpse he was working on and put away his apparatus.

"I can't think what's come over me," he said to the demonstrating surgeon, and described his symptoms.

"What's happened is clear enough," said the surgeon. "You must have cut yourself while dissecting. You have malignant fever."

"Impossible. I took great care and neither cut nor scratched myself."

"But you must have done."

The surgeon examined Taylor's hand, but found nothing. Then Taylor remembered pricking his finger the previous evening.

"Could a prick from a needle received yesterday have been still open this morning?" he asked.

"Yes, that's almost certainly the cause of the trouble. Get a hansom, drive home as fast as you can, and arrange your affairs. For," said the surgeon, encouragingly, "you're a dead man!"

"Unless I'm greatly mistaken, I have work to do in China, and shall not die. But if I don't recover, then I look forward to going to be with my Master."

"That's all very well, but you get a hansom and drive home as fast as you can. You've no time to lose. You'll soon be quite incapable of winding up your affairs."

Hudson Taylor set off to walk home. Before long he gave up and travelled by horse-drawn buses back to Soho. At his lodgings he asked a servant for some hot water and tried "literally as a dying man" to persuade her to become a Christian. Then he bathed his head, and lanced his finger hoping to get rid of some of the poisoned blood. The pain grew intense and he fainted.

When he came round he found that someone had carried him to his bed. Dear Uncle Benjamin had arrived and sent for his own doctor.

"I'm afraid it's past the stage where medical help will be of use," said Hudson. "And I don't want to go to the expense involved."

"Nonsense," said Uncle Benjamin. "The bill will be sent to me."

Uncle Benjamin's doctor arrived and gave his verdict: "If you have been living moderately, you may pull through. But if you have been going in for beer and that sort of thing, there's no hope for you."

"Well," replied Taylor, "if sober living has anything to do with it, few could have a better chance than me. I have eaten little more than brown bread and water for months. I find it helps me to study."

"But now," said the doctor, "you must keep up your strength. It's going to be a hard struggle. You must drink a bottle of port every day, and as many steak chops as you can eat."

Of course Taylor couldn't afford such luxuries. However Uncle Benjamin, who had heard the instructions, saw to it that his nephew began to eat and drink exactly what the doctor ordered, and paid the bills himself.

One day the doctor came and found Taylor on the sofa. He was surprised to hear that he had walked downstairs without help.

"The best thing you can do now is get off to the country as soon as you feel up to the journey. You must take things easy until you've recovered a fair amount of health and strength. If you begin your work too soon the consequences could be very serious."

Taylor lay on the sofa after the doctor had gone, feeling

exhausted. He began to pray.

"Dear God, I've deliberately avoided telling anyone about my need, so that my faith may be strengthened. What am I to do now? I can't afford to travel home."

He felt that God was telling him to go again to the shipping office to enquire about Captain Finch's wages.

"But dear Father," he prayed, "I can't afford to take a bus or a cab; and it's most unlikely that I shall succeed in getting the money. Isn't this impulse I have just clutching at a straw, a mental process of my own, rather than your guidance and teaching?"

After more prayer, he felt quite sure God was telling him to go to the office. But how? He'd only just managed to walk downstairs unaided, and the office was two miles away. He recorded: "The assurance was brought vividly home to me that whatever I asked of God in the name of Christ would be done, that the Father might be glorified in the Son; that what I had to do was to seek strength for the long walk, to receive it by faith, and to set out upon it."

"Heavenly Father," he prayed, "I am quite willing to take the walk if you will give me the strength. In the name of Jesus please give me the strength now."

He set off for Cheapside. At every second or third step he was glad to lean against the shop windows, and take time to examine the contents before moving on. He had never before taken so much interest in shop windows. Eventually he reached Cheapside, turned into the street where the office was, and sat down exhausted on the stairs leading to the first floor.

City gentlemen hurrying up and down glanced curiously at the exhausted figure slumped on the stairs. But after a rest and more prayer, Taylor succeeded in climbing the stairs and was glad to find the same clerk there. The clerk was alarmed at Taylor's appearance.

"Are you well, Sir?"

"I've had a serious illness," Taylor replied, "and have been advised to go to the country to convalesce. I thought I would call at your office to see whether there have been any developments about the seaman who had run off to the gold diggings."

"I'm so glad you've called. It turns out it was an able seaman of the same name who ran away. Captain Finch is still aboard and the ship has just reached Gravesend. It will be up very soon. I shall be glad to give you the pay up to date, for doubtless it will reach his wife more safely through you. But before I give you the money, won't you join me for lunch?"

Taylor gratefully accepted the invitation. With ready cash to hand, he caught a horse-drawn bus back to Soho.

Uncle Benjamin's doctor refused to take any money from Taylor on the grounds that he was a medical student.

"Would you allow me to speak freely?" Taylor asked the doctor.

"Go ahead."

"I feel that, under God, I owe my life to your kind care," Taylor began. "I do so wish that you would come to share the same precious faith in God that I possess. I'm in London undergoing medical training so that I may serve God in China. Before I go I've been trying to learn to trust God completely, and I therefore declined offers of help towards my support from both my father and the Chinese Evangelization Society. All my needs have been supplied. Yesterday God gave me the strength to walk from Soho to Cheapside."

"Impossible! I left you lying there more like a ghost than a man."

"I assure you I walked it. And now I've just enough money to go home to Yorkshire to convalesce."

"That's good. I'd give all the world for a faith like yours."

The two men never met again. Next day, Hudson Taylor was back in Barnsley being thoroughly spoilt by his mother, and under strict instructions never again to try to live on such an absurdly inadequate diet. He never did.

TANTALIZING NEWS FROM CHINA 6

Hudson Taylor and Marianne Vaughan became engaged at about this period. They had her father's approval, though he was still unhappy about her going to China.

But Hudson was depressed and nostalgic for the good times when Marianne used to play the piano and he and Amelia would stand side by side and sing. Despite the engagement, he noticed that whenever he suggested a meeting somewhere with Marianne, she always produced some reason why she couldn't make it. He felt sure she didn't love him as much as she once did; and she had told him that her friends were against the idea of their marriage.

Hudson returned to London during January 1853. Tom Hodson, who under Hudson's influence had become a Christian, was ill with rheumatic fever, and Hudson lost a lot of sleep looking after his cousin at nights. His depression deepened. When he prayed, "the heavens seemed as brass". He wrote to Amelia telling her he longed to see her and that if she were there he would give her "such a squeeze". He went on, "I think sometimes I love you too much."

To make things worse, his funds were exhausted. He prayed about this and again God answered: he was offered the post of assistant to a Dr Brown of Bishopsgate in the City of London. The offer included board and lodgings at the surgery and would allow him the morning and early afternoon free to attend The London, with late afternoon and evening duties at Dr Brown's. It would also cut his daily walk from four to two miles. Hudson accepted, moving at the end of March, 1853.

His routine now was: The London Hospital from 8 am to 3 pm; back to Bishopsgate to eat, dispense, visit patients or work on the doctor's accounts; study anatomy by himself, practise chemical analysis; and then perhaps make more late visits to patients. An absurdly busy day for anyone!

He spent Sundays happily at Brook Street Chapel, Tottenham, usually entertained by a former Quaker lady, Miss Stacey, who became a lifelong friend. The young people in the Tottenham assembly knew they would always be welcome in her home. She noticed how tired and pale Hudson looked and took care that whenever he needed to be alone he could. When summer came he spent many hours enjoying her garden, and often stayed in her house over the Sunday night, going straight to work from there.

Hudson Taylor was now grappling with a tricky decision. The CES was talking of paying another hundred pounds to cover his full qualification as a member of the Royal College of Surgeons. But if he accepted this offer and established a hospital in China under their auspices, he wouldn't feel free at a later stage to leave them and move on into the interior of China. He asked his parents to pray about this.

Meanwhile, he had a meeting with Marianne back at Ruffles.

"You know that I'm very much in love with you," Hudson told her, "but I'm not sure how you feel about me."

"My mother is ill," Marianne replied. "My father is worried that she may die at any time. He's afraid that I'll go off with you to China. Although he gave his consent to our engagement, I know that he's most unhappy. It's a terrible dilemma for me."

"Then we must write to him," said Hudson, "to see what he really feels. How can we continue our engagement if we don't have his approval?"

The news from China was tantalizing. In *The Gleaner*, the CES had appealed for missionaries to come without delay. And most intriguing of all were accounts of the progress of the extraordinary Taiping Rebellion, which during the fifties and early sixties was to dominate political events in China. *The Times* called it "the greatest revolution the world has yet seen", and many Christians felt it improved the prospects for the evangelization of China.

The Taiping rebellion was a response to the unpopularity of the Qing dynasty (1644-1911). The Manchus, who had established this dynasty, were still regarded as aliens by the Chinese. They had become lazy, weak and oppressive, and during the first half of the nineteenth century discontent grew; secret societies flourished and armed uprisings increased.

The founder of the Taiping rebellion was Hong Xiu-quan. Hong had been influenced by a series of Christian books written by Liang A-fa, who had become a Christian through the missionaries Robert Morrison and William Milne. In 1843, Hong Xiu-quan and his cousin baptized each other and began to preach to their relatives, some of whom were converted. Hong met the American missionary Issacher Roberts, who studied the Bible with him.

Later, as a result of Hong's preaching, a sect calling themselves Worshippers of Shangdi (God Worshippers) appeared on the scene and by 1849, Hong was accepted as their leader. He kept in touch with Issacher Roberts who reported these developments in optimistic letters home.

Some of the local leaders who emerged among the Worshippers of Shangdi were less well-taught and more militant than Hong. They began to drill fighting units and make common cause with members of a secret society, the

Triads, whose ambition was to overthrow the Qing dynasty and restore the Ming.

Hostilities between Hong's followers plus associates and the Imperial Manchu Government began in 1850. The rebels saw themselves as the founders of a new dynasty, the "Heavenly Kingdom of Great Peace". Hong was the emperor, the *Tai Ping Wang*, hence the name of the rebellion.

The Taipings set out their aims and objectives and established a system of belief and codes of conduct. They would overthrow the Manchus, abolish idols, and stamp out the abuse of opium. In the early days they honoured the Bible, attached great importance to the ten commandments, used the Lord's Prayer, held daily services at which they sang hymns in honour of the triune God, recited creeds and listened to sermons. They baptized adults. Although they permitted polygamy, their moral code was in many ways strict and wherever they went they destroyed idols.

These developments in China naturally aroused intense interest and excitement among Christians in England, Europe and America. A Christian dynasty and the abolition of idolatry and heathenism appeared possible. Even more encouraging for Christian missionaries was the apparent attitude of the Taipings to foreigners. "The great God," one Taiping leader said, "is the universal Father of all under heaven. China is under His government and care. Foreign nations are equally so. There are many men under heaven, but all are brethren."

In March, 1853, the Taiping army arrived in Nanjing, the ancient capital of China under the Ming Emperors, and heavily defeated the Manchu garrison. Nanjing, the heart of the Empire, was theirs — the key to the main north-south waterway, the Grand Canal.

The Gleaner led the way in reporting details of what was going on and Hudson Taylor was strongly tempted to abandon his medical course and sail for China at once.

The normal practice was for missionaries to marry shortly before sailing so that the couple could start their new life together. So the reply to his letter to Marianne's father would be crucial.

"... Were you to remain in England," wrote Mr Vaughan, "nothing would give me more pleasure than to see you happily united to Marianne. But though I do not forbid your connection, I feel I can never willingly give her up, or ever think of her leaving this country ..." And so the engagement was, in Hudson's words, "mutually and honourably" broken off.

For three years and three months he had loved Marianne, and had hoped and prayed that she would go with him to China. "I must say," he wrote to Amelia, "I think it very wrong of Mr V to countenance our engagement for so long a time, and then not to give his consent ... I cannot help loving her and believe she loves me." It was a sad time for Hudson. The two pet squirrels he now kept were good companions but a poor substitute for the lovely Marianne and her music. As he took a stroll in Finsbury Square with Dr and Mrs Brown's baby in his arms, he reflected on the joys of family life and prayed that one day they would be his.

Throughout the Christian world, interest in China continued to be intense. The editors of *The Gleaner* believed that Beijing would soon fall into the hands of the Taiping rebels. "The light of day is dawning on China ... We have a prospect of very shortly sending out some medical gentlemen of decided Christian character."

That same June, events began to move fast. Charles Bird contacted Taylor urgently. "If you're sure you don't wish to complete your full medical qualification, then we feel you should go almost immediately to China," Bird told him. "We should like you to go under our auspices. You should sail by early September to avoid the autumn gales.

"The committee will impose no obstacle to your progress inland, should the way ever be open. If any circumstances should arise in which you could not work happily with the Society, the committee would not think it dishonourable or unchristian for you to leave them. Think and pray about it. If you do decide to go you should complete your application at once."

Hudson Taylor decided to go.

The application papers consisted of a lengthy questionnaire and statement of his beliefs. For two nights in succession he worked from one till three in the morning drafting his replies. His answers were totally honest. He believed that he had stated his unorthodox views so freely that he would not be accepted. According to the clerk to the committee, the part which caused eyebrows to be raised the highest was where he said, "I do not believe in the division of the Church into clergy and laity. I believe all Christians have a right to preach, baptize and administer the Lord's Supper ..." The committee's reaction is hardly surprising, for the majority of them were clergymen or ministers holding the opposite view.

Three weeks went by, and Hudson Taylor heard nothing from the committee. His parents approved of his decision to go to China as soon as possible, though his mother was concerned that he had given in his notice to Dr Brown before the CES had made up its mind. Actually Brown offered Hudson strong inducements to stay, and tried to persuade him to take another year to pass the College of Surgeons' exams. But Hudson Taylor's mind was made up: "If in the time and with the expense required to make me MD, MRCS or both, I am instrumental in leading any poor Chinese to the feet of Jesus — how much better would that appear in eternal ages!"

Then came a note from Charles Bird. The committee had made its decision. They were prepared to send him to China as soon as he could make the arrangements for the journey.

✳ ✳ ✳ ✳ ✳

In August, Hudson Taylor spent a few delightful weeks at home in Barnsley. The family talked and sang together —

and he gave one of his pet squirrels to Amelia and the other to Louisa, now thirteen.

At the end of the month he was back in London, racing around collecting and packing medical equipment, clothing, and a hundred and one other things he would need in Shanghai.

In September, he was asked to tell the Brook Street congregation about himself and what he would be up to. "I was not very collected in my thoughts" — but he was received warmly, and dear Miss Stacey instructed him to get a warm dressing gown made and send the bill to her. At the CES office he was commended to the protection of God and told to proceed as soon as possible to Nanjing, thought to be the current headquarters of the Taiping rebels.

From the CES office he went straight to Euston and caught the night train to Liverpool, where he joined his mother and George Pearse. His father and Aunt Hannah arrived and met up with the other members of the family at Owen's Hotel. Then Hudson's drugs and surgical equipment were delivered to the wrong station and it took several days to track them down.

After four days away from the shop, James Taylor had to return to Barnsley and the family went to the station to see him off. Hudson never forgot the agony of that parting. The whistle blew, there was a huge belch of smoke and steam and the train began to move. Hudson hung on and ran along beside the train. Father and son looked into each other's eyes, their hearts breaking, until the speed of the train dragged them apart.

Hudson's ship, the *Dumfries*, was to sail on the 19th. Among letters he dashed off during his final days in Liverpool were several to his darling Amelia and one to John Hodson, still working for Dr Hardey in Hull: "Come to Jesus," he wrote, "see all your sins laid on Him ... I write thus because I love you — but how much more God loves you." John died at 29 but not before Hudson's prayers for his conversion had been answered.

SLOW BOAT TO CHINA 7

Monday, September 19, 1853: the little three-masted clipper *Dumfries* was almost ready to sail. Built in 1837, she weighed less than five hundred tons. As the crew carried the last of the cargo aboard, four people met in Hudson Taylor's cabin in the stern: Hudson and his mother, another missionary named Arthur Taylor (no relation), and an elderly minister whom the Taylors had met in Liverpool. The cabin was roomy and had been freshly painted in honour of the young man of 21 who was off to the other side of the world, perhaps never to return.

Hudson suggested they should sing John Newton's hymn—

"How sweet the name of Jesus sounds
In a believer's ear!
It soothes his sorrows, heals his wounds,
And drives away his fear."

Then he prayed. His voice was firm until he commended to God those he loved, when it faltered for a moment. He paused, steadied himself, and then, referring to the difficulties which almost certainly lay ahead, he concluded: "None of these things move me, nor do I count my life dear to myself, so that I might finish my course with joy, and the ministry which I have received from the Lord Jesus to tell the gospel of the grace of God."

The others prayed in turn and Hudson Taylor read a psalm. Amelia Taylor smoothed her son's bed for the last time. Neither mother nor son expected to meet again.

They went up on deck to find that the crew had already cast off, and the *Dumfries* was beginning to edge away from the wharf. Three of the four were helped off the ship.

Mrs Taylor sat down on the dockside and began to shake all over. Hudson leaped ashore, and put his arm around her.

"Dear mother, don't cry. We shall meet again. Think of the glorious object I have in leaving you! It's not for wealth or fame, but to try to bring the Chinese to the knowledge of Jesus."

As the ship drifted further from her moorings, he managed to jump aboard again and ran to his cabin. He found a pocket Bible and scribbled on the flyleaf, "The love of God which passeth knowledge — JHT." Returning to the deck he threw the Bible to his mother.

The first mate arrived late at the dockside and shook Mrs Taylor's hand.

"Keep a brave heart," he said. "I'll bring good news back again."

The *Dumfries* drew closer to the wharf and the mate climbed aboard. Hudson was able to grasp his mother's hand again.

"Farewell, God bless you."

As the three on the Liverpool dockside waved their handkerchiefs, Hudson climbed into the rigging, doffed his hat and, holding it high above his head, returned their signals with all his energy until the forlorn figures disappeared from his view. Meanwhile, in London, the Bible Society passed a resolution to print a million copies of the Chinese New Testament.

With Hudson Taylor aboard the *Dumfries* were Captain

Morris, two mates, a steward, bosun, cook and carpenter, seamen, boys and apprentices: making a crew of 23. Apart from a little Chinese boy from Macao, Taylor was the only passenger — except for a number of live pigs, hens, ducks, dogs and two cats.

In his cabin, Taylor fastened and arranged his possessions, played his concertina and sang. Then, as the ship began to roll, he took a "creosote pill" and fell asleep. When he awoke, he spent some time watching his cabin lamp swing lazily in all sorts of curious shapes.

But as the *Dumfries* headed into the Irish Sea, the gentle breeze turned into a westerly gale. For three days they tacked to and fro making little real progress.

On Saturday, the wind dropped for a while but all day the barometer kept falling. When darkness came the wind freshened again.

As they battled their way south off the west coast of Wales, Captain Morris abandoned his normal Sunday practice of reading prayers. Hudson Taylor visited the crew and gave them tracts to read. By noon the wind was blowing hard and the men took in all the sail they could.

Feeling sick, Taylor returned to his cabin. The barometer was falling still and the gale became almost a hurricane.

Between two and three in the afternoon, Taylor struggled up to the deck again. He never forgot what he saw. The sea was white with foam, and the waves were towering above the *Dumfries* on either side, seeming about to swamp it.

"I've never seen a wilder sea," shouted the captain. "Unless God helps us, there's no hope."

The wind was blowing the *Dumfries* towards the lee shore.

"How far are we from the coast of Wales?" Taylor asked.

"Fifteen or sixteen miles. We can do nothing but carry all possible sail. The more we carry the less we drift. It's for our lives. God grant the timbers may bear it."

The *Dumfries* was racing — one moment high out of the water and the next plunging headlong into the sea as if about to go to the bottom. The ship was leaning at a sharp angle with the sea pouring over her lee bulwarks.

With a loud crack, the spar which joined the foremast to the upper corner of the square-rigged sail split. But it held.

Taylor watched the sun set. He thought: *Tomorrow the sun will rise as usual, but unless the Lord works miraculously for us, only broken timbers will be left of our ship.*

Without the sun, Taylor felt lonely and desperate. He went below, read a couple of hymns, some psalms and a passage from John's Gospel, and slept for an hour.

On waking, he looked at the barometer. It was rising, and he returned to the deck. They were sailing north, still off the Welsh coast.

"Shall we clear Holyhead?" Taylor asked the captain.

"If we make no leeway, we may just do it. But if we drift, God help us!"

They did drift.

First the Holyhead light was ahead of them, and then Taylor saw it to seaward. They were heading for the shore.

Captain Morris looked grim but calm. The barometer still rose, but too slowly.

Taylor thought of his family and friends. Tears came. He spoke to the steward, who was also a Christian.

"I am nothing, but Christ is all," the steward told him.

Taylor remembered the verse in Psalm 50, "Call upon me in the day of trouble; I will deliver you," and prayed to God to spare them.

There was a bright moon now, and they could see land. The barometer was still rising but the wind hadn't dropped. Taylor went below, took out his pocket-book and wrote his name and home address in it in case his body should be found. He tied some things together in a hamper which might float and help him or someone to land. After more prayer, he returned to the deck.

"Could the lifeboats survive a sea like this?"

"No."

"Could we lash the loose masts and booms together to make some sort of raft?"

"We probably shouldn't have time," replied Captain Morris. "We can't live half an hour. What of your call to work for God in China now?"

"I wouldn't wish to be in any other position. I still expect to reach China. But if not, my Master will say it was well that I was found seeking to obey His command."

They saw land close ahead, lit up by the moon.

"We must try to turn her and tack," said the captain, "or it's all over. The sea may sweep the deck as we turn and wash everything overboard, but we must try."

Morris gave the order and they tried to turn out to sea. They failed.

They tried the other way, and the *Dumfries* began to drift towards the shore.

Just as she did so, the wind changed direction and they were able to head away from the rocks. The ship cleared them by no more than twice her own length.

Gradually the storm blew itself out. Hudson Taylor saw the sun rise in the morning.

✳ ✳ ✳ ✳ ✳

Captain Morris's men were able to repair the damage to the *Dumfries* during the voyage. Some of the crew had received minor injuries, and Hudson Taylor had to put a stitch in the Swedish carpenter's eyebrow. The two men became firm friends. Taylor discovered that not only the Swede and the steward but also the captain were Methodists. Captain Morris gave permission for Taylor to begin regular services among the crew, and the steward helped him in arranging and conducting them.

On October 6, Taylor and the steward met for prayer in Hudson's cabin.

"Dear God," Taylor prayed, "please give us a favourable wind and sea for our voyage, for you alone rule the wind and the waves."

As they were praying they heard a great deal of tramping about on the deck above them. They discovered that the wind had suddenly veered round and the noise was that of the sailors squaring the yards (the horizontal poles which supported the sails). Many times during the voyage Taylor prayed about the weather and received remarkable answers. After a gale in the Bay of Biscay, the prevailing north-east wind helpfully blew them towards South America. They rounded the Cape of Good Hope on the westerlies and headed for Australia on the great rollers of the southern oceans.

There was so much of God's wonderful world to delight Hudson Taylor — the gentle light of the evening and morning skies, flying fish, birds resting in the rigging, magnificent sunsets seen from the mast-tops. When animals came his way — a dying ship's cat, a bonito, two albatrosses — he dissected them, taking measurements and keeping careful records in his journal.

Doctoring also kept him busy: opening abscesses in the captain's eyelid, on the cook's arm and hand, and on a sailor's back; removing part of one of the men's tonsils; and extracting the steward's last molar. In calm weather he sorted and labelled the chemicals he had ordered. He distilled water and alcohol for chemical analyses and photography, made photographic paper and tried unsuccessfully to construct a camera using a microscope lens. Captain Morris was doing algebra with him and he was also teaching the captain to play the concertina and the second mate the flute.

One hot day, he went on deck when the crew were washing it and they were quick to throw five or six buckets of warm water over him. He heartily enjoyed this and the sailors warmed to his sense of fun. On another day, the captain and he rowed around the *Dumfries* on a raft inspecting the ship's condition and then enjoying a swim together, keeping a wary eye open for sharks. Sometimes he helped the crew in their work, learning some of the techniques of managing the sails.

They celebrated Christmas, 1853, by killing the first of the pigs aboard. But in the light breezes progress was slow: the end of the year found them about five hundred miles from Australia and five thousand from China.

✳ ✳ ✳ ✳ ✳

Friday January 13, 1854. Hudson Taylor woke up at two in the morning. He wasn't superstitious but surely there was someone in his cabin? A shadowy figure was standing beside the bed.

"Get up, Taylor, and come with me on deck," said the Captain.

Taylor joined Morris on the deck in a bright moonlight. They were south-east of Sumba, in the Savu Sea.

"Do you see those islands?" Morris asked, with a blend of excitement and alarm in his voice "They're not correctly laid down in the chart. Navigating a route through them will be extremely dangerous."

But they succeeded, and next day they sailed north-east through the Ombay Straits. Ombay's forest and ravines looked beautiful and the sight of trees and fields made Taylor long to be on *terra firma* again.

Sunday January 29: danger threatened again. There was no breeze at all, and a strong four-knot current began to carry them towards the northern shore of Papua New Guinea. The shore was peppered with sunken reefs, and the mainland was the home of painted headhunters. They had drifted forty miles off course and were helpless, very close to land. All they could do was lower a longboat, and try to turn their bow into the current to reduce the drift and eventual force of impact.

Hudson Taylor held his morning service as usual. Morris attended but kept walking to the side of the ship, anxiously studying their position.

"We've done everything that can be done; we can only

await the result," he said to Taylor after the service.

"No, there's one thing we haven't done."

"What's that?" asked the captain.

"Four of us on board are Christians," said Hudson Taylor. "Let's each retire to his own cabin, and ask the Lord to give us a breeze. He can as easily send it now as at sunset."

Captain, steward, carpenter and passenger went to their cabins to pray. Hudson Taylor had what he described as a "good but very brief season of prayer", then felt certain that his prayer had been answered. He went up again on deck.

The first officer was in charge. Hudson Taylor saw that the corners of the mainsail had been drawn up to prevent useless flapping against the rigging.

"Let down the corners of the mainsail," he said.

"What would be the good of that?" asked the officer.

"We've been asking God to send a wind and it's coming immediately. We're so near the reef that there's not a moment to lose."

The first officer looked at Taylor with a mixture of incredulity and contempt. "I would rather see a wind than hear of it!"

But as he was still speaking, Hudson Taylor watched the first officer's eye and followed his glance up to the highest sail. There, sure enough, the corner of the sail was beginning to tremble in the coming breeze.

"Don't you see the wind is coming? Look at the royal!" said Taylor, who after four months at sea knew all the right nautical terms.

"No, it's only a cat's paw [a mere puff of wind]," replied the sailor.

"Cat's paw or not," Hudson Taylor cried. "Let down the mainsail, and let's have the benefit."

The first officer gave the order, and in a few minutes they were sailing at six or seven knots, leaving the sunken reefs and painted savages behind them.

With the right winds it would now be possible to reach Shanghai in a week or so. Hudson Taylor began to pack up his equipment and books.

On Saturday February 25, they anchored off Gutzlaff Island near the mouth of the Yangzi estuary, fifteen miles from Shanghai. For six months they had lost touch with the outside world, and now besieged an English pilot they had taken on board with questions.

"The Taiping rebels have had possession of Shanghai for four months, and are marching to Beijing," he told them.

On Wednesday March 1, 1854, they reached Wusong and a passing pilot boat took Hudson Taylor up the Huangpu river towards Shanghai. He saw European ships sharing the river and jetties with ocean-going junks, and British and French men-of-war. A dozen or more foreign business houses stood shoulder to shoulder with an ornate Chinese temple now used as a custom house. Upstream he could see the walls of the ancient city of Shanghai. Outside the walls were the colourful banners and tents of the imperial Manchu army, besieging the Taiping rebels within.

China. What he had read about in the pages of *The Gleaner* had become a reality before his very eyes.

THE SEARCH FOR MEANING 8

The glow of sunset behind bare mountain peaks; thunderclaps over fertile plains; evening twilight on a pagoda-topped hill above the quiet reaches of a river; the solid outline of an ancient city wall; the sound of a distant temple gong echoing through the night; the chanting of coolies in the sweltering heat of a summer afternoon; the meandering Yangzi; a monastery half-hidden in a bamboo glen; the well-proportioned contours of a lovingly tended garden; the magnificent colours of imperial palaces. China had cast her spell for many centuries before Hudson Taylor arrived.

But it was not primarily to enjoy the beauty and charm of this vast, intriguing land that Taylor had come. He had left his family and risked his life to travel halfway across the world believing not only that the Chinese were in error, but that millions of them were dying without hope. He came bearing what he believed was the message of truth and life to a land where various forms of religion had long been practised; where professional scholars had wandered from place to place discussing the meaning of life and debating political and economic theories.

The most famous of all these scholars was Confucius, who lived at about the same time as the Old Testament Ezra (551-479 BC).

Chinese religious beliefs in the days of Confucius seem to have had four main strands. The first was the idea of a divine Providence. Confucius himself had a sense of mission and felt that Heaven would protect him to carry on that mission. The earliest Chinese records spoke of *Shangdi* (a supreme deified being) who ruled the world in righteousness and required righteousness from men.

A second feature was the host of spiritual beings with which the Chinese peopled their world. There were house gods, for instance of the hearth or of the corner where the seed grain was stored, and spirits or gods of the rivers, of the mountains and of the stars.

Most deeprooted of all Chinese religious observances, however, was the third strand — ancestor worship. Nearly every household possessed a small shrine, like a shelf, where the family kept a wooden tablet with the name, date of birth and death of each family member. In wealthy households these were gilded or highly ornamented. The members of the family prostrated themselves (*kowtowed*) at regular intervals, lighting candles, burning incense and making ceremonial offerings of food. When a parent died the eldest son did the honours for the family, kneeling at the grave and praying: "Let the bones and the flesh return to the earth, and may the spirit reside with us in the tablet."

The Chinese regarded ancestor worship as the highest duty in family life. They believed it led to real communion with the spirit world, and that the happiness of the dead depended on the sacrifices of their descendants. Departed spirits had power to confer blessing or trouble on the living, and ancestor worship ceremonies resulted in family solidarity and helped to maintain social stability.

The fourth strand in the ancient religious system of China was the Imperial or Grand sacrifice made by the Emperor as representative of his people and Son of Heaven. He prostrated himself in front of a tablet to "The Supreme Ruler of Imperial Heaven", and in sacrifice and prayer to Shangdi expressed his sense of the nation's obligation to and dependence on higher powers.

Confucius always took these religious traditions seriously. He certainly believed in the reality of the spiritual world, and in a supreme power which governs and controls the destinies of men. But his main interest wasn't religion: he was an ethical teacher with a political aim.

Confucius preached what has been described as "a utilitarian gospel of common sense and homely virtues". To him learning was in order to further moral ends, and his aim was to reform the corrupt Zhou dynasty by means of the moral principles of the ancient worthies. He extolled the superior man, or gentleman: a person motivated by the highest moral standards and careful to observe the conventions of family and state.

The highest Confucian virtue was human-heartedness. Men should not do to others what they would not want done to themselves.

Confucius diverges from Christian ethics in his principle of meeting personal harm or injury with justice — not with mercy or forgiveness. And he mainly confined his teaching to a limited audience from the ruling class, leaving ordinary people to concentrate on worshipping their ancestors and to placating the spirits. This gap was filled by the growth of Daoism.

Daoism was founded by Laozi, an older contemporary of Confucius. Daoism as a philosophy was about the great reality underlying the universe. But as a religion of the peasants it degenerated into a hotchpotch of spiritism, exorcism, magic, geomancy and divination. At different times through the centuries Daoism seriously rivalled the more sedate and disciplined way of Confucianism. More than once it was more popular at the imperial court, although Confucianism was always needed to meet the requirements of State ritual.

The Han dynasty (206BC - AD221) eventually adopted the Confucian principle that China should be governed by the ablest and best, regardless of birth. So they established schools to teach the Confucian system, and introduced the civil service examinations through which mandarins were recruited and which became a major feature of Chinese life for centuries.

During the Han dynasty also, four centuries before the first Christians came, Buddhist missionaries arrived from India and established Buddhism as a major religion. It made great advances in China. Hudson Taylor was to discover that Buddhist monks and shaven-headed priests in yellow robes were a familiar feature. Buddhism never, however, displaced Confucianism or Daoism. Chinese religion was often an amazing mixture of the three.

Eventually the civil service examinations became so well established that the majority of China's best minds sought promotion, wealth and recognition in society through them. The exams tested knowledge of a well-defined curriculum, concentrating on a knowledge of the Confucian Classics. The system of governing China by educated and able men had its faults, but was actually very successful. Confucian philosophy inculcated high ideals in the relations of men to one another, producing an orderly and to some degree a prosperous society. It fostered an extensive and varied literature; it attached high value to good taste and an appreciation of manners, ritual and poetry.

During the Qing dynasty (1644-1911) Chinese culture began to have an influence on Europe. Roman Catholic missionaries translated portions of Chinese literature and their writings about China were widely read at home. In general, the missionaries admired Chinese culture and their enthusiasm was infectious. China became a fad: Rococo art reflected a knowledge of Chinese forms; the wealthy built Chinese gardens, pagodas and pavilions and stocked them with Chinese plants such as tea roses, azaleas, primroses in the greenhouse, chrysanthemums, mountain peonies and China asters; sedan chairs became fashionable, as did lacquer, incense, tea, Chinese colours and styles of painting and wallpaper.

And it was under the Qing that those intimate contacts with the western world began which had such revolutionary results for China. As its rulers became more incompetent and decadent China faced some of the most serious crises of its history, such as the Taiping rebellion — into the middle of which Hudson Taylor had now arrived with enthusiasm and anticipation.

SETTLING IN SHANGHAI 9

S tepping ashore at one of Shanghai's many jetties, Hudson made for a British flag flying in the distance. As he neared the British consulate, he was looking forward to reading letters from home and, he hoped, to finding a letter from CES authorizing him to draw cash from the society's agents in Shanghai.

"The office which handles the mail closed an hour ago. You must come again tomorrow," the consulate staff told him.

So Hudson turned to his letter of introduction to Dr Walter Medhurst of the London Missionary Society. Medhurst was about the most experienced of the British missionaries already in China, and an interpreter and adviser to the British consul.

The consulate staff gave Taylor directions to the LMS compound, and he set off along the raised bank of the Huangpu river, turning right along a mile of mud tracks flanked by deep drainage ditches. The Chinese man who answered Taylor's knock couldn't speak a word of English, but Hudson soon got the message that Dr and Mrs Medhurst were away from home.

Taylor then met a young English missionary, Dr Joseph

Edkins, who welcomed him and introduced him to the other missionaries in the compound. One of these was Dr William Lockhart, a surgeon who had established a hospital in Shanghai.

"Why don't you make my home your home for the time being?" Lockhart asked. Taylor accepted gratefully, but with some embarrassment that as a CES missionary he had to accept LMS hospitality. Lockhart agreed to let Taylor pay a fee to cover expenses.

The Rev and Mrs John Burdon of the Church Missionary Society, who lived in the LMS compound, invited Taylor to dinner that evening. They were young, their fireside homely, their company pleasant, and their conversation interesting: Taylor thoroughly enjoyed the evening. Burdon went on to become the first CMS missionary in Beijing and later Bishop of Victoria, Hong Kong.

From the room in Lockhart's house where Taylor spent his first night in China, he could see across no-man's-land between the Taiping rebel forces and the imperial army. Over to his right the government soldiers were camped; the city walls were lit up and he could see sentries on duty. Despite the sound of gunfire which shook the house, he managed to get some sleep. Before dawn the firing of a cannon made the windows rattle. But this was followed by the cheerful sound of birds singing. He went to his window. The green corn was waving in the fields and the plants in the garden were beginning to bud. He could smell blossom on the trees.

After breakfast Hudson Taylor went quickly to the consulate to collect his post. There was only one letter from home, written five months earlier, and a copy of *The Gleaner*. Nothing from the CES: no money, no credit notes, no guidance, no instructions. Foolishly or thoughtlessly, or both, friends and society seemed to be waiting until he reached Shanghai before writing.

Later that day, he collected his baggage from the *Dumfries* and returned through the crowded streets of the city at the head of a procession of coolies, all his belongings swinging from bamboo poles across their shoulders.

He also visited the hospital and listened to Dr Medhurst preaching to the waiting patients in their own dialect. Medhurst greeted him warmly.

"You have a choice," he said. "You could learn the Shanghai dialect: but that is only used and understood in this area. Or you could learn the language of the mandarins. This is used with variations by hundreds of millions of people all over China. My advice is to learn Mandarin — I could find you a teacher."

"I have no doubt you're right," Taylor replied. "Please be kind enough to find me a teacher." •

✳ ✳ ✳ ✳ ✳

Hudson Taylor now had to find a house, establish financial arrangements with the agents of the CES, and learn enough Chinese language and customs to be able to manage on his own without the help of LMS and CMS missionaries.

"I felt very much disappointed on finding no letter from you," he wrote to George Pearse, "but I hope to receive one by next mail. Shanghai is in a very unsettled state, the rebels and imperialists fighting continually ... There is not a house to be obtained here, or even part of one; those not occupied by Europeans are filled with Chinese merchants who have left the city ... The missionaries who were living in the city have had to leave, and are residing with others here in the settlement at present; so that had it not been for the kindness of Dr Lockhart I should have been quite nonplussed. As it is I scarcely know what to do ..."

On his first Sunday afternoon he went into the city with Alexander Wylie, the printer in charge of the LMS press and a keen evangelist. Realizing the importance of literature to the Chinese, he had studied their classical writings and written articles in Chinese to draw attention to the greatness of the One who created the galaxies. Hudson Taylor found him stimulating company.

Wylie showed Taylor the city under siege. They walked

around the outside of the city wall and saw row after row of wrecked houses and the misery of those who had once lived in them. They spoke to some rebel soldiers guarding the entrance to the city. All were dressed in richly embroidered long caps, tied on with red scarves, rich silk coats with brightly coloured lapels, green silk trousers and boots.

As they wandered through the city, Wylie talked to the people in Chinese and both men gave away tracts, even going into some of the temples and speaking to the priests. Reaching the LMS chapel, they found it packed; Dr Medhurst was preaching. After he had finished, LMS missionaries distributed rice to homeless people.

At the north gate of the city they saw fierce fighting outside the walls. One man was brought in dead; another had been shot through the chest. Taylor examined a third and found a cannon ball had gone right through his arm, breaking the bone in the process. The man was writhing in agony, but there was nothing they could do unless he came to the hospital.

"If we treat him here," said Medhurst, "someone will only pull our dressings off."

Further on they met soldiers bringing in a small cannon they had captured. Another group of soldiers were dragging prisoners along by their pigtails. The prisoners cried out to Taylor and his companions to help them, but there was nothing they could do.

✳ ✳ ✳ ✳ ✳

The other missionaries in Shanghai were all highly educated and connected with either the Anglican church or large and well-established missionary societies. Taylor was connected with no particular denomination and had been sent out hurriedly by the CES before his medical course was finished, in the hope of reaching the Taiping rebels in Nanjing. Misled by optimistic reports of the Taiping movement, the CES had adopted a strategy which the practical men already working in China regarded as absurd. Some of them openly ridiculed the CES and its journal, *The Gleaner*.

Taylor was coming to recognize the CES's shortcomings and suffering from its inefficiency; but he never lost his respect for many members of the committee or for the society's secretaries. He respected their spirituality, their love for the Word of God and anxiety to see men and women converted to Christ.

Many Europeans lived in luxury in Shanghai at this time; it was a new world to western enterprise. Even some of the missionaries were, in Taylor's eyes, "worldly"; they were in great demand with government officials as interpreters and came into frequent contact with officers from gunboats stationed at Shanghai to protect the international settlement. The general atmosphere of hearty sociability came as something of a surprise to the child of a strict Methodist upbringing.

Taylor was bright and adequately educated, but he had no university or college training, and had taken no medical degree. He expected to do medical work, but he was not a doctor. He was able to preach and exercise pastoral care, but he was not ordained. He adamantly refused to accept the title "Reverend" which many wished to thrust upon him. His salary of eighty dollars a year from the CES was hopelessly inadequate — the CMS allowed single men seven hundred dollars besides paying their rent, medical expenses and a sum sufficient to cover a Chinese teacher and books. Taylor looked shabby compared with those around him.

When he unpacked his crates and cases, he found that during the voyage ink bottles had broken and stained his books and papers, and salt water had ruined his shoes and some clothing. The *Dumfries* had left Shanghai for home but never made it: she was totally wrecked on the Pescadores though all aboard were saved.

Early in March Taylor's Mandarin teacher, a northerner, arrived and they began to work together every day. Hudson Taylor prayed that while his teacher was teaching him Chinese, the Holy Spirit would influence his heart and bring him to Jesus.

After four days the two men could talk to each other in very basic Chinese. Taylor tried out phrases with the soldiers and ventured into shops, finding that he had some success both in understanding and making himself understood.

The imperialist commander-in-chief in Shanghai, Koer-hanger, had instructions to blockade the city: but it was open in the north to the foreign settlements, and foreigners were providing the citizens with enough food and arms to make the siege virtually useless. Foreign merchants were giving money and other help to the rebels and city-dwellers, hoping for an eventual change in dynasty following a Taiping victory. The missionaries were distributing rice and meat to those in need.

On April 4, 1854, the Battle of Muddy Flat was fought. Hudson awoke to the sound of gunfire. As he went outside, a cannon ball shot past and embedded itself in the wall of William Muirhead's house. Muirhead was a tall Scottish Presbyterian whom Taylor was getting to know and admire.

At 6.30 am Taylor and Muirhead walked through the international settlement to the riverside. Chinese war junks were weighing anchor and beginning to move downstream towards the settlement where the British, French and American frigates were lying. They were commanded to stop, but paid no attention and attempted to enter the Suzhou river. A British ship fired on them.

On shore the consuls were demanding that imperialist camps and cannon move out of the foreign settlement. The British consul, Rutherford Alcock, sent General Koer-hangar an ultimatum. "If you do not begin to move your troops by three pm the marines will be landed on shore, and if by four pm your men have not withdrawn, they will be driven out and their camps destroyed."

Three o'clock came and there was no movement. British and American marines and merchant sailors went ashore. With flags flying and drums beating they marched under Alcock's command to the racecourse, where the imperialist troops were assembled close to the international settlement.

At four o'clock Hudson Taylor heard the din of American guns and saw the first shell explode, as American and British soldiers attacked the camps. Chinese imperialists fled in all directions. A sea of red turbans appeared on the scene — triad rebels had seized the opportunity to join in the fun.

It turned out an easy victory for the British and Americans; they lost only two. lives in the whole battle. The rebels had a marvellous time supplying themselves with arms and ammunition from the imperialist camps after the Manchu soldiers had fled.

Repercussions for the missionaries, however, were not so good. The defeat angered the imperialist forces, and not until the autumn could missionaries safely venture into the countryside to preach. Attempts to live outside the international settlement were out of the question. Hudson Taylor would continue to live under obligation to a mission other than his own for some time to come.

SINGING FOR THEIR LIVES 10

Hudson Taylor was writing a heart-to-heart letter to Amelia when a letter from his mother arrived Reading it brought tears to his eyes. How he missed them all! He wasn't feeling well — his eyes were inflamed and he was getting bad headaches. If only his family would write more often; his father never wrote.

If only he had a wife to share his life. "I wish you would give me father's opinion of Miss Sissons ... Give her my love," he wrote to Amelia. Elizabeth Sissons was a friend both of Amelia and of Hudson's former fiancee Marianne, and had taught at his aunt's school. When Hudson visited Marianne, Elizabeth had told friends that she loved him. She had given him some drawings, and they had exchanged mementos.

She was interested in China, and he had some hopes that maybe she would one day become his wife. He treasured a lock of hair she had given him at his request. At the same time, he wrote home asking for news of Marianne. "She may get a richer and handsomer husband — but I question whether she will get one more devoted than I should have been."

✳ ✳ ✳ ✳ ✳

With the spring, the weather in Shanghai grew warmer and the countryside lost its greyness. "The view from this house is very beautiful," Taylor recorded, "garden, fields of corn, city walls, and showing over the nearer houses, masts and rigging of ships on the river." A few weeks later, anemones bathed the scene with colour.

In an extraordinary development, the Triad rebel chiefs announced that they were going to follow the example of the Taipings and become Christians. They exhorted everyone to worship God the heavenly Father. But the leading Triad chief was an opium smoker, and the rebel leaders were fond of taking any woman they fancied, threatening torture or death if she was not handed over to them. In reality they had no understanding of Taiping or Christian teaching. The Taipings were at the height of their success and there were rumours that Beijing was about to fall to them or, some said, had already fallen.

Years later, George Pearse admitted that the CES had no idea just how bad conditions in Shanghai were at that time, and that war-induced inflation was making Taylor's salary totally inadequate. Taylor sent them careful lists of all his items of expenditure, explaining how it would be impossible to live on anything less. "Our society must provide better for its missionaries," he told his parents. "This sort of thing will not do." He told the CES, "the total expense of my first year will be little under two hundred pounds, and even so I feel confident that there is no other missionary in Shanghai who will not have cost considerably more."

In June the heat and humidity became intense, with temperatures often in the low hundreds by day and rarely less than eighty at night. "We are all sweating like bakers," Taylor said as he continued to work for five hours a day at the Chinese language. From time to time, with John Burdon or Alexander Wylie or both, he loaded up with tracts, Bibles and medical bag and ventured into the countryside. The others would preach while Hudson Taylor examined the people, sometimes performing simple operations. He pursued his medical studies and experiments, read chemistry, and watched and assisted in operations. For all of this work and study, the Royal College of Surgeons in London gave him full credit in due course.

He was now easily able to go shopping on his own, make himself understood and begin to bargain with the shopkeepers. He watched Chinese printers at work and decided that the Chinese were an ingenious people, doing things in the most simple but at the same time the most effective way.

As the war dragged on, morale fell in the Chinese city. The people were beginning to lose faith in their idols and some gave them away. The missionaries were treated with respect and their chapels attracted packed congregations. Hudson Taylor decided to make a real effort to leave the comfort and safety of Dr Lockhart's home and look for housing in the no-man's-land between the rebel and imperialist forces. In this dangerous and battered district, property might be on offer at a price he could afford. At last he found a suitable house, at a rent of eight dollars a month.

The wooden house, near Shanghai's north gate, had twelve rooms with a multitude of doors and passages. Taylor decided to live upstairs and had all the rooms cleaned and whitewashed; he took one room for a bedroom and another for a dining room and study. He planned to use the downstairs rooms as a dispensary, schoolroom and chapel.

Having the house repaired, cleaned and painted tested his patience. He hired men to remove all the rubbish, but when he arrived he discovered them watching the bricklayers. He gave them plenty to do and went away for a while; when he returned an hour later he found one man writing, another smoking and the rest asleep! So he decided to bring his desk and chair to the house so that he would be on hand to supervise the work.

"Now this must be thoroughly washed," he said.

He listened for a while to the sound of splashing and

scrubbing, and then silence. He went to investigate.

"But you have only cleaned the outside!"

"Oh, you want within-and-without washing?"

"Yes, I do."

The splashing and scrubbing began again until the next diversion or misunderstanding brought work grinding to a halt.

At last, on August 30, he was able to move into his new home permanently. After breakfast on the first morning two jars of delicious chutney arrived from Dr Lockhart, and later in the day two bottles of wine. Burdon showed him how to check his cook's daily purchases and avoid being over-charged. He made up his mind to have family prayers in Chinese twice a day, with his servants and neighbours. Employing a cook and a water-carrier ensured that he was respected by the Chinese and taken seriously as a teacher.

He also employed a local Christian named Si to teach him the Shanghai dailect, and a Mr Dzien became his new Mandarin teacher. Si helped him at family prayers, reading portions of the Bible to the servants and the growing number of neighbours who began to join them. Taylor soon opened a day school, initially for ten boys and five girls. Si did the bulk of the teaching, while Taylor was still learning the language. After a few weeks, he took to questioning the children on what they had learned. Every day, too, patients came to his dispensary; he gradually learned the Chinese expressions he needed for questioning them and telling them how to take their medicines.

It was a dangerous area to live in. Every evening the planks forming the bridge to the international settlement were taken away, so at night Taylor kept a light burning, and had his swimming belt blown up so that at a moment's notice he could take to the water.

❈ ❈ ❈ ❈ ❈

In mid-September Taylor made a trip down the Huangpu river with Joseph Edkins and a young American Presbyterian,

John Quarterman. They travelled by boat, taking a large supply of Bibles and tracts which they handed out on the big junks from the far north and south of China. It was a good way for the gospel to reach inaccessible parts of the country.

The three men left for home in the evening aboard the same boat, anxiously wondering how they would pass the Chinese imperial fleet in safety. The imperial forces were well known to be somewhat random with their fire after dark, and might easily have mistaken them for Taiping or Triad rebels.

"Why don't we sing loudly as we pass them?" suggested Edkins. "Then they'll know we're foreigners."

"Good idea!" chorused Hudson Taylor and Quarterman.

As they approached, they began to sing lustily. Just as they were about to congratulate each other on their success, the boatmen shouted to them to begin again. What they thought was the fleet had not been — only now were they coming within range of the imperial ships' guns.

So they burst into song again, this time with a rendering of "The spacious firmament on high" to the tune *Creation*. Unfortunately, they finished the last verse just opposite the largest ship in the fleet.

"What next?" shouted Edkins. "There's not a moment to lose!"

Edkins began to sing something which Taylor had never heard in his life Quarterman struck up a magnificent American tune and Hudson Taylor raised a third tune as loudly as he could. The men on the warship were shouting loudly, and the crew of the westerners' boat shouted even louder. Taylor burst out laughing.

"Who goes there?" shouted a man from the imperial ship.

"*Bai gui*" (white devils), yelled the boatmen.

"*Da Ying-guo*" (Great English Nation), shouted Taylor and Edkins.

"*Hua qi guo*" (Flowery Flag Country or America), yelled Quarterman.

The government sailors let them pass, and Edkins and

Quarterman then began to scold the boatmen for calling them "white devils."

"We're most terribly sorry," said the boatmen. "We were so frightened we didn't really know what we were saying. We shall be most careful to refrain from such discourteous expressions in the future."

"YOUR WORDS ARE TRUTH" 11

At last, the CES increased Taylor's allowance to sixty pounds a quarter — but the committee's instructions to their Shanghai agents were ambiguous. Hudson Taylor sought clarification and suggested improvements in the arrangements, but of course his queries took months to reach London and the CES reply would be equally slow. Pioneer missionaries certainly needed the patience of Job, he reflected, as he discovered that his second Mandarin teacher, Dzien, was stealing from him and had to be dismissed.

In the autumn cholera struck Shanghai. John Burdon's wife was one victim. Burdon himself was unwell, and Hudson Taylor spent as much time as possible at their house to let Burdon get some sleep. Mrs Burdon died on September 26, and Hudson made all the arrangements for the funeral. In John's desolation and loneliness the two men took long walks together, Hudson trying to comfort his friend as best he could.

At the end of October, Burdon decided to give up his house in the LMS compound and Taylor was asked if he would like it. Cannon balls now fell close to his North Gate

Shanghai Hinterland

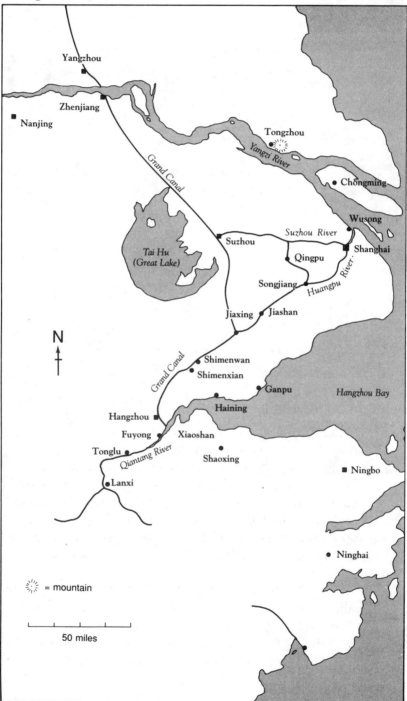

Yangzhou

Zhenjiang

Nanjing

Tongzhou

Yangzi River

Chóngming

Wusong

Suzhou River

Suzhou

Qingpu

Shanghai

Grand Canal

Songjiang

Huangbu River

Tai Hu
(Great Lake)

Jiaxing

Jiashan

N

Grand Canal

Shimenwan

Shimenxian

Ganpu

Hangzhou Bay

Haining

Hangzhou

Fuyong

Xiaoshan

Tonglu

Qiantang River

Shaoxing

Lanxi

Ningbo

Ninghai

= mountain

50 miles

home with frightening regularity, and with new CES missionary Dr William Parker and his family due almost any day, the offer of the Burdons' house was a marvellous development.

In November, he moved into his newly acquired property, but continued to use the North Gate house for evening meetings with the neighbours and staff who now attended regularly. He also breakfasted there and held his morning meetings and dispensary.

He still had no idea when the Parkers would arrive. Provided accommodation problems could be solved, it would be tremendous to have a colleague and companion. He knew the Parkers' ship, the *Swiftsure*, was at sea but had no idea where it was or even if it had been lost.

Fighting between the imperial forces and the rebels grew fiercer and conditions in the North Gate suburb more dangerous. Very reluctantly, Taylor was forced to close his school and move all his belongings back to the settlement.

At the end of November he was paying a return visit to his neighbours in the North Gate area when an urgent message came from Dr Lockhart: "Return to the settlement at once." Quickly he made his way to Lockhart's house and was delighted to find him lunching with none other than Dr William Parker. His wife and children were still aboard the *Swiftsure*.

William Parker was a canny Scot. Although sent out by the CES, he was supported entirely by its Glasgow auxiliary and felt independent of the main society. He was a man who quietly formed his own opinions, knew where he wanted to go and calculated the way to get there. When the CES had urged him to go to China at the height of optimism about the Taiping rebellion, he had refused, saying he wasn't ready.

Taylor and Parker had never met in England, and knew very little about each other. The differences were considerable: Parker was a Presbyterian, Taylor wouldn't accept any denominational label. Parker was a fully qualified doctor with an MD from Glasgow; Taylor had not yet completed his training. Their membership of the same society in an alien land and their common commitment to win the Chinese for Christ was to draw them together in a working relationship, but never into a close friendship.

Taylor had received no official notification of their departure, and no authorization from the CES to go to any expense to prepare for their arrival. Nor had he had heard anything from Parker himself. Consequently the rooms which he intended for them were still almost entirely unfurnished. Dr and Mrs Medhurst solved the immediate accommodation problem by opening their own house to the Parkers. But Hudson Taylor's apparent unpreparedness for their arrival put him in a bad light with the other missionaries, and the strain of this is evident in his sharp reaction to reading criticism of the LMS in *The Gleaner*. He wrote to the CES: "Irrational statements such as that ... 'we want the Bible and not Chinese classics', would be better avoided for the credit of the society and *Gleaner* ... You should not voluntarily irritate those who are more thoughtful for the shelter and support of your missionaries, than the society which sends them out seems to be ..."

No doubt with thoughts of Christmas firmly in mind, Hudson Taylor sent home a trunk full of gifts for family and friends. Treasures in the trunk included a spent cannon ball which had struck his house, fans, necklaces of carved peach-stone beads, chessmen, Buddhas, Chinese puzzles and padlocks, tea caddies and chopsticks, Chinese books and medicines, pots and pictures. Of course Elizabeth Sissons was not forgotten: for her (with love) a folding fan and carved ivory abacus, books and Scriptures in a new translation. His accompanying letter well illustrates his skill in writing and in parodying flowery Chinese phraseology, as well as the irrepressible sense of humour which never failed him even when times were at their blackest: "... you may enjoy the fruits of that exalted benevolence which, high as heaven and boundless as the ocean, has induced me to remember even you poor outside barbarians, who by the grace of heaven's Son, are permitted to eke out a miserable existence in some barren isle in the remotest corner of the earth."

✷ ✷ ✷ ✷ ✷

In the twelve years since the signing of the Treaty of Nanjing in 1842, foreigners had become a regular feature of life in the five treaty ports and missionary work was establishing itself. But still hardly anyone had dared to venture into China's vast interior. Joseph Edkins and Hudson Taylor now planned to travel a hundred miles inland to see how the mandarins would react, and whether the Chinese people themselves and any troops encountered would be hostile.

They hired a junk with a covered cabin and a crew of three men and a boy. The British and Foreign Bible Society had supplied three thousand Chinese New Testaments, and the two men loaded many of these on to the junk, together with drugs, medical instruments, food, clothes and bedding.

Early on a Saturday in December, 1854, they hoisted sail and the British flag. When wind and current made progress impossible they tied up and, with bags of Bibles and pamphlets on their shoulders, visited hamlets along the banks of the Huangpu river, preaching and looking for people who could read. When the tide turned in their favour they set off again, and woke on Sunday morning riding anchor near Songjiang, thirty miles south of Shanghai.

Songjiang was an old city and Taylor and Edkins made straight for one of the Buddhist temples, the normal place for public gatherings. The extraordinary appearance of two foreigners drew crowds of excited people who followed them into the temple. Edkins preached and Taylor handed out leaflets, as shaven-headed priests in yellow robes looked on.

As they moved on through the city, a crowd of men and boys began to jostle them. Edkins turned down a side street to what he thought was a ferry pier, but it turned out to be a private wharf. They were trapped. The crowd cheered with delight at the prospect of some sport at the expense of two barbarian devils. They closed in behind them, shutting the gates to prevent their escape. Several boats were passing along the narrow stream and Taylor and Edkins called out for a lift. To the great amusement of the crowd, none would stop to take the two men on board. Taylor finally managed to leap aboard a moving boat; he pulled it to the bank and Edkins joined him.

The boatmen were only too pleased to put the missionaries ashore on the opposite bank. Their own junk was waiting at a bridge further down the river and they now made their way to it. But the mob was soon after them and caught up just as they reached it. At that moment, Hudson Taylor saw Dzien, the language teacher he had dismissed. Dzien was one of the city's respected scholars and, apparently bearing no serious grudge against his former employer, calmed the mob and escorted the two men to safety.

Hudson Taylor and Edkins were not deterred, and after lunch toured the city with more literature.

Moving on next day towards the small town of Jiashan, they discovered how efficiently the authorities of neighbouring areas collaborated. A passenger who asked to travel with them turned out to be an officer of the Songjiang magistrate, who obviously had instructions to keep his eye on them, and was carrying a message about them for the Jiashan magistrate. The two men therefore decided to leave the boat and walk quickly ahead so that they could begin to distribute books before being intercepted. Their shadow followed them, in Taylor's words, "puffing away famously".

At Jiashan they met an imposing procession, which stopped as the two men walked towards it. Two men with gongs led the way followed by men wearing red cloth caps and carrying flags. Then came a man with a large umbrella, and four men bearing an enormous sedan chair.

Hudson Taylor and Edkins walked up to the chair and the chief magistrate himself emerged with great pomp.

"May I ask you please what your intentions are?"

They told him.

"I have read your literature. May I suggest that you would be ill-advised to go to the prefectural city of Jiaxing."

"We have every intention of going there."

"Then I will provide an escort."

Jiaxing was the oldest place they had yet visited, with a history going back to 2000 BC. They sailed to an island on a lake and tied up near the spot where a former Chinese emperor had built a beautiful summer residence. Even there the crowds followed in ferries, and the ferrymen did a thriving business as Hudson Taylor treated patients and Edkins preached. Several people including mandarins came to talk to them about books or pamphlets they had received earlier in the day. One of them, with a crystal globe in his cap denoting high rank, lowered his voice and said, "Your books are true. Your words are truth."

In two days, they were back in Shanghai. Nothing on their two-hundred-mile round trip suggested they had wandered too far from the treaty limits of thirty miles from Shanghai. They decided to attempt further journeys inland and Hudson Taylor bought an old boat complete with furniture for twelve pounds. The future looked promising.

TEA WITH THE VENERABLE CHEN 12

Hudson Taylor and the Parkers now shared the house formerly occupied by the Burdons in the LMS compound. Taylor and William Parker talked late into the nights about how they wanted the CES work in China to develop. The plan they eventually submitted to London was a bold one. They wanted a hospital; a school; permanent buildings for the headquarters of the CES in China; three or four village schools with dispensaries attached; and the employment of two colporteurs to assist Hudson Taylor on his travels. Now came the long wait while the submission travelled to England, the committee gasped and deliberated, and their response travelled back to China.

That wasn't the only letter which Hudson eagerly awaited. Bachelorhood didn't agree with him and he was pleased to learn that his mother's opinions of Elizabeth Sissons coincided with his own. He wrote two other letters to England — one to Elizabeth and one to her father. Would Elizabeth come to China, marry him and work with him? He begged her father not to oppose her coming. Chinese women needed the gospel and Hudson Taylor wanted a wife.

* * * * *

In January 1855, a deputation from the CES committee went to the Foreign Office in London to see Lord Clarendon, the Foreign Secretary. They argued that the Nanjing and other treaties of 1842-43 had secured rights in China for merchants but had not clearly set out equal rights for missionaries. The treaty between France and China of October 1844 won concessions which favoured French subjects and their Chinese converts; and the "most favoured nation" clause in a later supplement to the Treaty of Nanjing stated that all immunities and privileges granted to other nations should also apply to British subjects. The CES urged that full privileges for missionaries and their converts should be clearly set out in revised or new treaties between China and Britain. Other societies made similar approaches to the Foreign Office.

Lord Clarendon promised that the subject would be carefully considered. The noble earl was as good as his word: the Treaty of Tianjin (Tientsin) and the Peking Convention of 1858-60 specifically allowed foreigners freedom to travel freely to the interior of China and gave toleration for Christianity, so that those who taught or practised it should be entitled to the protection of the Chinese authorities.

But for the moment, in 1855, a strict interpretation of the Treaty of Nanjing made the mandarins responsible for arresting any foreigners who strayed away from the five treaty ports into the interior. Despite this, merchants and smugglers ventured inland to size up the potential for trade, and missionaries to spread the gospel. Taylor, Parker and the rest tested the mandarins and the people and often found them tolerant if not welcoming. But one barrier to acceptance of the gospel remained: the fact that England was associated in the Chinese mind with the trade in opium.

* * * * *

Shanghai was now completely surrounded by imperialist and French troops. The desperate Triad rebels debated their next moves. It was unlikely that they could hold out for as long as a month. The rest of China was also very unstable. Early Taiping successes had not been repeated, but their rebellion provided an opportunity for all sorts of men with other aims and grievances to take up arms. The Manchu dynasty was as weak as ever with little sign of reform. Meanwhile Taylor's views on the nature of the Taiping rebellion were changing. He told his mother, "I am afraid their success would do more harm than their destruction. Their errors are great and their impostures so numerous."

Taylor, Alexander Wylie and John Burdon obtained permits for a week of evangelism inland, and headed south-west. One Sunday morning in February, 1855, they climbed a hill to a ruined pagoda and sat there singing hymns and reading the Bible. Looking back they saw in the distance a great pall of smoke rising above Shanghai: realizing they had no hope, the Triad rebels had set fire to the city and fled.

The three men returned at once. The South Gate had been blown up; the city was a mass of smoking ruins. Hudson Taylor lost count of the number of headless corpses he saw. Familiar places were unrecognizable. Women and children were stripped naked before being executed, and then left lying where they fell. The citizens had taken vengeance against the rebels, their collaborators and their families. Shanghai was now at peace — but it was the peace of death.

✳ ✳ ✳ ✳ ✳

As the Chinese sought to rebuild, so too did the missionaries. Taylor and Parker bought a site for their hospital and headquarters buildings, although no word of approval had come from the CES. "Young societies tumble men into the field, careless whether they fall on their head or feet," Taylor was told. Management of the CES was appalling. Perhaps for this reason, W T Berger of Hackney donated ten pounds specifying that it was to be forwarded to Hudson Taylor and the Parkers for use at their discretion. The two men used the money to support a single Chinese boy in need. They saw this as the first step towards a permanent boarding school in Shanghai.

In April, 1855, Hudson Taylor and John Burdon hired two junks and sailed to the point where the Yangzi estuary narrows away from the sea. They instructed the boatmen to enter the nearest inlet so that they could climb the mountains on the northern shore.

The countryside was exceptionally fertile; a fresh breeze blew over fields of flowering peas and beans. They counted five peaks, the highest topped with a fine newly painted pagoda; nestling at the foot of the hill and running up its slope was an enormous Buddhist temple and monastery.

The mountainside was covered with rock interspersed with grass, flowers and trees. As they climbed, Hudson Taylor noticed the colours of the leaves "from the deep, gloomy cypress to the light, graceful willow, mingled with orange, tallow and other trees." At each turn of the path, new shrines and pavilions greeted them.

At the temple, a team of workmen were busy painting and gilding; thousands of colourfully dressed worshippers were celebrating a festival. Taylor and Burdon saw hundreds of brightly painted idols. The air was thick with the smell of incense. The streets echoed with the noise of people throwing coins into baskets, the sound of music, the buzz of conversation, the tramp, tramp, tramp, of hundreds of pairs of feet.

At last they reached the summit and climbed to the top of the pagoda. As Hudson Taylor looked at the breathtaking view, he thought: *Here, nature is offering that worship to her Creator which man is refusing.*

The air at the top was clear and through their telescope they could make out distant objects on the other four mountains. Below them, early spring crops grew richly green following recent rain. Orchards of peaches, apricots, plums, apples and cherries were surrounded by fields of wheat already in the ear. Streams lined with drooping willows wound their way through the fields. The farmhouses had neat willow fences, and cypress trees cast their shade over tiny cemeteries. Beyond lay the Yangzi, fifteen to twenty miles wide at this point, and on the distant bank the Sacred Mountains, crowned with their monasteries and temples. To the north-west lay the city of Tongzhou.

On their way down, a priest stopped Hudson Taylor, inviting him to kneel on a stool in front of his Buddha, burn incense and give some money. Taylor promptly stood on the stool, and spoke in Mandarin about the folly of idolatry. He told the crowds that God loved them. Burdon then preached in the Shanghai dialect, and both men judged that the priests understood the significance of what they were saying.

"Tell us if we say anything which is contrary to truth," said Burdon. No one took up the invitation.

They returned to their junks and decided that the following day they would visit Tongzhou, a city known as "Satan's seat", and notorious for its unruly mobs. The town was bound to give foreigners a rough reception.

The day dawned dull and wet. The two Chinese teachers with Taylor and Burdon tried hard to persuade them not to go.

"Stay here in one of the boats," the two missionaries said to the frightened teachers. "If we don't return tonight, try to find out what has happened to us, then return as quickly as possible to Shanghai in one of the boats with the news. Leave the other boat here, so that if we cannot return tonight we can follow you to Shanghai when we can."

Taylor and Burdon set off with their books and one servant for Tongzhou. They decided that walking was out of the question because of the state of the roads, and hired two "wheelbarrows" driven by coolies.

They hadn't gone far before their servant asked if he might return to the junks. He too had heard reports of the ugly mood of the Tongzhou mob. The two men agreed to his return. Then a respectable-looking man approached them.

"I beg you not to enter the town. If you do, you will find to your sorrow what Tongzhou people are like."

"We're very grateful for your kind advice, but we can't

take it as our minds are made up."

After this, Hudson Taylor's wheelbarrow driver announced that he would go no further. Taylor found another prepared to do the job for a fat fee.

As they approached the city, they told their wheelbarrow men where to wait for them and walked the rest of the way. They were amused to hear themselves described as *hei guizi* (black devils), due to the colour of their clothes.

As they approached the West Gate, a powerfully built man walked towards them. He was drunk, and grabbed John Burdon by the shoulders. Burdon tried unsuccessfully to shake him off. They were now surrounded by a dozen violent-looking men, who began to hurry them towards the city.

"We demand to be taken to the chief magistrate," shouted Taylor and Burdon.

"We know where to take you and what to do with your sort!" replied the men, who had mistaken them for Taiping rebels.

The large man who had seized Burdon now left him, and caught hold of Taylor instead. He knocked him to the ground several times, pulled his hair, gripped his collar until he nearly choked, and grabbed his arms and shoulders until they were black and blue.

John Burdon, undaunted, tried to give away a few books as they were walking along. This infuriated the big man who demanded that handcuffs be brought: fortunately none could be found, but Burdon decided to abandon his attempts at literature distribution for the time being.

Then a quarrel broke out among the two men's captors.

"Take them to the magistrate's office," cried the moderates.

"Kill them now!" shouted the extremists.

For a moment Taylor and Burdon were thrown together.

"Remember that the apostles rejoiced they were counted worthy to suffer in the cause of Christ," Taylor said.

He managed to get a hand into his pocket and produce his identity card, a sheet of red paper bearing his name. After this they treated him with more respect.

"The card must be given to the chief official in the area," Taylor demanded. "Lead us to his office at once."

They were led on until they came to a mandarin's residence. Totally exhausted, drenched with sweat, his tongue sticking to the roof of his mouth, Hudson Taylor slumped against a wall.

"Please bring us some chairs."

"You wait," replied their captors.

"Then please give us some tea to drink."

"You wait."

A large crowd gathered and John Burdon found the strength to preach to them.

Their identity cards and books were taken in to the mandarin. He kept them waiting for some time, and then referred the case to his superiors in another part of the town.

When Hudson Taylor and Burdon heard this they got tough.

"We shall not walk a single step further. Bring us chairs."

After some discussion, chairs were duly brought and the two men were carried off into crowded streets.

"They don't look like bad men," some of the onlookers said. Others, Hudson Taylor recorded, "seemed to pity us". At last they arrived at the chief mandarin's residence, or *yamen*. They were led through two sets of gates and saw a large tablet with the inscription *Min zhi fu mu* (the father and mother of the people).

Once more their cards were sent in. Then they were ushered into the presence of *Chen da laoye* (the Great Venerable Father Chen). He wore on his cap the opaque blue button of a lieutenant-governor. His attendants fell on their knees and bowed to the ground, signalling to the two Englishmen to do the same. Taylor and Burdon declined the invitation. Fortunately Chen had previously been prefect of Shanghai and knew the importance, under the terms of the treaties, of treating foreigners with courtesy. He came forward to meet them and spoke to them politely, then took them into an inner more private room, followed by a small team of officials.

As the best Mandarin speaker of the two foreigners, Hudson

Taylor did most of the talking. He explained the purpose of their visit, and asked to be allowed to give Chen copies of their literature. The mandarin thanked him and Taylor handed him a copy of the New Testament and some tracts. He explained a little about them, and briefly attempted to summarize Christian teaching. Chen listened politely and, taking their cue from the chief mandarin, so did his officials. Chen then ordered refreshments to be brought, which he ate with them.

After a long stay, Hudson Taylor and John Burdon asked permission to see something of the city, and to distribute the remainder of the books they had brought with them. The permission was given.

Then Taylor looked Chen in the eye and addressed him politely but firmly: "As we entered your city we were most disrespectfully treated. We don't wish to attach much importance to the fact, as we know that the men knew no better. However we have no wish to go through such an experience again. May we therefore ask you to give orders that we are not further molested."

"I will certainly do so," answered Chen.

He walked with them to the door of his *yamen*, and instructed several runners to go ahead of them and ensure that they were treated correctly. Taylor and Burdon quickly distributed their books. They were amused to see the use to which the runners put their long pigtails; when the streets were blocked by the crowd, they turned them into whips to clear a path! One of Chen's officials returned with them to the river where their junks were waiting. And so they left the city in a very different state and with a very different status than they had entered it.

WHEN IN CHINA ... 13

Hudson Taylor soon planned another journey inland, encouraged by the support of the British and Foreign Bible Society. They not only supplied him with as many Bibles as he could distribute but also agreed to meet the bulk of his travelling expenses. Once again the route would be by boat up the Yangzi estuary.

Taylor stopped at Zhangjiasi where, as far as he knew, no foreigner had ever been seen before. The people were astonish-ed to find that he could understand their language, and when he took out his watch to look at the time, a lively debate began.

"I've never before seen such spectacles!" said one.

"Nonsense," said another. "That's not spectacles. It's a telescope. Western men are famous for making such things."

"No," said a third. "What we have seen is a clock. It tells the hour by striking a bell. What the foreign devil is wearing on his nose is a telescope, not spectacles. How ignorant some of you are!"

But it was Taylor who found himself on the receiving end of wisdom when he visited the home of a former mandarin in Zhangjiasi. He was shown into the guest-hall and noticed these words over the entrance: *"Act morally and you will obtain happiness."*

When Hudson offered the old man some books the compliment was returned.

"I also have books to give you."

He gave Hudson Taylor ten beautifully bound volumes on a whole range of subjects from astronomy to meteorology, and geography to mathematics. A wealth of wisdom from the most intelligent nation on earth.

Then the old man leaned forward in his chair.

"I have one supreme idea which I am delighted to have the opportunity of disclosing to you. There are three great kingdoms in the world, England, Russia and China, but this discovery is as yet unknown in any of them. Confucius himself was ignorant of it as were all our great philosophers. It is a truth known to only one person — myself. And I am now eighty years of age. Let me tell you what it is."

Hudson Taylor waited, eager to know what the old man's insight was.

"The sun stands still," he said with great solemnity. "And the earth travels around it."

The younger man smiled as politely as he could.

"I believe you are right," he said, and a bond of friendship was established.

Next day, Hudson Taylor returned to the home of the old mandarin.

"Jesus is your sage," he told Taylor. "Confucius is ours."

"Jesus was not an Englishman," Hudson Taylor said, to the old man's astonishment. "He was born into a race known as the Jews. But he was no mere man, but perfect God and perfect man in one."

As proof of the divinity of Jesus, Hudson Taylor described the miracles and the resurrection. The old man listened.

"I am coming to Shanghai in a few weeks and will return your call. Meanwhile I will read your books. Make sure that you read mine!"

✳ ✳ ✳ ✳ ✳

Hudson Taylor spent his 23rd birthday, May 21, 1855, on Qingdaosha Island in the first great westward bend of the Yangzi. It was Mandarin speaking and he preached without difficulty. He was now eating his meals with chopsticks and beginning to wean himself of all sorts of European customs. His boatmen were delighted at his gradual adaptation to their ways.

"You should have your head shaved and change into Chinese clothes," they said.

"But you cannot change your eyes and nose," said one, thoughtfully.

Towards evening, he was taken to see a sick person and prescribed some medicine. The news spread, and before he could return to his boat a hundred or more people had gathered. Half of them had illnesses which he was able to relieve.

On this trip he bought a cat and two kittens. At home in Shanghai, rats had the impertinence to eat his candles and jump on to his bed while he was in it; now they would have three new enemies to reckon with, and Hudson would have company.

The local women reminded him of Amelia, and Hudson often thought of her and of Elizabeth. *But how can I ever marry if the society which is supposed to support me is so unreliable?* he reflected. *I wish that when I was in England I had been able to procure a medical diploma independent of the CES. If I had, I could easily have got a position offering £300 or more per annum without preventing my doing missionary work.*

✳ ✳ ✳ ✳ ✳

In June, 1855, Hudson Taylor, John Burdon and William Parker made a visit to Ningbo, another of the five treaty ports. It was Taylor's first visit to the important missionary centre which was to have a major influence on his future life. Ningbo was one of the finest cities in China, with beautiful temples and gardens, spacious mansions and in its centre a moon-lake. Its main streets were broad and clean. The river Yong, still navigable at Ningbo twelve miles from the coast, formed a natural moat from the city's north to south gate. A ring of hills formed an outer bastion to the basin in which the city was built. An inner circle of defence was provided by granite walls with a road running around the top, solid enough to withstand a British bombardment in 1841. Many of its citizens were well-educated and cultured. Members of the missionary community there were to become Hudson Taylor's firm friends.

First to arrive had been the American Baptists and Presbyterians, represented by two medical men, Dr Macgowan and Dr McCartee. An indomitable Englishwoman, Mary Ann Aldersey, had arrived in 1843 and started a school near the centre of the city. With her, as teachers, were Burella and Maria Dyer, the two attractive daughters of the late Rev Samuel Dyer. Dyer had gone out to Penang in 1827 and was later described as "one of the most efficient missionaries ever sent forth to the heathen world ... He was a man of God."

The Church Missionary Society was represented by William Russell, later to become the first bishop of North China, and R H Cobbold and Frederick Gough, both skilled Bible translators. The remarkable American Presbyterian, William Martin, had arrived in Ningbo in 1850 and was to spend 57 years in China.

Burdon, Parker and Hudson Taylor were made welcome by Dr Macgowan and next day toured the city with Frederick Gough. But after some days an urgent message arrived from Shanghai to say that John Burdon's son was seriously ill. For the second time in a year Hudson Taylor was able to support Burdon at a time of personal crisis. The two men hurried back to Shanghai without stopping by day or night; two or three weeks later, the child died.

* * * * *

The missionary and merchant community in Ningbo now formally invited William Parker to move there as community surgeon. Both Parker and Taylor had been impressed by the way in which the Ningbo missionaries worked together, though from a variety of different backgrounds and societies. In a letter home, Taylor wrote: "I do wish I had a pious companion, with whom there would be some sympathy of mind and feeling, with whom I could take counsel." Parker had never been such a companion; he was a man who knew his own mind and did his own thing, while cooperating pleasantly enough with others. The following month he accepted the invitation to go to Ningbo, while Taylor remained in Shanghai.

All through July and August Hudson Taylor carried on a daily service in the Shanghai dialect for between thirty and forty teachers, servants and others who wished to come. After a sudden death in the neighbourhood from cholera, he stressed the importance of immediate salvation from sin and its consequences.

"Jesus died for you and atoned for your guilt. Have any of you prayed to God to pardon your sins?"

He paused for a moment, hardly expecting an answer.

"I have," said Guihua, a young cook and brother of the pupil they had adopted with William Berger's gift.

"Though not without faults," Taylor wrote of Guihua later, "he is greatly changed for the better." Guihua became the first convert Hudson Taylor baptized in China. "If one soul is worth worlds," Hudson wrote to his mother, "am I not abundantly repaid, and are not you too?"

✳ ✳ ✳ ✳ ✳

Walter Medhurst had advised Taylor to wear Chinese clothes when travelling in the country; he himself had done so on a journey to the green tea district in 1845. Catholic priests regularly did so.

Since his Yangzi journey, Taylor's own thoughts had been moving in this direction. It wasn't that he wanted to disguise himself — he wanted to do the Chinese the courtesy of dressing, speaking and living like them all the time. But he knew that the merchant community would regard this as demeaning his "superior race" — and some in the missionary community would take a similar view.

On July 27, Hudson Taylor made his big decision. He would rent a house in the country, start regular medical and evangelistic work, dress in Chinese clothes and wear the *bianzi* (the pigtail or queue). If the experiment failed, he would rejoin the Parkers in Ningbo. Meanwhile he ordered a set of Chinese clothes.

In September, the CES response to Taylor and Parker's proposals for establishing elaborate headquarters in Shanghai arrived. By then the two men had guessed the answer. "Our professed intentions," wrote the CES, "are not to work in free ports, but in the *interior* ... We don't want to spend money in Shanghai." Despite the society's infuriating inefficiency, was it possible that they were actually right in maintaining this policy? Many people in Shanghai were convinced it was impossible. Taylor was about to put the matter to the test.

On an intensely hot day, at the CES residence in Shanghai, Parker sat down to write a letter of protest to George Pearse. Couldn't the society understand that however well intentioned their policy might be, settled residence in the interior was quite out of the question at this time and in this part of China? The dour Scotsman didn't pull any punches: "How can persons at the distance of many thousand miles judge as well as those on the spot as to the state of the country or what is the best course to pursue?"

While Parker's pen was flowing, putting his employers in their place, Hudson Taylor was downstairs making up medicines and concocting a dye to blacken his fair hair as soon as it had grown enough to plait into a *bianzi*. He took down a giant bottle of ammonia from a shelf, and because of the intense heat loosened the cork with special care. But not carefully enough: he had underestimated the pressure which had built up inside. The cork blew out of his hand; gas and liquid ammonia gushed out. Frantically, he pressed his hand down on the mouth of the bottle. Ammonia spurted into his eyes, nose, mouth, hair and over his clothes. The fumes began to suffocate him.

He ran for his life, hardly able to see, but somehow managing to stagger into the kitchen and grope his way towards a large jar of water. At once he plunged his head, shoulders and arms into the jar. This saved his life. Over and over again he repeated the operation, feeling as if he were on fire. As soon as he could speak he yelled to the servants.

"Fetch Dr Parker at once!" he shouted — first, in his confused state, in English, then, collecting himself a little, in Chinese.

But Parker had heard the commotion and was already on his way. When he arrived on the scene, Taylor's face was so swollen that Parker could hardly recognize him. He quickly applied castor oil to his eyes and face, then administered a very large dose of opium which Taylor found difficulty in swallowing. Next he put Taylor's feet in hot water and applied ice to his face; finally Parker and the anxious Chinese servants got the patient to bed and continued to apply ice to his body all the next day. Taylor lived to tell the remarkable tale.

BREAKING THE MAGIC RING 14

F ive days after the ammonia incident Hudson Taylor was back in action. But then he and the Parkers received notice to be out of their house as a family of new LMS missionaries was expected.

Parker was now ready to move to Ningbo and asked Taylor to go part of the way with him. This would be a good time, Taylor thought, to take on his Chinese appearance. He had a month's growth of hair to plait into a *bianzi*, and his Chinese clothes had arrived He would be able to test the reaction of both Chinese and Europeans to his radical step.

First he went to hire a boat; while making enquiries he heard of a vacant four-roomed house in the Chinese part of Shanghai, near the South Gate. Taylor advanced six months' rent and could move in in ten days.

Late that night, he called a Chinese barber. In addition he paid for the barber to travel with him and attend daily to the tricky business of managing a new *bianzi*.

Having your head shaved for the first time is a painful business, especially if your skin is already irritated by prickly heat, as Hudson's was. And the subsequent application of hair-dye for five or six hours didn't do much to soothe the irritation. To complete the agony the barber set to work combing out the remaining hair which Hudson had allowed to grow.

Next day, he put on his new clothes. First the socks, made of calico with thickened stitched soles and without elastic. Then the enormous *han ku* or breeches, two feet too wide for him round the waist, but he folded them in front of him and kept them in place with a strong girdle. The legs were huge like bloomers — he tucked them into his socks just below the knee with coloured garters. Then a cotton shirt, and on top of this, a heavy but colourful silk gown with wide sleeves reaching twelve or fifteen inches beyond the tips of his fingers — he had to get used to folding the sleeves back when using his hands. Last he put on the cloth shoes with upcurled toes, big enough to leave room for his bulky socks.

William Parker looked him up and down, his eyes coming to rest on the breeches. He smiled.

"You could store a fortnight's provisions in those!"

The two men walked to the jetty, the Scotsman his usual confident self, the Yorkshireman looking self-conscious and struggling to get used to the extraordinary socks and shoes. At the boat, the barber and servants were already on board with the crew, and Parker's luggage was stowed away. A messenger handed a note to Parker, which read; "For founding a hospital in Ningbo, from a friend, per Rev J Hobson. This is the money promised to assist in opening one in Shanghai." The friend was in fact Hobson himself, CMS chaplain to the British community in Shanghai, and the money amounted to a hundred dollars.

They cast off and headed south down a maze of canals. It took four days to reach Hangzhou Bay, stopping on the way at canalside towns to give away Bibles while William Parker attended to patients on the boat.

At Ganpu, where Hudson was to leave them, they engaged in tough negotiations with the captain of a sea-going junk who insisted on receiving payment in advance. Taylor knew the captain might take advantage of Parker's inexperience once he had parted with a substantial sum of money. So there was deadlock.

"How can I be sure of my money when you have reached the other side of the bay?" the captain asked.

"Because," replied Parker's servant, "we three are disciples of Jesus. Disciples of Jesus don't cheat or lie and defraud. What the doctor says he will do."

Parker and Taylor were thrilled. It was the first they knew of the servant's faith in Jesus. The deal was struck and Parker sailed away.

✳ ✳ ✳ ✳ ✳

Hudson Taylor was now left alone for the first time in Chinese clothing. At the first town on his journey back to Shanghai, he went ashore and walked through the town. No one guessed that a foreigner was near. Not until he began to distribute books and see patients did they realize: then his men were asked where he came from and the news soon spread. At first he was treated with less respect, but a little medical work soon put that right. Indeed women and children were more ready to come to him for treatment than before. He concluded that wearing Chinese clothes was going to be a great help for work in the interior.

Back in Shanghai, he wrote to his mother revealing something of his inner thoughts at this time. "I must wait on God and trust in Him and all will be well. I think I do love Him more than ever, and long increasingly to serve Him as He directs. I have had some wonderful seasons of soul-refreshing lately, unworthy of them as I have been." And to Amelia, "The love of God is indeed wonderful to contemplate ... Dr Parker is in Ningbo, but I am not alone. I have such a sense of the presence of God with me as I never before experienced, and such drawings to prayer and watchfulness as are very blessed and necessary."

But there were other thoughts on his mind as well. The mail brought letters from Elizabeth Sissons and her parents. Elizabeth's have not survived but he reported that they were "very satisfactory". But her father, like Mr Vaughan before him, began a tiresome saga of prevarication — "had I been labouring in or near England, he thinks there would have been little or no objection" — and so on, and so on. Poor Hudson Taylor. He poured out his love for Amelia: "I love you with a love so intense ... No words can tell the intense fervency of my love to you my sister. I love you more than life ...."

* * * * *

His new South Gate house was ready: two up and two down, with an outside kitchen across a little yard. The floor of beaten earth and rubble was damp; the walls were made of planks nailed to a rough framework with cracks through which the wind whistled; and the roof was of thin tiles with no interior lining. But it was in a good position, and the best he could afford on the CES's salary.

Every day now he wore his Chinese clothes and his *bianzi* was a respectable length. The reaction in Shanghai to the step he had taken was well described by George Woodcock in his book *The British in the Far East:* "A belief in the equality of all men before God, too literally acted upon, can produce patterns of behaviour which no imperial society can accept with equanimity. To the *taipans* and all the other people who believed that the white man's dignity rested in strict adherence to British dress and British habits, Hudson Taylor's action was deeply shocking. He had gone native. He had lost face. He had broken the magic ring of white solidarity. The word *traitor* was not too harsh to describe him." To pay this small compliment to the Chinese people by adopting their culture was too revolutionary, however often it had been done by others down the centuries.

Perhaps some compensation came in a letter from William

Berger enclosing two gifts. First, ten pounds, with a promise to repeat it every six months to provide entirely for the care and education of Hudson Taylor's adopted pupil. Second, forty pounds to be used as he thought best in his work. Berger's growing practice of sending funds direct to Taylor suggests that he, like many others, had lost confidence in the CES.

✳ ✳ ✳ ✳ ✳

Every day Hudson Taylor gave time to teaching three new Chinese Christians, Guihua, Si and Tsien; also he spent time preaching to as many as his house would hold, and going out and preaching on the streets of Shanghai. Si now shared some of the preaching with him, and Tsien joined Guihua in ask-ing for baptism. But Taylor only thought of Shanghai as a base: as soon as possible he wanted to put down roots in the interior.

In October, Taylor, Tsien and Guihua sailed to Chongming Island at the mouth of the Yangzi estuary. They managed to rent six rooms on two floors above a shop for an initial period of a month. It was ideal for the busy evangelistic and medical work which they now began. "I wish you could pop in and see how snug I am, in the midst of these people," Hudson told his mother.

On their return to Shanghai to restock with fresh provisions and medical stores, they found good news and bad. The good news was another gift from William Berger — this time of fifty pounds. The bad news was a writ from the chief magistrate of Chongming against Taylor and everyone associated in the rental of the property on the island. Later in the month, he was summoned to appear before the British consul, Rutherford Alcock, who wanted to investigate the incident.

"I'm afraid I have to prohibit you from living in Chongming. If you disobey, it will mean a $500 fine," Alcock told him.

Hudson Taylor knew that if he didn't give up the rental on the property he would get his Chinese friends into far worse trouble than he, as a foreigner, would suffer. He would have to do as he was told, but felt the consul had been unfair, since two French missionaries had built a Catholic chapel on the island. The "most favoured nation" clause in the supplement to the Treaty of Nanjing should have extended the same privilege to him.

"Come again, come again," his neighbours said as he reluctantly left his Chongming property after six weeks' occupation. "The sooner you return the better. We shall miss the good doctor and the heavenly words."

"It is hard indeed to leave them," Taylor wrote, "for I had hoped a good work would be done there. Much seed has been sown, and many books are in the hands of the people. It rests with the Lord to give the increase. May He watch over them."

Things grew worse. A letter arrived from Elizabeth Sissons. She said she was afraid she didn't love him He wrote her a long letter trying to prove that her fears were groundless because, he argued shakily, "if she did not love me she would not be tormented with the fear that she did not love me."

Later a letter came from his old friend, Miss Stacey of Tottenham. She reported that when the news of the consul's action reached England, some took the view that Hudson should have disregarded the threats, stayed in the rented property and, like the apostles, waited till they fetched him out. But dear Miss Stacey supported him: "You did right to act upon the words 'If they persecute you in one city, flee ye to another.'" And then some words of much needed comfort and encouragement from this stalwart of the Brook Street assembly: "God has given you, dear brother, a remarkable place amongst us at Tottenham in not being forgotten in our prayers: no name comes in so often ... Farewell dear brother in Jesus and fellow partaker in the hope of glory ... Rich the promises to him that *overcometh*!" He needed that!

In London, the CES took up the cudgels on Hudson Taylor's behalf. A spirited statement in *The Gleaner* said that the course the British consul had taken was "contrary to the law, as by residing in Chongming Mr Taylor was beyond the British jurisdiction; and if he chose to expose himself to the dangers, the consul had no authority to interfere ... any British subject is, according to the treaty, to be allowed to do the same (as the French priests do). The matter is so important ... it will be duly brought before the British government."

The CES may have been inefficient and unreliable but it was by no means without influence. On its General Committee sat the Earl of Cavan, two other members of Parliament, a baronet and a future bishop of Ripon: names likely to catch Lord Clarendon's eye when the society's complaint arrived at the Foreign Office.

THOSE HAPPY MONTHS 15

"He is one of those holy men one seldom meets with," Hudson wrote to his mother, "who do possess a single eye to God's glory ... The secret is easily learned and told — he is a man of prayer — added to which he possesses an iron frame, and a strong will, which would not be easily moved from its purpose."

Hudson Taylor had at last found a like-minded friend. The Rev William Burns had been the first British Presbyterian to go to China. Seventeen years older than Taylor, he was already a household name to many Christians. The Scottish revival of 1839 had occurred as a result of his powerful preaching and he was experienced in evangelism in Ireland and Canada, using his natural wit to advantage in open-air preaching.

Since arriving in China in 1847 he had learned the language of ordinary Chinese people, written popular hymns and translated *Pilgrim's Progress* into Chinese. After pioneering the English Presbyterian Mission in China, he had tried to develop a work among the Taipings at Nanjing but, like others, had failed.

When he arrived in Shanghai in 1855 and moved into a houseboat, his hair was already going grey. But he had lost none of his youthful evangelistic zeal. He and Hudson began to see a good deal of each other, Taylor visiting Burns' houseboat and Burns preaching in Hudson's South Gate home.

Hudson Taylor learned three things in particular from William Burns — seed-thoughts which were to prove fruitful in the subsequent organization of the China Inland Mission. The first was the way he often pointed out God's purposes in trial so that life assumed "a new aspect and value"; second were his views about evangelism as the great work of the church; and finally the importance of lay evangelists.

As their friendship grew, the two men began to serve the Lord together. In December, 1855, they set off in two boats, with a teacher named Song as well as servants and boatmen. Tsien and Guihua were to join them later.

Hudson had a comfortable boat with a good-sized cabin to himself. It had an oyster-shell window which gave light but prevented people peeping in, a little table on which he wrote and took his meals, and a locker above which his bed folded at night. He slept under two thick *pugai* — wadded Chinese quilts. Two spare seats were available for receiving visitors. Another cabin housed his servant and Song; a cabin for the boatmen held the books and was used for cooking.

At Nanxun, just south of the Great Lake, Burns heard that an immoral play was being performed outside the city among the rice-fields. A percussion and string band was playing when they arrived at what seemed to be a vast camp site with thousands of people. Seductively dressed prostitutes, brothels, and gambling booths surrounded the stage. "Satan's camp" and "Vanity Fair" was how Hudson later described the scene.

Burns didn't hesitate: he jumped on to the stage and stopped the play.

"What you are doing is very wrong. This sort of behaviour will land you in hell!" he told them.

He and Taylor were not roughly handled, but were simply

taken hold of and led away. Next day they returned and, without attempting to stop the play, preached from a ladder. The people crowded around them at first, but after a while they were again led away. Despite all the immoral behaviour, Taylor wrote, "I feel a great love for these dear people — Oh! that the Lord would reveal Himself to them — I should be sorry to have to leave them for any reason."

Respectable people in Nanxun asked them to try to stop the goings on at the play. The two men prayed, and decided that Taylor should make the second attempt. In his Chinese clothes he passed the gambling booths unrecognized and made his way through the crowd. Climbing on to the stage, he ordered the actors to stop and the people to listen. As he began to speak, he noticed Burns in the crowd; when men moved forward to stop Taylor, Burns told them to sit down.

"Pity your own souls. Don't be the bait to allure others to endless damnation," Taylor shouted to the actors.

He was dragged off the stage. When they let him go, he moved to a different part of the crowd. A prostitute got up from a stool she was sitting on and Hudson immediately stood on it.

"What you see all around you is wrong," he shouted. "Isn't what I am saying true?"

Many people agreed that it was, then Taylor was led away.

"Would you like your own daughters to be in the state of these women?" Burns shouted. He heard his question repeated in the crowd and there was some agreement that they wouldn't.

"Then why buy other men's daughters for immoral purposes?" he asked.

The two men returned unharmed to the canal and preached to groups of prostitutes in boats. "Thank you, Father," they prayed aboard Hudson's boat, "for keeping us from injury while doing such perilous service among the people."

The citizens of Nanxun generally approved of what the two men had done. One man followed them everywhere, and took them into a teashop.

"What you were preaching was the truth," he said. "I will pay for your tea."

Burns' lantern began to attract attention. It had glass on three sides and a mirror to reflect the light, common in England at the time but unusual in China. A group of men gathered round them at a table.

"Are all idols false?"

"What benefits arise from believing in Jesus?"

"If Jesus is in heaven, how can we worship Him here?"

"Take me to see God and Jesus," said one, "and then I can believe on them."

As he went about filling the cups, the tea-boy would put his kettle down on the table, fold his arms over it and listen intently to what was being said.

"Do you believe the barbarians' doctrine?" Taylor overheard one man whisper to his friend.

"Yes, I do," came the reply.

A reflective young man from Beijing who couldn't understand the Shanghai dialect said to Hudson Taylor, "I think we are very much alike. We are both far from home, alone without friends among people of a strange language. Do you feel lonely, or does God your Father prevent it?"

"There are times when I feel this," replied the reflective young man from Barnsley, "particularly when I am unwell. Often I long for my dear parents and relations. But then I kneel down and pray for them and God puts a little heaven into my heart. Although the desire for home is not removed, I am enabled to wait until I meet them again, wherever that may be."

"Oh! That's good."

"You should have your head shaved," some of the men said to William Burns, "and wear a Chinese cap like your friend. You would look much better!"

Burns took the hint and decided to follow the example of the young man. He wrote to his mother: "A young English missionary, Mr Taylor, of the Chinese Evangelization Society, has been my companion during these weeks — he in his boat, and I in mine — and we have experienced much mercy, and on some occasions considerable assistance in our work.

"Four weeks ago, on December 29, I put on the Chinese dress, which I am now wearing. Mr Taylor had made this change a few months before, and I ... concluded it was my duty to follow his example."

✳ ✳ ✳ ✳ ✳

Taylor was talking to some Chinese guests in the cabin of his boat, still moored at Nanxun.

"It's foolish to worship idols. We are indebted to the one, true and living God for every good gift."

"But surely you are too sweeping in your statement. There are good idols as well as many that are good for nothing."

"And which are the good idols?" Taylor asked.

"They are in there," he said, pointing in the direction of a nearby temple. "Many years ago two men came to our town with a boatload of rice to sell. It happened that it was a time of famine. There had been no harvest and the people were hungry. Seeing this, the strangers took the rice and gave it away among the poorest people. Then they couldn't face going home again."

"Why not?"

"Because they had given away the rice instead of selling it."

"It wasn't their own?"

"No, it belonged to their master. And as they were afraid to meet him again they both drowned themselves here in the river. The people said they were gods and made idols to represent them. They built that temple and the two men have been worshipped there ever since."

"Then your idols were only men. And men who stole their master's property and did wrong by taking their own lives." Taylor went on to tell his guests for the first time about the true and living God who gave His only Son that whoever believed in Him might not perish but have everlasting life.

Of this time in Nanxun, he wrote to his sister, "I wish I could tell you of an outpouring of the Holy Spirit on the place. The Lord has not been pleased to grant this. But there are many who have learned a good deal of the way of salvation, and some have bowed the knee with us in prayer, confessing that they believed in the truth of our teachings."

And looking back on the times he had spent with Burns, Hudson wrote: "Those happy months were an unspeakable joy and privilege to me. His love for the Word was delightful, and his holy reverential life and constant communings with God made fellowship with him satisfying to the deep cravings of my heart."

❊ ❊ ❊ ❊ ❊

Back in Shanghai, Hudson Taylor and William Burns attended the weekly prayer meeting at Dr Medhurst's one wintry night. A Christian captain was there, named Bowers, whose ship had just arrived in Shanghai from Shantou (Swatow). He asked the group to pray for Shantou and stressed the potential of the port as a centre for missionary work.

"Merchants and traders of all nationalities live there," he said, "so why can't missionaries? But the missionary who went there would have to be prepared to cast in his lot with some of the dregs of Chinese society."

Shantou lay eight hundred miles to the south of Shanghai. Although it was not a treaty port and therefore not legally open to foreign traders, foreign merchants in large numbers were occupying Double Island at the entrance to its harbour, unchallenged by the Chinese government or their own consuls. Moral standards among the merchants and people of Shantou were as low as could be found anywhere. The major commodities traded were opium and human beings; the coolie trade involved women and girls as well as thousands of men.

Taylor couldn't forget what Captain Bowers had said and felt that God was calling him to Shantou. But what a sacrifice it would involve! "I had never had such a spiritual father as Mr Burns; I had never known such holy happy fellowship; and I said to myself that it could not be God's will that we should separate."

Feeling most unhappy, he went some days later with Burns to the home of a Rev Reuben Lowrie. After they had eaten, they gathered round the piano while Mrs Lowrie sang a piece which Hudson Taylor had never heard before, entitled "The Missionary Call":

> And I will go!
> I may no longer doubt to give up friends, and idle hopes
> And every tie that binds my heart ...
> Henceforth, then, it matters not, if storm or sunshine
> be my earthly lot, bitter or sweet my cup;
> I only pray, God, make me holy,
> And my spirit nerve for the stern hour of strife.

Hudson was so moved by the song that he was scarcely able to speak when Mrs Lowrie finished. At the end of the evening, he asked Burns to go with him to his South Gate home, where he broke down in tears.

"God has been telling me to go to Shantou to work for Him. But I have been very rebellious, and unwilling to go. I couldn't bear the thought of parting from you and bringing our period of service together to an end."

Burns listened with a surprised expression on his face, though not of pain but of pleasure.

"I too have heard the Lord's call to Shantou. But my one regret has been the prospect of severing our happy fellowship."

Captain Bowers was thrilled with the news and offered them free passages. And so they left Shanghai on March 6, 1856, wondering what lay in store for them in Shantou.

SLEEPING ROUGH 16

The voyage south took six days. Shantou was in a beautiful part of China with high ranges of hills and small fertile valleys cultivated in terraces. There were tropical trees and shrubs, cacti, palms and banana plantations. But the behaviour of the people didn't match the beauty of the landscape.

"The people are poor, miserable and vicious," wrote Hudson Taylor. "They are wild, violent, and in a lower state of civilization than any Chinese I have yet seen."

Neither missionary could understand a word of the local dialect, Chaozhou. Burns could speak Cantonese, though, and they met a Cantonese man who happened to be a relative of the most senior official in Shantou. Delighted to be addressed in his own dialect, he used his influence to find them somewhere to live — a room above an incense shop, entered by a ladder through an open hole.

They divided the room into three smaller areas — two running east to west and one north to south. Taylor's bedroom was in the south, Burns took the north side, and they used the strip on the west as a study. They made the partitions out of sheets and a few boards. The landlord promised to install the luxury of a trapdoor. Their beds were a few deal boards, and their table the lid of a box supported on two bags of books.

"Surely, Mr Burns, you can find a better place to live in!" said Captain Bowers when he visited them.

Burns laughed. "I would rather live in the midst of the Chinese people than be at home surrounded by every comfort."

"How much do they charge you for the room?" Bowers asked.

"Ten dollars a month."

"Ten dollars a month!" cried Bowers, "Mr Burns, that wouldn't keep me in cigars!"

* * * * *

One night, Hudson Taylor heard piercing screams from two women not far away. He asked what it meant.

"It's almost certainly from women who have recently been taken into a nearby brothel. They have a horror of working as prostitutes and are being tortured into submission. It's very common here," he was told. The screams went on for about two hours. How Shantou needed Christ!

Towards the end of March they found an old farmer who could read well, which was unusual. They secured his services as a Chaozhou teacher for Hudson. Talking and reading with him for several hours every day, Taylor began to make rapid progress and by the middle of April was able to work on his own.

Once when he was out with his servant in the hills, they came to a village.

"Is there a teacher in the village, and a school?" he asked.

"No," said an old man, who had just left his work in the fields. "Last year we had one, but now we are too poor. We have scarcely any clothes to cover us." He pointed to the very scanty pair of trousers he was wearing.

It wasn't Hudson Taylor's style to pull any punches.

"If you wouldn't smoke opium, and spend so much money

worshipping dead relatives and the Queen of Heaven and other idols, you'd be far better off than you are at present. You hope to be preserved, enriched and prospered, but it's obvious that you are disappointed. Your idols have eyes, but do they see? They have ears, but can they hear when you pray? They have mouths, but do they speak? Can they preserve you from robbers, from quarrels, sickness, or disaster?"

By this time, about thirty or forty people plus children had gathered and were listening under the shade of a magnificent banyan tree.

"True! True!" some of them said. "Our idols are certainly not much use."

"Well, there is one you ought to worship," said Hudson Taylor. "That's the great Father who made heaven, earth, men and women, and all things. If you would turn to Him, He would forgive your sins, for Jesus' sake. Believing in this precious Saviour, you would find peace in life or death, and possess something truly satisfying."

❋ ❋ ❋ ❋ ❋

Taylor never forgot those long hot summer months in his room above the incense shop. The roof of the building got so hot that it was impossible to touch the tiles even from the inside. He rigged up a *punkah*, a sheet suspended from the rafters; the beauty of this device was that he could lie in his bed or sit in his chair, pull a string, and gently fan himself.

Letters from home did something to relieve his loneliness. One from his old friend Benjamin Broomhall brought the good news that he and Amelia were about to get engaged, and what's more they were thinking of coming to China as missionaries! He was delighted and wrote to congratulate them. If Benjamin did come to China, he advised him to get ordained or he would be handicapped among his fellow-missionaries. This was a major departure from the view he had expressed in his own application form, that he did not believe in the division of the church into clergy and laity. He now regarded the Church Missionary Society as one of the societies that he would be happy to serve. "The *mode* of worship is of small importance, the *power* is the main thing. And I believe there is more real liberty in the Church than in most of the dissenting bodies."

After further reflection, and in a later letter, he thought that perhaps the London Missionary Society would suit Benjamin better. The society's valuable mission libraries of Chinese books would suit the intellectually minded Benjamin, and he wouldn't be "annoyed by the whims of a bishop".

He was disappointed to learn that neither Amelia nor Elizabeth Sissons approved of his decision to dress like a Chinese. "If the Chinese costume seems so barbarous to you," he replied, "the English dress must be no less so to them ... Without it we couldn't be here for a single day."

There was another depressing letter from Elizabeth. Her mother was still opposed to their marriage, but she and her father were still in two minds about it. This was a very curious love affair indeed.

For six months the CES had sent him no money at all, apparently taking advantage of the knowledge that William Berger was occasionally sending personal gifts. In fact, after a boom period when donations had been generous, the society was now in debt. Taylor had privately hinted to George Pearse that he might resign. Berger sent him another fifty pounds.

Some years later Dr De la Porte, a Christian doctor who practised among the merchant community, recalled meeting Hudson Taylor during this period at Shantou. "I have seen him come home at the close of the day footsore and weary, his face covered with blisters from the heat of the sun. He would throw himself down to rest in a state of utter exhaustion, and then get up again in a few hours to face the toil and hardship of another day. It was clear to me that he enjoyed the highest respect from the Chinese, and was doing a great deal of good among them. His influence was like that of a fragrant flower, spreading the sweetness of true Christianity all about him."

✳ ✳ ✳ ✳ ✳

✳ ✳ ✳ ✳ ✳

The local mandarin fell ill, and his own doctors could do nothing. He had heard from friends that they had received help from a young Englishman, and so sent for him. Hudson Taylor recorded, "God blessed the medicines given and, grateful for relief, the mandarin advised our renting a house for a hospital and dispensary. Having his permission we were able to secure the entire premises, one room of which we had previously occupied."

Taylor had left his main stock of medicine and surgical instruments in Shanghai. Another Christian captain offered him a free passage to fetch them, and on July 5 he boarded the *Wild Flower*. Burns came to see him off; both men had high hopes for the future.

The voyage north in the *Wild Flower* lasted ten days and did Hudson a power of good after the debilitating intense heat. He went straight to the LMS premises, totally unprepared for the shock which greeted him. Fire had destroyed the warehouse and its contents, thirty thousand New Testaments and most of his own medical equipment apart from a few surgical instruments! If he was to return to Shantou with the medical supplies he needed, he would have to go to Ningbo to see what Dr Parker could do to help.

And that was not the only shock. A letter from Elizabeth Sissons finally rejected his proposal of marriage.

✳ ✳ ✳ ✳ ✳

Hudson set off for Ningbo intending to take the normal route via the Grand Canal and Hangzhou. He took with him his two watches, and, in a large bamboo box, his camera and photographs, his insect collection, a few surgical instruments, a concertina, some expensive books on the Chinese language, and the indispensable *pugai*.

After fourteen days travelling, he and his servant, Youxi, reached a large town called Shimenwan where, as the Grand Canal had dried up, he hired coolies to carry his luggage as far as Haining, eighteen miles away. But by the time they had gone six miles he discovered that the coolies were heavy opium smokers with no strength, and Youxi announced that he wanted to visit a friend who lived in the town of Shimenxian. Hudson objected to this, and leaving Youxi to hire more coolies he walked on ahead. He waited for them in Changan but they failed to join him. After spending an uncomfortable night in a dirty inn, he walked the following day to Haining to follow up a report that his luggage had been carried there. But at Haining there was no trace of coolies or luggage; and finding no accommodation he slept in the open air on the steps of a temple, narrowly escaping being robbed.

Next day there was nothing for it but to retrace his steps. Arriving at Changan at noon, he made fruitless enquiries. After a meal in a teashop he washed thoroughly and bathed his sore feet, and then slept until four in the afternoon.

Feeling much better, he set off for Shimenxian where two days previously he had parted from Youxi and the coolies. On the way he began to reflect on the goodness of God, and remembered that he had forgotten to pray that God would find him lodgings the previous night. He felt guilty that he had been so much concerned about the few things which were missing, and so little concerned about all the unevangelized people around him.

"Dear Father," he prayed as he walked along, "I come to you as a sinner and plead the blood of Jesus ..."

"Oh, the love of Jesus, how great I felt it to be!" he recorded. "I prayed for myself, for friends in England, and for my brethren in the work. Sweet tears of mingled joy and sorrow flowed freely, the road was almost forgotten, and before I was aware of it I had reached my destination."

Outside the South Gate of Shimenxian he drank a cup of tea, made yet more unsuccessful enquiries about his belongings and managed to get in a little preaching. About to set off for the six-mile walk to Shimenwan, he met one of the original coolies and learned that Youxi and his luggage were last seen heading in the direction of Hangzhou. The only thing to do was to try to get back to Shanghai by boat.

Hudson Taylor spent the night on a passenger boat stranded in the dry bed of the river. At sunrise he committed the day to God.

"If it is for my good and your glory, I know that my things will be restored to me. If not, all will be for the best."

At the boat office in Shimenwan he found to his dismay that no passenger boats would leave that day or perhaps even the next, due to the shallow state of the river.

"What about letter-boats?"

"They have already left."

At this point Hudson saw a letter-boat in the distance at a bend in the canal. It must have been unexpectedly detained. He ran for about a mile and caught it up.

"Are you going to Jiaxing?" he shouted breathlessly.

"No."

"Are you going in that direction?"

"No."

"Will you give me a free passage as far as you are going in that direction?"

"No."

Hudson Taylor fainted and lay unconscious on the grass.

✳ ✳ ✳ ✳ ✳

"He speaks pure Shanghai dialect," Hudson Taylor heard someone saying as he recovered consciousness.

The voice was coming from a large passenger boat on the other side of the canal. A group of men there had heard his shouts before he fainted, and he knew by their accents that they too were from Shanghai. They sent their small boat to fetch him and he went on board.

The boat was on its way south away from Shanghai, though temporarily stranded in shallow water. The crew gave him tea and food, and hot water to bathe his blistered feet. On hearing his story they felt sorry for him, and hailed every passing northbound boat to see if it was going to Shanghai. None was.

"I haven't enough strength to walk to Jiaxing," Taylor told them, "nor enough money to get there by letter-boat. I don't know how the God I serve will help me, but I've no doubt that He will. And when He does, that will show you that the religion which I and the other missionaries in Shanghai preach is true! My job now is to serve Him where I am."

He then went ashore with the captain, intending to preach in the nearby temple. As they walked towards the town the captain said:

"Look, there's a letter-boat. Maybe it's going to Shanghai."

"Maybe," Taylor replied, "but, as I said, I don't have enough money to pay the fare."

Nevertheless, the captain hailed the boat. It was heading for a town about nine miles from Shanghai.

"This gentleman is a foreigner who lives in Shanghai," the captain shouted. "He has been robbed and hasn't enough money left to get him home. If you will take him as far as you are going and then engage a sedan chair to carry him the rest of the way, he will pay you in Shanghai. You see my boat is lying over there in shallow water and cannot get away. I will stand surety: if this gentleman doesn't pay when you get to Shanghai, I will do so on your return."

"We agree to your terms," the crew of the letter-boat shouted back, and Hudson Taylor was taken aboard.

Letter-boats were long and narrowly built, surprisingly fast, and operated by two men sculling with their hands and feet. Accommodation was limited: you actually had to lie down all the time the boat was in motion because a clumsy movement could tip the whole thing over. But Taylor didn't mind: he was glad of the chance of rest and quiet, and reached Shanghai safely.

DRAMA ON THE CANAL 17

What was Hudson Taylor to do about Youxi who had apparently made off with his belongings? Wondering if Youxi was in detention in a mandarin's *yamen*, Taylor sent a messenger to Shimenxian to make enquiries. It turned out to be a case of deliberate theft.

He found it hardest to be without the little things — Amelia's photograph; his concertina; his hymnbook; a Bible his mother had given him; to say nothing of all his maps, much-loved hobbies and clothing.

It wouldn't have been difficult to go to law to recover the property and he was strongly urged to do this. But the more he thought and prayed, the more he shrank from it. He had often prayed for Youxi's conversion: to hand him over to the authorities, who would probably have thrown him into prison, would not have been in keeping with the teaching of Christ.

He decided to send him what he described as "a plain, faithful letter". He told Youxi that he knew what he had done; that at first he had considered handing the matter over to the *yamen*, but remembering Christ's command to return good for evil he had not done so. "You are the real loser," he wrote. "I freely forgive you and urge you to flee from the wrath to come." He added that while Youxi was unlikely to give up the possessions which were of use to a Chinese person, the foreign books and papers could be of no use to him, and he ought to send these back.

Excerpts from Taylor's letters home describing the incident, and the course he had decided to take, were published in *The Gleaner*. George Muller of Bristol read them. Muller was firmly convinced that Christ's radical demands should be taken seriously: that the Sermon on the Mount was irksome if followed half-heartedly but thrilling if put into practice by the totally committed disciple. Here was a young man who appeared to believe this and had acted upon it. Muller prayed for him and wrote a warm letter enclosing forty pounds, which he understood to be the amount of the loss Hudson Taylor had sustained. It was the first of many gifts.

❇ ❇ ❇ ❇ ❇

Hudson Taylor set off for Ningbo again to seek help from Dr Parker in replacing the medicines lost in the fire; this time the journey was safe and uneventful. On this visit he met John and Mary Jones for the first time. John Jones now represented the CES in Ningbo. The couple had sailed for China agreeing to accept whatever the CES could send them but holding the society under no obligation, trusting in God to supply their needs whether through or apart from the CES. Hudson Taylor and John Jones hit it off well and quickly became close friends on trips they took together in the country around Ningbo.

For nearly two months Taylor joined in the work of Parker's Ningbo clinic. Every week the Parkers dined with Miss Aldersey and the Dyer girls who worked with this remarkable lady. Some of the Chinese citizens of Ningbo believed that just as England was ruled by a woman, Queen Victoria, so Miss Aldersey had been delegated to be the head of the

British community in China; they said that the British consul took his instructions from her!

When the vibrations of an earthquake alarmed the people, they put it down to Miss Aldersey's magic powers, alleging that they had seen her climb the city wall before dawn and open a bottle in which she kept strong spirits which shook the pillars of the earth. It was actually true that at all seasons of the year Miss Aldersey would walk on the city wall at 5 o'clock in the morning, in the winter preceded by a man carrying a lantern. A bottle she carried did really contain strong spirits — spirits of hartshorn which she used regularly to relieve headaches and as "an antidote for ill odours". As far as we know, however, it was not capable of producing earthquakes.

The school which she ran with the help of Burella and Maria Dyer, the only unmarried young ladies in the Ningbo missionary circle, was the first girls' school to be established by Protestant missionaries in China. Burella and Maria, who had spoken Chinese from childhood, had become expert in the Ningbo dialect and added a little brightness and glamour to the foreign community in Ningbo. There is no record of Hudson Taylor's first impressions of the two girls, but we know that nineteen-year-old Maria was so attracted to him that she "took the matter at once to God."

* * * * *

On September 15, 1856, the post brought twenty pounds from William Berger, and Hudson Taylor was able to buy his replacement drugs and instruments from Parker. Three days later another forty pounds arrived from Berger, and in thankfulness to God Taylor gave fifty dollars to Parker's hospital building fund.

Later in the month, Taylor left Ningbo for Shanghai with John Jones and his son Tom, who was recovering from an attack of dysentery. After Hudson left, Maria Dyer was startled to find how much she missed him being around.

Back in Shanghai, the post brought yet another gift from William Berger. Berger had sent three hundred pounds in a year, whereas the CES had sent no more than a fraction of what they had promised.

Just as he was about to sail south to Shantou again, a letter arrived from William Burns not from Shantou but from Guangzhou. Burns said that he and two Chinese colleagues had been arrested and imprisoned. They had been held in custody for six weeks and then handed over to the consul in Guangzhou. In this uncertain situation it would be unwise for Hudson Taylor to return to Shantou for the time being. Many years later Taylor wrote: "Thus hindered, I could not but realize the hand of God in closing the door I had so much desired to enter."

In fact, there were good reasons for Hudson Taylor to make a more permanent move to Ningbo. That was where his CES colleagues were — William Parker, now well-established and preparing to build his hospital, and John Jones, becoming more familiar with the Ningbo dialect and in need of a more experienced companion evangelist. Could another factor have been the presence in Ningbo of Burella and Maria Dyer? Whatever the reasons, conscious or subconscious, Hudson Taylor, Jones and his son decided to return together to Ningbo.

They set off by junk with a young Chinese named Peter, not yet a Christian, whom William Parker had met in England and employed as a servant and teacher on his voyage to China. (It was in England that he had acquired the name by which the missionaries knew him.) Peter had written to Parker asking if he could come to Ningbo and work for him, and Parker had accepted.

One morning, Taylor was in his cabin preparing tracts and books for distribution. Peter was pottering about the junk. He had been warned several times about his silly habit of clambering along the narrow ledge past the cabin when moving from one end of the boat to the other.

From his cabin, Hudson Taylor heard a cry and a splash.

He rushed on to the deck. Peter had fallen head first into the canal. The water was still low; Peter was held fast in deep sludge somewhere under the water. The boatmen were looking helpless. A strong wind was carrying the junk quickly forward in spite of a heavy current running in the opposite direction. The bank was featureless, with no landmark to indicate how far behind they had left Peter.

Taylor quickly lowered the sail and then leaped into the water, thrashing about in a frantic search. Then he saw a fishing-boat with a drag-net and hooks.

"Come!" he shouted "Come and drag this spot. A man is drowning!"

"It is not convenient," the fishermen replied.

"Don't talk of *convenience*. A man is drowning, I tell you!"

"We are busy fishing and cannot come."

"Never mind your fishing. I'll give you more money than many a day's fishing will bring. Just come. Come at once!"

"How much money will you give us?"

Hudson Taylor couldn't believe his ears.

"We can't discuss that now! Come quickly, or it will be too late. I'll give you five dollars."

"We won't drag for that. Give us twenty dollars, and we will drag."

"I haven't got that much. Come quickly and I will give you all I have!"

"How much will that be?"

"I don't know exactly. About fourteen dollars, I think."

At last, but even then slowly, the fishermen brought their boat over and let down the net. In less than a minute they brought up Peter's body. Although Peter had been under the water all the time these negotiations had been going on, Taylor tried artificial respiration — to a chorus of complaints from the fishermen that they weren't being paid immediately.

His lengthy efforts to revive the man failed. Peter was dead.

Taylor was well aware of Chinese attitudes to death and

their fear of departed spirits, and he knew that a difficult time lay ahead. He set off, back towards Shanghai. The weather was against them. The corpse became more and more offensive. In Shanghai he searched for Peter's relatives. His widowed mother refused to receive her son's body, but tried to get as much money out of Hudson Taylor as possible. Many hours later, after much yelling, howling and haggling, they took the body. Taylor gave them five dollars to pay for the funeral.

Hudson Taylor wrote later that to him, "this incident was profoundly sad and full of significance, suggesting a far more mournful reality. Were not these fishermen actually guilty of this poor Chinaman's death, in that they had the means of saving him at hand, if they would but have used them? Assuredly they were guilty. And yet, let us pause ere we pronounce judgment against them, lest a greater than Nathan answer, *Thou art the man.* Is it so hardhearted, so wicked a thing to neglect to save the body? Of how much sorer punishment, then, is he worthy who leaves the soul to perish, and Cain-like says, 'Am I my brother's keeper?' The Lord Jesus commands, commands *me*, commands *you*, into all the world, to preach the gospel to every creature."

A PLOT FOILED BY PRAYER 18

E nter Ningbo from the Salt Gate in the east, follow the main streets past the ancient pagoda, cross the canal by a rough stone bridge, enter a narrow street which leads to the Sun and Moon lakes, and pass a large Confucian temple. Then, Hudson Taylor told his friends at home, "go straight on down the stone-flagged main street for half a mile. If you see a man beating a large bronze bell, go up and you will hear him inviting everyone in to hear the gospel. Cross a well-flagged courtyard into the large guest hall and there you will see us about to start."

A few weeks after arriving back in Ningbo with John Jones and his son Tom, Taylor moved into an attic above a schoolroom in Bridge Street used by William Parker. When the children left, the hall was used as a chapel.

Although the winter was a fairly mild one, Taylor never forgot tracing his initials in the snow which had collected on his bedclothes overnight. "The tiling of an unceiled Chinese house may keep off the rain — if it happens to be sound — but it does not afford so good protection against snow, which will beat up through crannies and crevices, and find its way within." The barn-like attic was divided into four or five smaller rooms by wooden walls which Taylor whitewashed, papering over the cracks where he could.

Parker now had a well-paid contract for being on call as a doctor to merchant vessels, and had begun to lay the foundations of a new hospital on a riverbank site outside the Salt Gate. His reputation in the city and countryside was bringing him scores of patients.

While Hudson Taylor helped Parker in his medical work, John Jones took to joining Frederick Gough of the CMS, preaching in the open-fronted tea-shops. Mary Gough took Mary Jones visiting Chinese women in their homes. Often Taylor would join Gough and Jones, picking up more of the Ningbo dialect as he worked.

The Joneses rented a house from the American Presbyterians in the heart of the city near the East Gate. A few streets to the west was Miss Aldersey's home and school.

Miss Aldersey invited John and Mary Jones and Hudson Taylor to dinner. She rather disapproved of the eccentric young man who, as far as she knew, was connected with no recognized Christian denomination and, horror of horrors, actually dressed as a Chinese. To crown it all, he had grown his hair long and plaited it into a fully fledged *bianzi*. What she didn't know was that the younger of the two Dyer girls was fascinated by this absurd young man and was praying that he would notice her.

Hudson's friend, the widowed John Burdon, was getting on famously with Burella and was shortly to become engaged to her; forty-year-old Joseph Edkins had proposed to Maria, but this had only reduced her to giggles and Edkins had been too bashful to persevere. Some thought that John Burdon's success might encourage Edkins to try again.

After the dinner at Miss Aldersey's, Hudson Taylor described Maria as "a good looking girl, despite the slightest cast of the eye". He noted that she spoke the second best Chinese of all the Europeans in Ningbo (the top award was probably taken by a young civil servant, Robert Hart); that she had been dedicated to mission work by her father on his deathbed; and that he had been told she was very earnest and zealous. Others described her as vivacious, witty and intelligent, with fine light-brown hair and a slim figure. The Dyers were a gifted family — Maria's father had studied law at Trinity Hall, Cambridge, before going as a missionary to Penang in 1827.

One day, Maria was at the Joneses' house when Taylor dropped in, fresh from whitewashing and papering his Bridge Street home.

"You'll soon be ready for a visitor!" said Mary Jones with a twinkle in her eye.

Maria looked as grave as an embarrassed nineteen year old could and a Victorian young lady should.

"Yes," said Taylor solemnly, "I hope I shall have a good many visitors."

Mary Jones, the matchmaker, was obviously going to have a lot of work to do!

Taylor's spirits were low. Although most of the Shanghai missionaries were warm in their dealings with him, he had discovered that being neither ordained nor a fully qualified doctor did make a difference. Ordained ministers were invited to preach at English and Chinese church services, but so far he had been invited only rarely, although he was now fluent in a number of Chinese dialects. Miss Aldersey's hostility towards him was plain to see. He toyed with the idea of going home to England, qualifying as a doctor and marrying before coming back to China. He even thought of giving up as a missionary altogether. After all, Elizabeth Sissons' father had said that he would withdraw his objection to their marriage if Hudson lived in England.

For a time over Christmas he forgot his troubles. The Goughs threw a party for the fifteen English missionaries in Ningbo, with beef and plum pudding — and a special treat. Frederick Gough had a first-rate piano and he invited Burella and Maria to entertain his guests. Hudson Taylor mightily enjoyed the duets they played. But, oh, how it reminded him of that stolen concertina!

"The American missionaries here all have harmoniums ... very sweet instruments," he wrote to his mother next day. He asked her to find out whether portable harmoniums were made in England. If one could be had for twelve to fifteen pounds would they please buy one and send it to him? It must have five or more octaves so that he could play duets with the wife he hoped one day to marry.

That same day, Mary Jones took Maria Dyer with her visiting Chinese homes. On their return Taylor took tea with them, and afterwards escorted Maria home: she was delighted.

When Hudson Taylor told the Joneses, who by now were like brother and sister to him, that he was thinking of returning to England, they were amazed.

"I know perfectly well what would make you settled," said Mary Jones. "A nice wife! I'm going to use what influence I have in the direction of Maria Dyer."

"That's all very well," replied Hudson, "but the CES doesn't send enough money to keep me *alone* in European style."

"You are supplied by the Lord with what you now need," said Mary Jones sharply. "If your need were greater, so would be your supply."

So Taylor began to pray that God would guide him about Maria.

Meanwhile, he and Jones heard that the CES was in debt and they were drawing borrowed money. It was a blow to them both. "To me," wrote Hudson, "it seemed that the teaching of God's Word was unmistakably clear: 'Owe no man anything'. To borrow money implied, to my mind, a contradiction of Scripture — a confession that God had withheld some good thing, and a determination to get for ourselves what He had not given."

❈ ❈ ❈ ❈ ❈

After Burella and Maria's mother had died in 1846 and the two girls had left Penang, their stepfather, J G Bausum, had married again. Then, a few years later, he himself had died, and his widow had continued his work until Miss Aldersey, approaching sixty, had invited her to Ningbo in preparation for taking over the school from her. Mrs Bausum had arrived in October 1856.

Maria Dyer found that Mrs Bausum was motherly and wise. In January, 1857, Maria told her about Joseph Edkins' proposal. Mrs Bausum was forthright.

"A lady ought not to expose a gentleman to ridicule because he loves her and the love is not returned, or to despise him for thinking highly of her. You should neither refuse him nor accept him hastily or without prayer."

"I cannot think of accepting him," replied Maria. She explained her feelings towards Hudson Taylor.

"I haven't seen anything which would lead me to think that Mr Taylor is interested in you," said Mrs Bausum.

Maria was much in demand. The new interpreter to the British consulate in Ningbo was an eligible young man named Robert Hart. Hart found time in his busy life to meet and be charmed by the young English lady who could speak such excellent Chinese. The day came, early in 1857, when he proposed to her. Maria turned him down. Her thoughts were in another direction.

✳ ✳ ✳ ✳ ✳

Meanwhile, there was the very real threat of war between England and China. Hostilities had been sparked off by a silly incident in October, 1856. Chinese ships registered in Hong Kong were entitled to fly the British flag, which gave them immunity from their own customs officers and anti-opium mandarins. On October 8, a Chinese ship, *The Arrow*, busy smuggling opium, was boarded by Chinese officials in Guangzhou waters while flying the British flag; they hauled down the flag and carried off the crew.

The British consul demanded of the viceroy of Guangzhou that the men be released and the flag rehoisted. The viceroy refused. The Governor of Hong Kong, Sir John Bowring, then announced that unless within 24 hours the crew were released, an apology issued and an undertaking given that such an action would never be repeated, Guangzhou would be bombarded. No apology was issued and the bombardment went ahead.

Actually, the British had made an error. *The Arrow* had no right to hoist the British flag because the ship's licence had been issued before such licensing was legal; the licence had in any case expired some days before the incident. Chinese officials had acted properly and the viceroy's refusal to apologize had been justified.

But the whole affair was turning into a matter of honour. The British public was eager to see a British ambassador installed in Beijing and China opened up to foreigners.

A British naval force under Admiral Seymour attacked Guangzhou and took possession of the *yamen*. Tension increased and the Chinese plotted retaliation against foreigners. The Guangzhou viceroy vowed vengeance for the desecration of his palace and the bombardment of his city. He put a price on every barbarian head, and foreigners were in mortal danger wherever the news reached Cantonese anywhere in China.

Traditionally, relations between the people of Ningbo and foreigners had been good. But many of the mandarins, who came from other parts of China, didn't have much time for foreigners; and many Cantonese worked in the Ningbo area. Although the missionaries (including Hudson Taylor) denounced the British action, they were seen as tarred with the same brush as merchants and military men.

Early in January 1857 the Cantonese in Ningbo hatched a plot to destroy all foreigners in the city and neighbourhood. Everyone knew that many Europeans — consuls, merchants and missionaries — attended the meeting for worship held every Sunday evening in CMS missionary William Russell's house.

The plan was to surround the house at a prearranged time, and massacre the barbarians within. Any foreigners who were not in the habit of attending would be attacked at the same time. Permission for the operation was obtained from the *daotai*, the chief magistrate of the city.

Mercifully, however, one of those involved in the plot grew anxious for the safety of his friend who worked as a servant for one of the missionaries. He warned him of the planned attack and urged him to resign his position for his own safety. This servant at once told his employer who quickly told the other missionaries.

The missionaries promptly arranged a prayer meeting to seek guidance and protection. As they prayed, a junior mandarin went to see the *daotai*.

"With respect," said the young mandarin, "I must tell you that you are foolish to allow this attempt on the lives of the foreigners in Ningbo. If successful, it will cause foreigners in other parts of China to come with armed forces to avenge the death of their countrymen, and raze the city to the ground."

"When they come for that purpose," replied the *daotai*, "I shall deny all knowledge of or complicity in the plot. This will direct their vengeance against the Cantonese, who will in their turn be destroyed. Thus we shall get rid of both Cantonese and foreigners by one stroke of policy!"

"Such attempts to evade the issue and deny responsibility will be useless," insisted the mandarin sensibly. "In fact I have reason to believe that the foreigners are already aware of the plot and your complicity in it. I believe they are fully prepared for it."

That did it. The *daotai* agreed to withdraw his permission and sent a message to the Cantonese forbidding the attack.

A few streets away, the missionaries began to make their way home from their prayer meeting, not knowing that their prayers had already been answered.

❋ ❋ ❋ ❋ ❋

With feelings running so high, all foreigners in Ningbo were still in great danger. Foreign merchants and some missionaries had their houses guarded by armed men. So plans were made to evacuate the women and children to Shanghai. Miss Aldersey suggested that Burella and Maria should join those going; but she herself and Mrs Bausum chose to stay and the two young ladies decided to do the same.

With the fewest commitments binding them to Ningbo, Jones and Hudson Taylor were asked to escort the women and children and look after them for as long as they needed to stay in Shanghai. It might be a very long time indeed.

Maria went down to the wharf to see them off. On board the *Foam* were two American families. On board the *Japan* were the Martins (American Presbyterians), John and Mary Jones and their children, Mary Gough and hers, and Hudson Taylor. Hudson sat on deck with the Gough's baby on his knee.

Maria watched and waved as the *Japan* was towed down river to the bay before hoisting her sails. Looking after the "darling babe" for most of the journey, Hudson later recorded, "helped me to conceal my feelings on leaving Maria in Ningbo." And Maria wrote to her brother in England, "Mr Taylor went up to Shanghai, against his own inclinations, at the request of a friend to take care of his friend's wife and family. Before he left, I had some little reason perhaps to think that he might be interested in me, but I thought I had better not be too sanguine ..."

Neither knew whether they would see each other again.

THE COURSE OF TRUE LOVE ... 19

In Shanghai Hudson Taylor and John Jones spent their
time preaching and distributing Scriptures in the Chinese city and in the countryside. For some weeks they didn't
know when, if ever, they would be able to return to Ningbo,
or whether they might even have to join a general exodus
from China. They heard that three new CES missionaries
would be arriving in Shanghai but they didn't know when
or how the CES could possibly support them.

By the end of February, the scare in Ningbo seemed to
be over. Parker reported that people and mandarins were
friendly. Most of the refugees returned but Mary Gough, the
Joneses and Hudson Taylor stayed in Shanghai. He wrote,
"the Lord who brought us here has not taught us to go back
and so we are still remaining, till the pillar move."

More and more Taylor realized that he missed seeing Maria.
"I do so long for someone to have unrestricted communion
with — for someone to love and confide in," he wrote.
Encouraged by John and Mary Jones, he sat down on March
21 and wrote Maria a letter. The letter no longer exists
but it is clear that in it he expressed his feelings about her;

asked that he might be allowed to get to know her with a view to marriage; begged Maria not to send him a hasty refusal; inferred that ridicule would be painful to him; and asked her to burn the letter if she found it unacceptable. Quite correctly, according to the rigorous standards of Victorian society, he wrote at the same time to Frederick Gough explaining the proposals he was putting to Maria.

In Ningbo, on the morning of April 8, Maria was busy at the school when Mary Gough, home again by then, called with a letter for her. The handwriting was not familiar. She didn't read it at once but carried on with her work until she was free. Then she went to her room and opened it. It was from Hudson Taylor.

As she read, she could hardly believe what was happening to her. It seemed that her prayers had been answered. At the first opportunity she told Burella.

"That's marvellous," said her sister. "Congratulations!"

Then she told Miss Aldersey.

"I suppose you will not think of accepting him," said the formidable lady.

When Maria indicated that she might, Miss Aldersey said, "We had better write to Mr Tarn and ask him to find out more about Mr Taylor." William Tarn was Maria's uncle and guardian in London.

"I must ask you," Miss Aldersey continued, "to decline Mr Taylor's proposals and ask him never at any time to refer to the subject again. You yourself must put the subject entirely out of your mind."

Here was a dilemma for Maria. She was under no legal obligation to do as Miss Aldersey said, but she obviously had to respect the wishes of the lady she loved despite her domineering nature, and who had done so much for her over the years. Mary Gough was very sympathetic but urged obedience.

"I feel that Miss Aldersey stands in the place of a mother to you. Whatever your own feelings may be, you would not feel it right to follow a course to which she is so directly opposed."

Miss Aldersey proceeded to write to William Tarn disparaging Hudson Taylor. Maria began a letter to her uncle and aunt saying how she felt about Hudson and seeking their approval. But then she received a message via Burella that Miss Aldersey was very much against her writing.

Maria thought and prayed much about her reply to Hudson Taylor, which Miss Aldersey would probably insist on seeing. In her own heart and mind she wanted to encourage him. But in view of what Miss Aldersey had said, and her wish to be seen to respect her, the reply would have to look like a rebuff. The letter she eventually wrote was a masterpiece: the choice of words, and the course the letter steered, were magnificent. There was more between the lines than in them.

April 16, 1857
My dear Sir

I have to acknowledge receipt of a letter from you dated March 21st, which was put into my hands yesterday week, April 8th by Mrs Gough — and to thank you for the kind Christian spirit which breathed throughout it.

I have made the subject of your letter a matter of earnest prayer to God, and have desired I think sincerely only to know His will, and to act in accordance with it. And although it gives me no pleasure to cause you pain, I must answer your letter as appears to me to be according to God's direction. And it certainly appears to be my duty to decline your proposals. But think not dear Sir that I do so carelessly, and without appreciating the kind feelings which you express towards me. And I have too great a respect for those feelings (although my duty requires me entirely to discourage them) to expose you and the subject of your letter to ridicule.

It was right that I should acquaint Miss Aldersey and my sister with the matter, and Mrs Bausum is the only other person besides the parties through whom your letter came, who knows anything about it — as far as I am aware. And it is my desire that no one else except my own immediate relations, and those to whom you have thought or may think proper to acquaint with the matter, should ever know anything about it. Before I close this letter, I shall take an opportunity of burning yours as you desired me.

I regard you dear Sir, as a Brother in Jesus, and hope ever to bear towards you those feelings which disciples are commanded to bear to one another. But ask me not for more. I request you not to refer to the subject again as I should be obliged to return the same answer. You will perceive by the tone of my letter that I have not lightly sent you a refusal. I have written with less reserve to you than I should have done to one to whom I did not feel bound by ties of Christian fellowship. And now may Jesus Himself bless you abundantly, and make you a blessing. And may you be the honoured instrument of leading many souls to Jesus, and have many crowns of rejoicing in the day of Christ.

I remain,

Yours in Jesus,

Maria Jane Dyer

Would the letter get past the censor? Disciples are of course commanded to *love one another*. She had *requested,* not forbidden, Hudson to raise the matter again. Would Hudson take the hint that she saw it as her duty to obey Miss Aldersey's instructions?

The letter did get past censor Aldersey and off it went to Shanghai. "After I had sent the letter," Maria wrote, "I felt that I could not wish one way or the other: I could only leave the matter in God's hands, praying Him to do what He saw best."

✳ ✳ ✳ ✳ ✳

Early in May, Hudson Taylor received Maria's reply. He read it over and over again. He soon saw that it could be taken two ways; but, at least at its face value, it was saying, for some reason, *No, and please don't try again, at least for the moment.* He strongly suspected that Miss Aldersey might have something to do with the ambiguity of the reply.

Before the next twist in the tale of his romance, there was another matter to be settled. On May 29, 1857, a week after his 25th birthday, Hudson Taylor resigned from the CES. He had often warned them that he might take this step. The CES had failed to send him the full quarterly amounts it had promised. It was continuing its operations with borrowed money, a state of affairs which he believed to be unscriptural. Not only was the society unsatisfactory, but his connection with it was actually a hindrance to him as, for example, its rules forbad its missionaries to earn separate money to supplement its own meagre supplies.

He had proved in Hull and in London that God would supply his needs in answer to prayer; he had been inspired by the example of George Muller. Now, once again, he would act according to these principles. "If the Lord blesses you," he told the society, "and leads you to send anything to me, either in the way of counsel, pecuniary aid, or otherwise, I hope to receive it as from *Him*, and with thankfulness to Him and you." John Jones resigned a few days later. On the whole, the break with the CES took place with friendly feelings on both sides.

After many hours of reflection and prayer, Taylor and Jones had decided that they would work together in a treaty port until a fellowship of Chinese Christians was formed. They would aim to develop the gifts of those Christians and encourage them to take the gospel to their own people. They would pool their resources, living as one family and sharing a common purse. They would return to Ningbo and work with William Parker and other missions while establishing and training the Chinese church.

On June 7, word reached them that the ship carrying the

expected three new CES missionaries — Charles Hall, his wife and Miss Magrath — had arrived at the mouth of the Yangzi after six months at sea. Taylor and Jones went to welcome them, and after a week of preparations, the whole party travelled to Ningbo. For the time being, the Halls and Miss Magrath moved into the Parkers' home in the fields beyond the foreign settlement; the Jones family and Hudson Taylor took over the Russells' old house inside the Chinese city near the Salt Gate.

With Maria's letter never far from his thoughts, Hudson Taylor dutifully tried hard to avoid meeting her. For her part, Maria dutifully avoided calling on her friend Mary Jones lest she should bump into the young man who lived in the same house. Hudson Taylor and John Jones plunged themselves into the work they believed God was calling them to do, planning a short journey into the country which would keep them away from home for a few nights.

So far so good. But sparks began to fly when Mary Jones asked Maria to visit Chinese homes with her and keep her company in the house while the two men were away. Maria must have mentioned it at home, for in no time Miss Aldersey confronted Mary Jones, determined to demonstrate her famous ability to create earthquakes.

"I do not wish," she began imperiously, "Maria to go with you on your proposed visits. Moreover," she continued, even more imperiously, "I have to tell you that I am aware of Mr Taylor's proposals to her and that I strongly object to them. I am asking you not to promote a meeting between these two young people. Finally I want you to promise not to tell Mr Taylor what I have said."

Dear Mary Jones. She reluctantly agreed not to promote a meeting, afraid that if she did not do so, she might be prevented from working with Maria altogether. But then, mustering all her courage, she said to Miss Aldersey:

"I cannot undertake not to tell Mr Taylor what you have said. Furthermore I am bound to say that it is a very serious thing for you to tamper with the affections of two young people in this way."

After this highly-charged interview, Mary Jones told Hudson all about it. This was the first time either of them had had firm evidence that Maria's rejection of Hudson was not on her own initiative.

Miss Aldersey also called on Mary Gough and extracted a similar promise from her not to play the matchmaker.

Hudson Taylor decided that there was only one thing to do. He must speak to Miss Aldersey himself.

... NOT RUNNING AT ALL SMOOTH 20

Mary Ann Aldersey had recently handed her school over to Mrs Bausum and now lived with the Russells near the North Gate of Ningbo. On July 7, 1857, she was told that Mr James Hudson Taylor wished to speak to her. Perhaps because a part of her respected the courage and directness which had brought him there, she received him politely.

"I have come to ask why I have offended you. Is it because when I wrote to Miss Dyer I sent a covering letter to Mr Gough and not to you?"

"No. It is because you wrote directly to her in the first place without seeking my permission."

"Oh, I'm sorry! Are you still Miss Dyer's guardian?"

"No, strictly I am not. But she is, in some measure, entrusted to my charge. I feel sure that your engagement to Maria would not meet with the approbation of her legal guardians, Mr and Mrs Tarn, to whom I have referred the matter. It is for this reason that I cannot approve of something for which they might reproach me."

"I see that you are seeking to perform a difficult duty as you see it best. But you have now handed Miss Dyer over to Mrs Bausum's protection. What are the objections to me which have made you intervene so strongly?"

"You should in courtesy have consulted me first."

"But," replied Hudson Taylor, "that would not have been a proper step before I knew the feelings of Miss Dyer herself. If she had been disposed to entertain the question, that surely would have been the time to consult others. What other objections do you have?"

"I don't think it necessary to tell you."

"I'm very anxious to know what they are and believe you owe it to me to tell me."

"I will just mention two things. Is it not a fact that you are a member of the -er *Plymouth Brethren?*" There was a note of disdain in her voice, as if she could hardly bring herself to say the words. "And didn't you desecrate the Sabbath by travelling on a Sunday during your journey to Ningbo?"

"I am well able to answer these points. If by Plymouth Brethren you mean the followers of J N Darby[1], I have never been a member of that group. I was brought up a Methodist. The congregations I joined in Hull and Tottenham were independent churches meeting according to what they considered to be New Testament principles. As to the Sabbath — I prefer to call it the 'Lord's Day' — I prize, love, and respect the duties and privileges of this day. It is true that when I returned to Ningbo with John and Tom Jones in October last year, we were forced to travel on a Sunday in order to get both father and son urgently-needed medical attention in the city. The objections which you have expressed are based on erroneous reports. What else have you against me?"

"I will not say any more." Miss Aldersey brought the interview to a close.

✳ ✳ ✳ ✳ ✳

[1] now known as Exclusive Brethren

Hudson Taylor reflected on what had happened and spent long hours praying about it all. After a week he made a decision. It would, he thought, be right for him to visit Maria and ask her permission to write to her guardians in London.

On July 15 he took a sedan-chair to the school and was shown into the courtyard. It was an all-female establishment. Mrs Bausum, Burella and Maria were about to leave for the Goughs'. A tactful servant showed him into an ironing-room; he handed the servant a note for Maria which he had that day carefully composed. Hearing Hudson's voice, Maria hurried out of the way; the servant handed her the note.

"The foreign gentleman who gave it to me is waiting for a reply."

Her hands trembling, Maria read the note.

My dear Miss Maria

Last week I had an interview with Miss Aldersey and learned from her that she had written to your guardians on the subject of my letter from Shanghai and that till an answer was received her objections (which she would not name) could not be removed and from prayer-ful consideration of that which then occurred, it has appeared to me that a further step might be desirable. Neither am I alone in this opinion, but before taking steps I of course wish to see you upon the subject and most earnestly beg you to grant me an interview of a few minutes — and I may add that the importance and desirability of this is fully agreed in by those who have favoured me with their prayer and counsel.

Maria showed the note to Mrs Bausum and Burella.

"You mustn't see him," said Burella. "Miss Aldersey wouldn't approve."

Mrs Bausum agreed. Burella and Maria slipped away to the Goughs. Mrs Bausum went to speak to Hudson Taylor.

"Come upstairs to the living quarters," she said.

Mrs Bausum was a woman of wisdom and experience. She

wasn't unduly frightened of Miss Aldersey, having taken over her responsibilities. Taylor told her about his interview the previous week.

"Before I write to Maria's guardians," he concluded, "I need to know whether my affection for her is reciprocated."

Mrs Bausum hesitated and then replied: "It is."

✳ ✳ ✳ ✳ ✳

Next day, July 16, Maria wrote a long letter to her aunt and uncle explaining how she had written in April but had not been allowed by Miss Aldersey to send the letter. She said that she had been interested in Hudson Taylor for nearly a year; had prayed much about him; saw in his letter an answer to her prayers for guidance; and found it difficult to appreciate Miss Aldersey's opposition to their friendship. "I think Mr Taylor has acted in a Christian manner throughout the whole matter. Since his return to Ningbo, now nearly four weeks ago, we have not exchanged a word ... Though I sometimes feel that the greatest earthly pleasure that I desire is to be allowed to love him and to hold the closest and sweetest intercourse with him spiritually as well as temporally that two fellow mortals can hold, I desire that he may not hold the first place in my affections. I desire that Jesus may be to me the Chiefest among ten thousand, the altogether lovely ..."

On a sultry day in July, Maria and Mrs Bausum spent some time talking about Hudson Taylor. They read Psalm 69 together: "Do not hide your face from your servant; answer me quickly, for I am in trouble ..." Then Maria prayed, "Dear Father, if it is not wrong, please grant that Mr Taylor and I may have an interview." She wrote, "I could easily have arranged an interview, but preferred that it should be of God's overruling and not my arranging."

Late that afternoon, the ladies' prayer meeting was held at the house where the Joneses and Hudson Taylor lived. Maria went with Mrs Bausum. Hudson Taylor didn't think it right that he should be at home that evening, and decided that he would visit a merchant some way out of the city to see about some boxes of New Testaments which had arrived for him from Shanghai. But as evening came on it began to rain heavily. Not the sort of weather in which to carry books about the place.

So he took his writing materials to the top of the house, intending to stay there until the supper bell rang. And then the thought came to him: *Has this rain perhaps been sent to bring about the meeting I so much need by preventing me from venturing out?*

"Dear God," he prayed, "please give me an unmistakable indication whether I should leave the room before Maria goes home."

Shortly before the prayer meeting ended, there was a knock on his door and a servant entered. A fellow missionary had called: would Mr Taylor come down to see him? He did. His colleague couldn't stay and left after a few minutes. Mrs Bausum and Maria hadn't left, their sedan chairs delayed by the rain.

Taylor believed he had received his guidance.

"Would you tell Maria that I should like to speak to her," he said to John Jones.

Maria's head was bowed in prayer when she realized that John Jones had walked into the room. He beckoned her.

"Mr Taylor begs that you will allow him to have an interview with you," he said.

"It is what I of all things wish," said Maria. "Is it to be private or may another person be in the room?"

"It is to be as you wish."

"I should like Mrs Bausum to be present."

The two ladies were taken upstairs and shown into John Jones' study. A few moments later, a young man entered the room and Maria and Hudson found themselves standing face to face.

Hudson Taylor saw how pale and anxious Maria looked.

"I am sorry to have caused you so much distress," he said.

"I wanted to see you so that I might ask your consent to my writing to Mr and Mrs Tarn."

"You have my consent," said Maria. "I have already written to them telling them how I feel. I intend to write again. I must tell you that it was Miss Aldersey who compelled me to reject your proposals. Since then I have suffered agony. Now I think it would be good if we prayed together."

There was no suggestion with which Hudson Taylor would have more heartily agreed. The three of them knelt while he prayed.

A HAND TO SOOTHE HIS FOREHEAD 21

Hudson Taylor wasted no time in writing to the Tarns. He concluded his letter: "Gladly therefore do I commit the matter to Him who has the direction of all events in His hands, and pray that He may guide you to a right decision — and hope you may be led either to sanction our union, or to permit Miss M D to act for herself in the matter as the Lord may lead her ..." He gave the names of friends who could be consulted as referees, including the CES. He sent a copy of the letter to Maria under cover of a note which began, "Dearest Maria". Probably no one else knew that Mrs Bausum also wrote to Mrs Tarn in Maria's favour.

Having despatched the letter, life had to go on while he waited for the reply. He was renting the Bridge Street house again, both as a preaching point with a tight schedule of meetings which he shared with John Jones, and as a dispensary; he had begun to help opium addicts break their addiction.

Less than a week after his meeting with Maria, Taylor received a letter from none other than Miss Aldersey herself. She had heard about the meeting, and her wrath and indignation knew no bounds.

Sir, when you favoured me with a call you remarked ... that you were not aware ... that Miss M D was a minor ... When you did know from me that Miss M D was a minor, you went to (the Ladies' House) determining if possible to take advantage of her youth to induce her to trample on the prohibition which had been laid upon her ... In the absence of myself or of the elder sister you have availed yourself of a meeting concerned exclusively for religious exercises ... to obtrude upon Miss M D the forbidden subject. While I am astonished at the offensive indecorum of this last step, it (with all other like acts) makes my path of duty more clear with reference to your proposals; and now I beg to say that if you persist in continuing your addresses, not awaiting the permission of Miss M D's aunt, I shall be constrained to take steps of a more formidable character than you are prepared to meet ... It was surely a bad thing that a person calling himself a missionary should be found industrious as you Sir are in endeavouring to lead the daughter of deceased missionaries to take a step which all who know them must know would be displeasing to them!

Hudson showed the note to John and Mary Jones. Mary Jones read it and was immediately taken quite ill with the shock of its style and unchristian spirit. He passed the note to Maria to prepare her for what might follow. Poor Maria: years later one of Mrs Bausum's children recalled that Maria was at this time constantly unhappy and often in tears.

Miss Aldersey had now said that she didn't think Hudson Taylor was a worthy suitor for Maria because he was "without education and without position". Maria herself answered this snobbish charge well in a letter to her brother: "Mr Taylor had a medical education of five years and wanted only six months more when he might have taken his diploma. But the society thought that the call to China was of more importance ... Our own Father had he completed one more term might have obtained a scholarship, but his view of the importance of missionary work led him to renounce his legal studies ... It seems to me that Mr T is just such a person as my dear Father were he living would approve for me ..."

The summer was a hot one. Hudson Taylor found it a little easier to endure than the previous two, partly because he was "regularly using a little pale ale".

Then came the news that John Quarterman, with whom Taylor had worked and made several trips into the country, was ill: Dr Parker diagnosed smallpox. When Taylor heard this, he offered to take over nursing him, arguing that he had no need to be concerned for wife and children, and that a recently discovered vaccine would protect him.

There was no hope of recovery. All Hudson could do was ease Quarterman's suffering as far as possible and try to help him anticipate the "joy that was set before him".

"For this corruptible must put on incorruption," he would say.

"And this mortal must put on immortality," Quarterman would respond.

After four days, Quarterman died: Hudson wrote to Amelia, "sweet was his end".

Then Taylor himself went down with a high fever. He was exhausted after caring for Quarterman, and believed he had absorbed a good deal of the poison. On the night of October 20/21 he had a curious experience — not, he was convinced, the product of delirium.

At 3 am he heard a noise in the street outside. In his fever he could not bear the sound of his watch ticking at the other end of the room and wrapped it up. Unable to sleep, he sat reading his Bible for a while; then lay down again. His heart, as he later recorded, was "fluttering like a frightened bird" and his mind was "too excited to sleep".

Then, "I became conscious of the presence of Dear Maria. She came in noiselessly as a breath of air and I felt such a tranquillity steal over me — I knew she must be there. I felt spellbound for a short time, but at length without opening my eyes I put out my hand, and she took it so tenderly and with such a soft warm grasp, that I could not refrain from a look of gratitude.

"She motioned me not to speak and put her other hand on my forehead and I felt the headache which was distracting and the fever retire before it and sink as thro' the pillow.

"'Don't be afraid or uneasy. I am your Maria, and you my dear Hudson. Keep tranquil and try to sleep,' she whispered.

"And so," recalled Hudson, "I did."

He woke at 8 am. The fever was gone but he was very weak. "It was a sweet dream, (I would call it, but I was as wide awake then as I am now, and saw and felt her plainly as I do pencil and paper) ... It would have been a severe case of smallpox, had not God, through the protection of my previous vaccination, preserved me."

❊ ❊ ❊ ❊ ❊

For some reason, Burella had now turned against the idea of her younger sister's marriage to Hudson Taylor. She was herself shortly to be married to John Burdon and a plan had been hatched that Maria would spend some time in Shanghai with the newly married couple after their wedding. Did Burella hope that during Maria's stay in Shanghai, which might have to be extended due to the difficulty of travelling between the two cities, her love for Hudson would cool? Maria must be warned not to go: Hudson decided to speak to Mrs Bausum about it. He believed that Maria was at the Russells keeping Burella company until her wedding: therefore he could visit Mrs Bausum without fear of a chance meeting which others would criticize.

But when he arrived at the house, he had a surprise.

"I suppose I can talk to you without fear of doing the wrong thing?" he said to Mrs Bausum.

"No you can't, for Miss Maria is now in the house. Miss Aldersey brought her home this morning. However you may come in."

She showed him into the sitting room.

"Wait here while I warn Maria not to come downstairs."

But it seemed to Hudson Taylor like an answer to prayer and a wonderful opportunity to warn Maria not to go to Shanghai with her sister.

"Oh, do let me speak to her!" he begged.

"No, I'm afraid there'd be a row," said Mrs Bausum.

Just after she had left the room, someone opened the other door. In walked Maria. She was as surprised to see Hudson as he was to see her. Then Mrs Bausum returned, and stayed while Taylor warned Maria of his suspicions about the proposed stay in Shanghai.

"I know about the plan," said Maria, "and I'm determined not to go."

"I think it would be a good idea, to prevent annoyance, to tell Miss Aldersey of the circumstances of Hudson's call," Mrs Bausum said. "We don't want distorted accounts to reach her ears. I shall tell her that the interview was entirely unpremeditated."

✷ ✷ ✷ ✷ ✷

Burella was hoping that the American missionary William Aitchison would court Maria. Taylor had heard that Aitchison — "on whom I looked with great respect and love in the Lord" was "much smitten" with her.

If I had been allowed to have open dealings with Maria, he said to himself, *poor Aitchison would not have come to cherish feelings which I know will be disappointed*. He decided to explain the situation:

"The fact is, that we are waiting for a reply from Maria's guardians. Meanwhile we consider ourselves conditionally betrothed already."

There must have been something quite irresistible about Maria at this time. Was it her slim figure? Her light brown hair? Or even that very slight cast in her eye which enhanced her appeal? A Dutchman named Gaillard arrived in Ningbo and Hudson Taylor invited him to stay at the Bridge Street house.

One evening as the two men were talking Gaillard leaned forward, obviously wanting to confide something very important.

"I have written to two ladies in Holland and Germany proposing marriage. But now the charms of Miss Maria Dyer have so attracted me that I would prefer to try to win her!"

Hudson Taylor was "inwardly furious".

"What would you do if all three accepted?" he asked coldly.

✳ ✳ ✳ ✳ ✳

Taylor then heard reports that Maria was after all going to Shanghai with Burella: if only the Tarns' reply would come! Meanwhile he was clearly going to have to speak to Maria again.

On November 14 he called on some American Baptist friends, the Knowltons, who lived near Maria. It so happened that they were planning to go to Shanghai themselves, and Mrs Knowlton agreed to send her a note:

> My dear Miss Maria,
>
> I understand you are talking of going to Shanghai and we are intending to start on Monday, and may I ask you if you will kindly come over here a little while, as I would like to speak to you of a little matter — if quite convenient will you come at once —
>
> Very affly,
yours L A Knowlton
>
> PS. If engaged, please mention when you can call.

Maria came at once. Mrs Knowlton showed her into the room where Hudson was and slipped away. For the first time the two lovers spoke to each other in private. They sat side by side on the sofa: Hudson put his arm around her slim waist and clasped her hand with his other hand. He recorded later: "She gave me a sweet kiss that would have alone paid for a dozen ... this has done me more good than half a dozen bottles of quinine, port wine, or any other strengthening medicine could have done — in fact I never felt in better health or spirits in my life ... She is a dear, noble, disinterested, devoted girl, and now I know all she has passed through, I love her more and admire her more than ever."

They spent six hours together and made a momentous decision: they would get engaged whether the Tarns' reply was favourable or not.

It seems from a letter Hudson wrote to Amelia that the "sweet kiss" was not the only one: "I was not long engaged without trying to make up for the number of kisses I ought to have had the last few months."

"SUCH A TREASURE AS MINE" 22

Hudson and Maria discussed how, out of respect, they should first inform Miss Aldersey of their engagement. So, on a Monday evening, Taylor called on Miss Aldersey and told her what had happened. The lady said little; Hudson Taylor thought it might be because she didn't trust herself.

Next day, Maria received a note from her which said:

> I require you to call on me, as your guardian, without delay.

Maria replied:

> I cannot look on you as my guardian. But I will gladly call on you as a respected friend at any time.

Maria then received another note from Miss Aldersey which referred to her "strange infatuation" and charmingly reported William Russell's view that Hudson Taylor "ought to be horsewhipped" and that Russell would refuse Taylor communion if he presented himself for it.

Then came the good news. Maria received the long-awaited letter from her aunt, Mrs Tarn. Her heart leaped for joy

as she read it and she at once sent a note to Hudson.
My own dear —

I have received a letter from my aunt, and she tells
me that she and my uncle certainly have not heard
anything to induce them to oppose my wishes. Do come
quickly,

Your own loving
Maria

In London, the Tarns had been reassured by George Pearse,
a personal friend of theirs, who evidently was in no way
bitter about Hudson Taylor's resignation from the CES. He
had told the Tarns he couldn't understand Miss Aldersey's
opposition and wondered whether it was because she didn't
want to lose Maria from her school. Pearse sent his greetings
and good wishes separately to both Hudson and Maria.

The Tarns told Maria "we fully approve of your choice";
and in a letter to Hudson they wrote "we entirely approve
of the proposed union". Now the couple announced their
engagement and spent every evening together. Miss Aldersey
remained strangely silent. The Tarns' only wish was that
they should not marry until Maria came of age — that would
be the following month, on January 16, 1858.

That Christmas was one of the happiest Hudson ever spent.
There were a number of parties. One, for the younger members
of the European set in Ningbo, was at the home of John
Nevius, the American Presbyterian. Hudson and Maria were
there plus Robert (later Sir Robert) Hart, one of the many
young men who had proposed to Maria without Hudson's
success.

They all sat around a table playing a game which involved
hiding their hands under the table. Maria thought how
attractive her husband-to-be looked and was compelled to
demonstrate her affection. To his surprise, John Nevius
received an unexpected squeeze. He guessed it was a case
of mistaken identity: enjoying the joke, he returned the squeeze
with enthusiasm. To her horror, Maria quickly realized her

mistake but when she tried to withdraw her hand, it was tightly held. She blushed. At last when John Nevius saw tears beginning to well up in Maria's eyes, he realized the joke had gone far enough, and released his grip.

✳ ✳ ✳ ✳ ✳

Another letter was on its way from England. It was addressed to Hudson Taylor and read:

> Bristol
> December 9, 1857
>
> My dear Brother
>
> It affords me much joy in the Lord to have it in my power to send you the enclosed forty pounds which I have obtained from the Lord simply in answer to prayer. Let this be a further encouragement to yourself, as to the readiness of the Lord to hear your prayers, when, in your need, you call upon Him.
>
> I was glad to find that you had resolved to trust in the Lord alone for the supply of all necessities. I have myself proved Him thus faithful for more than 27 years, during which time I have to Him alone made known my wants ... I would gladly write more, but have thousands of correspondents, besides all my other work.
>
> I remain, dear Brother,
> Yours affect. in our Lord,
> George Muller

Busy Muller may have been, but many similar letters and enclosures travelled out to China in the years ahead — each one a massive encouragement to faith.

Hudson and Maria began to talk about the wedding. Maria wanted him to wear English clothes so he began to grow the hair on the shaven front half of his head and was prepared to cut off his *bianzi*. Then Maria changed her mind: the hair wouldn't grow long enough in time, and she now began to feel that she would hardly like to see him in English dress anyway. They asked Frederick Gough to marry them.

"I wish you knew my precious Maria," Hudson Taylor wrote to his mother, "she is a treasure, she is all I desire ... May God give us His own rich blessing, and keep us from making idols of each other."

✳ ✳ ✳ ✳ ✳

January 20, 1858: the day of the wedding had dawned and the sun shone brightly.

Maria, just 21, looked stunning in her grey silk dress and bridal veil. Hudson wore a Chinese gown and sported his fine *bianzi*. Frederick Gough conducted the service, echoing the theme "Keep yourselves from idols". Sadly conspicuous by their absence were Miss Aldersey and the Russells. Poor Mary Jones, the successful matchmaker, had just received news of her mother's death and, to her great disappointment, was also unable to attend.

A civil ceremony followed at the British consulate. The American consul put his personal sedan chair at the couple's disposal: the biggest and best sedan chair in Ningbo. Twenty-four friends were there, including officers from a British ship-of-war. Thomas Meadows, the vice-consul, had signed the marriage certificate and was represented by his assistant Robert Hart. Hart got a magnificent kiss from the bride: it was some consolation!

Then it was back to the reception, provided by John Quarterman's sister. Later, when Hudson Taylor offered his fees for consular services at the wedding, vice-consul Meadows wouldn't hear of it.

"How often," he asked Taylor, "have you interpreted for me without accepting payment?"

✳ ✳ ✳ ✳ ✳

They spent their three-week honeymoon at a monastery,

a favourite retreat for Ningbo people escaping from the heat of summer. They travelled first by canal, then by sedan chair up into the hills, followed by their cook, a servant and coolies with their luggage on carrying poles. It was partly a working honeymoon, with the couple returning to Ningbo at weekends to take services because John Jones was ill. From the monastery, Hudson Taylor wrote: "We are so happy! ... He has answered all our prayers; over-ruled the opposition of those who would have separated us; and justified the confidence He has enabled us to place in Him.

"Oh, to be married to the one you *do* love, and love most tenderly! This is bliss beyond the power of words to express or imagination to conceive. There is no disappointment there. And every day as it shows more of the mind of your Beloved, when you have such a treasure as mine, makes you only more proud, more happy, more humbly thankful to the Giver of all good for this the best of all earthly gifts."

At a village near the East Lake, nine miles from Ningbo, Hudson and Maria rented a Chinese cottage. At the end of the honeymoon they invited their friends there for an "at-home", planning to work there during the week and Ningbo at the weekends.

But then came near tragedy. Maria contracted typhoid fever. Back at Ningbo, Hudson and Mary Jones nursed her but for some weeks she showed no sign of improvement. Then she turned the corner — but Hudson fell ill. It was April before they were both well enough to convalesce at Mrs Bausum's, enjoying her peaceful home and rose garden. That same month Hudson told his mother that, all being well, it wouldn't be long before she became a grandmother. Naturally he asked her prayers that all would go well. "I cannot tell you how much I love my precious wife. I am fully satisfied in her ... perfection is nearer come to in her than I ever expected ..."

They took over the old attic above the school and street

chapel in Bridge Street where Hudson had lived as a bachelor, and remodelled it, putting in new floors, dividing it into smaller rooms and fitting it out with Chinese furniture. Maria remembered Mary Jones' joke about Hudson being ready to receive visitors. Hudson reopened his dispensary and resumed his work of treating opium addicts, finding that bringing his patients to faith in Christ worked better than medical cures. Maria opened a school for nine or ten girls and was assisted by one of her former pupils. Funds came in adequate if not large amounts. Maria had a small private income which roughly met her own needs of food and clothing.

One of those who heard Hudson preach at the Bridge Street Chapel was Ni Yongfa, a Ningbo cotton dealer and leader of a reformed Buddhist sect which would have nothing to do with idolatry and was searching for truth. At the end of Hudson's sermon, Ni stood in his place and turned to address the audience.

"I have long searched for the truth as my father did before me. I have travelled far, but I haven't found it. I found no rest in Confucianism, Buddhism or Daoism, but I do find rest in what I have heard tonight. From now on I believe in Jesus."

Ni took Hudson Taylor to a meeting of the sect he had formerly led and was allowed to explain the reasons for his change of faith. Taylor was impressed with the clarity and power with which he spoke. Another member of the group was converted and both he and Ni were baptized.

"How long has the gospel been known in England?" Ni asked Hudson Taylor.

"For several hundred years," replied an embarrassed Hudson Taylor vaguely.

"What!" exclaimed Ni. "And you have only now come to preach it to us? My father sought after the truth for more than twenty years and died without finding it. Why didn't you come sooner?"

It was a difficult question to answer.

✳ ✳ ✳ ✳ ✳

In June, 1858, the second war of the European powers with China ended. Russia, America, Britain and France all signed the Treaty of Tientsin with China. Ten more ports and the whole of the Yangzi river were thrown open to foreign trade and residence. Diplomatic representatives of the four powers were to take up residence in Beijing; foreigners were to travel and carry on their business in peace outside the treaty ports; toleration of Christianity was guaranteed. Chinese Christians as well as missionaries were promised protection in the practice of their faith. It remained to be seen, of course, to what extent these concessions would be recognized by the mandarins.

The reaction of the CES *Gleaner* was typical of the jubilation in the Christian world. "Thanks be to God! Unfeigned, fervent thanks! All China is open! The prayers of half a century are receiving their fulfilment! ... A new era dawns upon the work of missions in China — new territories present themselves, provinces as large, and some of them more populous, than European kingdoms ..."

✳ ✳ ✳ ✳ ✳

Miss Aldersey and the Russells were now friendly, and Burella was writing affectionate letters from Shanghai. The harmonium arrived from England, damp and damaged, but Hudson managed to restore it and they relaxed playing duets.

But that autumn held a double tragedy for the young couple. At the end of August a short note from John Burdon reported that Burella was dead, a victim of cholera at 23. Burdon, at 32, had twice been bereaved of a wife and once of a child. He returned to his evangelistic journeys with William Aitchison, but long afterwards was always tearful when he spoke of his darling Burella.

Then, in October, Maria's baby was born prematurely at seven months, and died. "We did again and again," Maria told Hudson's mother, "dedicate the little unborn infant to

God and He ... surely accepted the intention of our hearts."

At Christmas, the birth of another baby eighteen hundred years earlier was celebrated by the foreign and Chinese Christians in Ningbo. Five new Chinese members had been added to their number during 1858. There were fun and games, hymns and talks by Hudson Taylor and John Jones and, to everyone's delight, one of the new Chinese Christians had become a local preacher and added his distinctive touch to the seasonal meditations. Where there had been death, there was also life.

※ ※ ※ ※ ※

Taylor continued to spend a lot of his time trying to help opium addicts, and was earning himself a reputation for successfully breaking people of their addiction.

Late one Sunday, after a busy day's preaching, a man was brought to him determined to die from an overdose of opium he had just taken. Taylor tried to administer an emetic, but the patient broke away several times from the people who held him. He ran like a madman, but each time was recaptured. It wasn't until after two in the morning that Taylor thought it safe to leave the man and go to bed. Next day, Hudson wrote: "He has been in this morning to thank me for saving his life."

Sunday morning, July 31, 1859: temperature 104°. John Jones conducted the morning service alone. In a room above, Maria, with Hudson and Mary Jones as doctor and midwife, safely gave birth to Grace Dyer Taylor. Informing his parents of the arrival of their first grandchild, Hudson wrote, "I had longed to have a little miniature of my precious Maria."

The following week, the intense heat brought on a bout of rioting and anti-foreign feeling, and William Parker persuaded Maria to leave the city for the safety of the hospital compound between the river and city wall. Maria wrote on arriving safely at the hospital:

My own precious dearest love,

Dr and Mrs Parker have kindly received your fugitive wife ... The people did not seem excited as I came along, but the Salt Gate was shut. Just before I arrived at the gate I met Mr Jones who kindly turned back and saw the two gates opened for me. No objection was made ... When shall I kiss you again and feel your loving arms around me? God bless you my own precious Hudson, my husband, and keep you from all harm ...

In August, Parker's wife contracted cholera. Hudson Taylor took charge of the hospital and outpatient clinic. After 36 hours, Mrs Parker died. Parker, left with five children, was shattered.

Out of more than two hundred men missionaries in China since the arrival of Morrison in 1807, over forty had lost their lives, and the wives of 51 had died. But John Jones' attitude was typical when he declared: "If we had to choose again, we would choose just this work in this place."

For the time being, however, Parker decided there was no alternative but to take his children home to their grandparents in Scotland. That would be the end of the highly successful private medical practice by which he earned enough money to run the hospital. Most people thought the hospital would have to close as well.

Hudson Taylor didn't agree. "A brand new hospital in running order," he said, "shouldn't lie empty. If it's God's will to keep it open, He will provide the means."

By mid-September Taylor had taken over from Parker. Hudson and Maria moved into the Parkers' house beside the hospital. "For funds to carry on this expensive work," said Hudson, "I must look to the Lord." For some weeks attendance at the hospital dropped, until Hudson Taylor established his own reputation. But the pressure of these new responsibilities, and the sheer hard work, began to tell on his health: Maria reported that his face was "long and thin".

The day came when Hudson's old friend and cook from

his early days in China said to him, "We have opened the last bag of rice."

"Then the Lord's time must surely be near to meet our need," replied Hudson.

Sure enough, a letter arrived. It was from William Berger. "I have inherited a legacy from my father," he wrote. "I shall not be altering my standard of living. The enclosed fifty pounds is to be used at your discretion. Will you kindly indicate how more can be used? ..."

Hudson Taylor and Maria called their assistants together and translated the letter to them.

"Hallelujah!" chorused the usually undemonstrative Chinese and rushed into the wards to tell the patients what had happened.

❋ ❋ ❋ ❋ ❋

By March, 1860, there were 21 members in the Bridge Street Church. Besides Ni Yongfa the cotton merchant, there was Tsiu the teacher and his mother, Feng the basket-maker, Wang the farmer and Wang the painter. Hudson Taylor had appointed two Chinese Class Leaders on the Wesleyan pattern to help teach the others and give them responsibility and experience. Attendance at the hospital was increasing and Hudson Taylor recorded, "my work exceeds my time and strength."

"... I should inform you that for some time past my health has been failing," he wrote to his mother, "and I have felt more and more unequal to my work. It is a very difficult thing to be one's own physician ... so that my conclusions may be treated with some reservations. I think, however, ... that my chest is affected with tubercular disease ... attacks of ague have more or less injured my liver and spleen ... It may be that I may be sent home for a season."

By April, he felt so ill that he doubted whether he would live through the summer. On the other hand, as he told his father, "a voyage home might either re-establish my health (if but for a time), or I might rouse others to go and take up the work I am unable to continue ..."

An independent medical opinion was that it was high time he left China, and by June they had decided to return to England. For all Hudson and Maria knew, they might never come back.

FULLY QUALIFIED 23

Hudson Taylor invited a Chinese Christian to travel home to England with them. Wang Lae-djun would assist the Taylors to translate hymns and books into the Chinese used by ordinary people and to revise the Ningbo New Testament, as well as helping any new missionaries learn the language. They hoped the experience would also be useful for Lae-djun.

Hudson managed to book their passages on the *Jubilee*, a sleek new tea-clipper with three square-rigged masts. His first impressions of the captain, named Jones, were that he looked irritable and might well make life difficult for them on the voyage.

Before they left, a letter arrived from Hudson's sister Louisa with some marvellous news. She had been converted. The Taylors were an independent lot, and despite the pressures of the family it had taken Louisa twenty years to decide — but now she was likely to stick to her decision. "Cleave to the Lord," Hudson wrote immediately, "my doubly dear sister (now doubly my sister) with true purpose of heart and you will find your joy to be full."

On July 18 1860, they moved down the Yangzi from Shanghai to anchor near the mouth of the estuary, ready to sail in the morning. Hudson was about to say farewell to China after six eventful years, Maria after seven and a half; he was 28 and she was 23. At daybreak on the 19th they were off — out into the China Sea.

Hudson's first impressions of Captain Jones were soon proved correct. In fact he was more than irritable — he was extraordinarily bad tempered. Little Grace, now a year old, was teething and inconsolable.

"I cannot allow your baby to cry in that way," said Captain Jones in one of the century's most unreasonable remarks.

Hudson Taylor's reply is not recorded, but on July 22 he bravely asked the captain if he might conduct services aboard the ship. To his great delight, Jones consented: maybe he thought the singing would drown the sound of Grace's crying! Every Sunday throughout the voyage Hudson Taylor preached the gospel.

The voyage was not an easy one. Many of those on board, including Hudson Taylor, picked up dysentery; Maria contracted gastroenteritis; their cabin became infested with bedbugs; and Hudson intensely annoyed the captain by refusing to translate and bargain for him on Sunday with traders who came out to the ship. The only consolation was that the voyage was a fast one, lasting four months and three days rather than the six months it would have taken an older ship. On Tuesday November 20 they woke off Gravesend.

While they had been at sea, the CES had finally been dissolved after ten years well-intentioned bungling and inexperience of the ways of the Far East.

Wang Lae-djun was intrigued as the little foursome travelled by train to London; he had never seen a train, let alone travelled in one. Taylor wore his Chinese clothes while Maria looked attractive but unfashionable with her bonnet worn "off the head", not at all the vogue in England in the 1860s. Sixteen-month-old Grace chose to wear her white drawers almost to her ankles.

Their journey ended at 63 Westbourne Grove, Bayswater in London, the home of Hudson's sister Amelia and her husband Benjamin Broomhall, whom she had married a few months before. To their delight, Louisa was there too, thrilled to see them but concerned about Maria's unfashionable clothes. She fixed her sister-in-law up with a stylish full crinoline black silk skirt and jacket to match — and persuaded Hudson to change into English clothes. During their five months in Bayswater they began attending Westbourne Grove Baptist Church, striking up a friendship with the pastor, W G Lewis.

"You should allow people to call you 'Reverend'," Lewis told him.

It was not a new suggestion, and this time Taylor agreed.

On December 8, Hudson, Maria, Wang Lae-djun and Grace left for the long-delayed reunion with the family in Barnsley. How everyone enjoyed that Christmas! Amelia and Benjamin came up from London, and Hudson's favourite aunt Hannah Hardey and his Uncle Richard arrived from Hull. It was a marvellous time and Hudson was beginning to feel better.

But then in the new year he consulted his former teacher at the London Hospital. Dr Andrew Clarke looked grave as he gave his verdict.

"You must give up all thought of going abroad for several years, if not permanently. Otherwise you will throw away your life. Your liver, digestion and nervous system are seriously impaired."

✳ ✳ ✳ ✳ ✳

Hudson Taylor was too busy to let this news depress him. He had schemes for translation work and encouraging the evangelization of China which would keep him busy whether or not he would be able to return himself. He sent a hymnbook in the Ningbo dialect to press, and soon other books followed. He wrote articles on China for magazines. He successfully persuaded the Bible Society to sponsor the reissue of the

Ningbo colloquial New Testament in romanized script[1]. He himself would undertake the necessary editorial work, assisted by Frederick Gough.

He also made the major decision to move near to the London Hospital and resume his formal study of medicine. He had experienced the drawbacks of not possessing a recognized qualification, and had been recommended to take the diploma of the Royal College of Surgeons, which would take between one and three years.

On April 3, Maria's first son, Herbert Hudson, was born in Bayswater. On the 9th, Hudson, Maria, Wang Lae-djun, Grace and Herbert moved to 1 Beaumont Street, Mile End Road. The house was a few minutes' walk from the London Hospital and its spanking new medical college building. Taylor was soon dividing his time equally between his medical work and studies and the revision of the Ningbo New Testament.

While in China, Taylor had written to his parents asking them to pray and look out for five young missionaries to come and work in Ningbo. His father heard of a young man from Norfolk named James Meadows, who hadn't long been a Christian but might well be suitable. In October, Meadows arrived at Beaumont Street to stay with the Taylors. They would see if he had the aptitude to learn Chinese, assess the genuineness of his vocation and his ability to fulfil it, and pray together for China as they tried to discern God's will for James and his fiancee Martha. After some weeks Hudson Taylor reported that James had given them total satisfaction. He would be the first of the five, and there was no need to delay his departure for China. The young man went home for Christmas and to be married.

On New Year's Eve Hudson Taylor heard of a fast first-class ship, the *Challenger*, in port and preparing to sail for China: he immediately contacted the ship's captain. A gift of a hundred pounds came from William Berger to pay for the Meadows' tickets. On the morning tide on Wednesday

[1]A phonetic system using combinations of western letters for each Chinese sound.

January 8, 1862, James and Martha sailed down the Thames bound for China and an unknown future. Four days earlier, Dr William Parker and his new bride had sailed from Glasgow for the same destination.

✳ ✳ ✳ ✳ ✳

In July 1862, Hudson Taylor passed his exams and at last became a fully qualified member of the Royal College of Surgeons, "MRCS, England". He could now give his undivided attention to the revision of the Ningbo New Testament. More good news was that the Meadows and Parkers had reached China safely.

The Taylors enjoyed a week's summer holiday at the home of his wealthy donor and friend William Berger. Berger was the owner of a starch factory and now lived at Saint Hill, near East Grinstead, a beautiful house with lawns and a lake set in rolling Sussex countryside. Berger's sound business sense well complemented Taylor's spirituality — not that either of them lacked the other quality.

In 1861 Hudson Taylor had attended a series of meetings at Christ Church, Barnet, arranged by its evangelical vicar, William Pennefather, author of the lovely hymn *Jesus stand among us in Thy risen power*. Pennefather has been described as "the George Muller of the Church of England ... a man who walked with God". Horatius Bonar, the hymn writer, George Pearse, and members of the Brethren from Tottenham including Miss Stacey were there to hear Pennefather expound the Scriptures. In July 1862, Hudson and Maria were at Christ Church again for these meetings which were the forerunners of the Mildmay Conference, the first of which Hudson Taylor was to attend in 1864.

The Mildmay Conferences led on to the Keswick Convention with its motto "All One in Christ Jesus". Hudson Taylor loved this openminded attitude — ecumenical in the best sense of the word — and during this period in England he gladly preached wherever he was invited, at Anglican, Baptist,

Methodist, Presbyterian, Brethren and many more churches, in the same spirit in which he worked with or for a great variety of missionary societies.

Later in the year he successfully passed the Royal College of Surgeons' Licentiate in Midwifery, enabling him to add "LM(RCS)" to the letters after his name. So Maria had a well-qualified attendant when their second son, Frederick Howard, was born on November 23.

Across the seas, China was continuing to take her cruel toll. William Parker died from injuries received falling from his horse off a bridge into the icy waters of a river. He had been one of China's most successful medical missionaries. And some months later, young Martha Meadows succumbed to cholera. James told Martha's mother, "An early death has been an early crown! You have a child in heaven!" And John Jones, having been forced through poor health to leave China with his family, died at sea and was buried at St Helena. News like this made Taylor long to get back to China to support those who were left.

✳ ✳ ✳ ✳ ✳

The Taylors plus Wang Lae-djun spent a memorable week in the summer of 1863 as guests of George Muller in Bristol. Muller was now director of three large children's homes on Ashley Down in Bristol, and pastor of the flourishing and popular Bethesda Chapel in the town centre. Hudson Taylor addressed the congregation at Bethesda and spoke to the children on Ashley Down.

In May 1864 Hudson, Maria and Lae-djun went to hear Charles Haddon Spurgeon at the new Metropolitan Tabernacle. They got to know London's most popular preacher well and Spurgeon invited Hudson to address a weeknight meeting. Each man greatly admired the other, and in years to come Spurgeon's portrait had an honoured place in Hudson's London office.

But now it was time for Wang Lae-djun to return to China;

he had been away from his wife and family for too long. In gratitude for this and all his work in helping in the revision of the Ningbo New Testament, Taylor wanted to make Lae-djun's last weeks in England as enjoyable as possible. He took him to Guy's Hospital museum, the Royal Geographical Society, the Houses of Parliament, and a service at Westminster Abbey. Then, after Lae-djun had spoken at a number of farewell meetings, a little party set off with him to Gravesend for the departure. On the same boat were two missionaries with their families: Edwin Kingdon of the Baptist Missionary Society and W R Fuller, a Methodist, both of whom had been trained for China by Hudson Taylor.

In June the Taylors spent a marvellous relaxed week in Yorkshire, fishing and playing on the sands at Scarborough. Then, on June 24, their third son, Samuel, was born.

✳ ✳ ✳ ✳ ✳

In China, Captain Charles George Gordon had appeared on the scene and under his "ever-victorious" leadership, Chinese national armies had established mastery over the rebels. During the summer of 1864, with the recapture of Nanjing by imperial forces, the Taiping rebellion was finally defeated after sixteen years. The movement which had originally given grounds for enthusiastic optimism in the Christian world had degenerated into a tragic caricature of Christianity and had in practice known little other than battle and blood. Some twenty million people had lost their lives as a result of fighting, reprisals, famine and disease.

In Ningbo, James Meadows was already earning quite a reputation for himself. Mrs Bausum, now married to the American Baptist, E C Lord, reported to Maria with friendly sarcasm that young Meadows "is growing very wise and can already suggest improvements in translation and in missionary plans which older (missionaries) never thought of! ... He gives (Mr Lord) much information, talking very knowing-ly of Chinese customs and habits. Mr Lord listens as a good little boy should ... withal I believe he is a very good missionary and as such deserves praise."

✻ ✻ ✻ ✻ ✻

Back in the East End, No 1 Beaumont Street was now much too small to hold all that was going on. The Taylors found No 30 Coborn Street, Bow (later No 1), three quarters of a mile further east, in a more residential area. It was at that stage really too large for them, but Frederick Gough offered to pay the difference in rent and so they took it, moving in on October 6, 1864. Hudson Taylor was on the verge of the decision which would assure his name a place in history.

BRIGHTON WORKS WONDERS 24

" The Chinese will make the best Christians in the world — they will thoroughly study the Bible as they do their own classics."[1] Hudson Taylor was aware of this claim but also knew that the Chinese would only become Christians if missionaries went there in large numbers and penetrated the interior.

One task he had set himself was that of trying to persuade the boards of missionary societies to send men to work in the eleven unevangelized provinces of inland China. He had interviews or correspondence with all the main English societies, who listened to him sympathetically but over and over again gave him the same answer.

"Our funds are not equal to current demands, let alone new commitments," the societies told him. "It is surely better to wait until in God's providence China is widely open to the gospel."

But where would European Christianity be, Taylor wondered, *if the apostles had waited for better conditions? If the existing*

---

[1] Said by "an intelligent Chinese" to missionary Evan Davies.

missionary societies cannot or will not rise to the occasion, then who will do so?

As he and Frederick Gough spent those long hours working at the revision of the Ningbo New Testament, they often looked up at a large map of China on the wall and thought of the millions who had never heard the gospel. *Thirty-three thousand people will die in China today without hope — without God,* Taylor thought.

* * * * *

Towards the end of 1864, Hudson Taylor began to draw up plans to return to China. But it was not to be just yet. The second of the five missionaries for whom he had been praying sailed for China on December 20, and Hudson Taylor saw her off from Southampton. Jean Notman was a well-educated young woman. Her outfit had been paid for by donations from a growing band of supporters — notably William Berger, George Muller and friends from Tottenham. Taylor kept detailed records of what the outfit consisted of and cost — "1 winter dress, 2 skirts, 1 crinoline, 3 print dresses, 3 petticoats, 6 nightdresses, 3 vests, 12 pairs drawers, 9 chemises, silk apron, 2 dozen handkerchiefs, 9 pairs stockings ..." The list goes on for another half a page and includes everything from a toothbrush to a writing desk.

Early in 1865, he wrote a small book which came to have an enormous influence, *China: Its Spiritual Need and Claims.* Actually much of it was produced as he paced up and down in his study dictating to Maria, just as his father had dictated sermons to his mother. He prayed about every paragraph and the resulting book was well done. For example, it graphically illustrated China's immense size: it told the reader that if all the Chinese "were to march past the spectator at the rate of thirty miles a day, they would move on and on, day after day, week after week, month after month; and over seventeen years and a quarter would elapse before the last individual passed by."

But it didn't make very comfortable reading: "Can the Christians of England sit still with folded arms while these multitudes are perishing — perishing for lack of knowledge — for lack of that knowledge which England possesses so richly, which has made England what England is, and made us what we are? What does the Master teach us? Is it not that if one sheep out of a hundred be lost, we are to leave the ninety and nine and seek that one? But here the proportions are almost reversed, and we stay at home with the one sheep, and take no heed to the ninety and nine perishing ones! Christian brethren, think of the imperative command of our great Captain and Leader, 'Go, go ye, into *all* the world, and preach the gospel to *every* creature;' think of the millions upon millions of poor be-nighted China to whom no loving follower of the self-renouncing One has 'brought good tidings of good', or 'published salvation' ..."

The book may have hurt to read, but it proved a best-seller. It was reprinted many times and by 1887 had already gone into seven editions. It seems to have been painful to write too. The research and thought that went into it led to a deep conviction in Hudson Taylor's mind that a *special agency* was essential for the evangelization of Inland China. He was obviously in a position to establish such an agency, but what form should it take? And what about the danger of cutting the ground from under the feet of the older societies? And wasn't there a danger of launching into a venture which would go tragically wrong, like the well-intentioned CES at whose hands he had suffered?

Despite the fears, he could see so clearly the sort of agency that was needed. It would be a mission composed of men and women from different denominations who would give themselves to evangelism, church planting and the training of church leaders. They would need to press into the interior of China, depending on God alone to guide and provide for them in answer to believing prayer. To reach each of the eleven untouched provinces would need a minimum of 22 missionaries.

Should he go ahead, or content himself with some less ambitious and costly form of Christian service? He had many long, earnest and prayerful conversations with Maria, William Berger, George Pearse and his friends at Tottenham, discussing possibilities and strategies for combining a trustful approach with sound businesslike procedures. For months so many thoughts and concerns were racing around in his mind that he rarely slept for more than two hours at a time, sometimes not at all. Was he willing to do what God was calling him to do? All this time, he believed, a million a month were dying without God in China.

"I thought I should lose my reason," he wrote, "yet I did not give in! At last I became quite ill. Maria knew something of it; but to no one could I speak fully. I did not want to lay on her a burden so crushing."

Seeing perhaps that he desperately needed a break, George Pearse invited Hudson Taylor to Brighton for the weekend of June 24-26. On the Sunday morning he heard the Presbyterian, J M Denniston, preach and was moved by what he said. Then, as he recalled, "unable to bear the sight of a congregation of a thousand or more Christian people rejoicing in their own security, while millions were perishing for lack of knowledge, I wandered out on the sands alone, in great spiritual agony; and there the Lord conquered my unbelief, and I surrendered myself to God for this service. I told Him that all the responsibility as to the issues and consequences must rest with Him; that as His servant it was mine to obey and to follow Him — His to direct, to care for, and to guide me and those who might labour with me.

"Need I say that peace at once flowed into my burdened heart? There and then I asked Him for 24 fellow workers, two for each of eleven inland provinces which were without a missionary, and two for Mongolia; and writing the petition on the margin of the Bible I had with me, I returned home with a heart enjoying rest such as it had been a stranger to for months, and with an assurance that the Lord would bless His own work and that I should share in the blessing.

I had previously prayed, and asked prayer, that workers might be raised up for the eleven unoccupied provinces, and thrust forth and provided for, but had not surrendered myself to be their leader."

The Bible in which Hudson Taylor wrote his prayer still exists, and a few days ago I held it in my hands. There, above Job 18, in Hudson Taylor's handwriting are the words: *Prayed for 24 willing, skilful labourers, Brighton, June 25/65.* A little later he recorded, "Conflict all ended — peace, joy. Felt as if I could fly up that hill by the station to Mr Pearse's house ... And how I did sleep that night! Mrs Taylor thought that Brighton had done wonders! And so it had."

At the first opportunity, he went with George Pearse to the London and County Bank and opened an account under the name "China Inland Mission". The opening amount was £10, not much, but as Hudson put it later, it was "£10 and all the promises of God."

❋ ❋ ❋ ❋ ❋

A busy period followed, dominated by two major objectives: encouraging his relatives and growing circle of friends to pray for those 24 missionaries, and speaking at a gruelling schedule of meetings up and down the country. The meetings were designed not so much to appeal on behalf of the new China Inland Mission or to beg for money, but to speak about China and how a great God could meet that country's needs. A Christian merchant who heard him described how Hudson Taylor spoke very quietly, choosing every word carefully. He was impressed with the deep feeling with which Taylor spoke of the need of China, giving details of what the various missionary societies were doing and showing how much remained to be done in the interior. No rhetoric or appeals for funds detracted from the spiritual impact of Taylor's address.

The qualities Hudson Taylor was looking for in the men and women to make up his first 24 missionaries differed somewhat from those sought by other societies. The CMS and LMS wanted ordained men, preferably from the universities. So Hudson Taylor took care not to draw away such men from their own church societies. He wanted intelligent, educated men and women, but was convinced that the crucial thing was the candidates' spiritual qualities. The door would be open to those with little formal education. And the most important spiritual quality needed would be the unshakable conviction that there is a faithful God — coupled with an ability and willingness to trust Him.

Few of the other societies gave much scope to women except as teachers. From the outset the CIM was to be open to women of the right kind — and the younger they were the quicker they would learn the language. Women would have an indispensable role in working among Chinese women.

The new recruits would have to accept Hudson and Maria as their leaders: they were the only ones with experience of living and working in China. In exchange, Hudson Taylor would give them basic preliminary training and provide them with an outfit.

Taylor intended that the CIM would have six distinctive features. First, its missionaries would be drawn not from any particular denomination but from all the leading Christian churches — provided they could sign a simple doctrinal declaration. In practice, as the mission developed, they would come from many different countries too.

Second, the missionaries would have no guaranteed salary, but trust in the Lord to supply their needs. Income would be shared. No debts would be incurred.

Third, no appeals for funds would be made; there would be no collectors; the names of donors wouldn't be published — instead each would receive a dated and numbered receipt by which he would be able to trace his own contribution into the list of donations and then into the annually published accounts.

Fourth, anxious to learn from the mistakes made by the CES, Hudson Taylor was determined that the work abroad would be directed not by home committees, but by himself and eventually other leaders on the spot in China.

Fifth, the activities of the mission would be systematic and practical. A comprehensive plan to evangelize the whole of China would seek to establish footholds in strategic centres. The aim would not be to secure the largest number of converts for the CIM, but rather to bring about as quickly as possible the evangelization of the whole Empire. Who actually garnered the sheaves would be regarded as of secondary importance.

Sixth, as a courtesy to the Chinese people, the missionaries would wear Chinese clothes and worship in buildings built in the Chinese style — unlike the Gothic-style church in Ningbo.

✳ ✳ ✳ ✳ ✳

By 1866, Hudson Taylor had completely recovered from the ill-health that had brought him home from China. In the spring he embarked on a tour of the West Country visiting Exeter, Torbay, Plymouth and Callington in Cornwall. In Torquay, a note reached him from a saintly and respected figure in the early Brethren, Robert Chapman, begging him to come to Barnstaple and speak at his assembly. This he did, and six or seven years later Chapman told him, "I have visited you every day since you went to China," referring of course to his faithful prayers.

In May, Taylor accepted an invitation to speak at Totteridge near Barnet as the guest of Colonel John Puget. As usual, he stipulated that notices announcing the lecture should state "No collection". Colonel Puget protested that he had never had that condition imposed before, but he accepted and the notices were distributed.

At the meeting Hudson Taylor used his large map of China and described to his audience the size, population and spiritual need of China. Afterwards Colonel Puget, sensing that many in the hall were impressed by what they had heard, rose to speak. "Mr Taylor requested that the notices announcing this meeting carried the words 'No collection'. However I do feel that many of you would be distressed if you were not given an opportunity to contribute to the work in China. As what I am about to propose emanates entirely from myself and, I'm sure, expresses the feeling of many in the audience, I trust that Mr Taylor will not object to a collection being taken."

Mr Taylor however jumped quickly to his feet.

"Mr Chairman, I beg you to keep to the condition you agreed to. Among other reasons for making no collection, the reason put forward by your kind self is, to my mind, one of the strongest. My wish is not that members of the audience should be relieved of making such contribution as might now be convenient, under the influence of emotion, but that each one should go home burdened with the deep need of China, and ask God what he would have them to do.

"If after thought and prayer they are satisfied that a gift of money is what He wants of them, it can be given to any missionary society having agents in China; or it may be posted to our London office.

"But in many cases what God wants is *not* a money contribution, but personal consecration to His service abroad; or the giving up of a son or a daughter — more precious than silver or gold — to His service. I think a collection tends to leave the impression that the all-important thing is money, whereas no amount of money can convert a single soul. What is needed is that men and women filled with the Holy Ghost should give *themselves* to the work. There'll never be a shortage of funds for the support of such people."

Over supper that evening Colonel Puget said to Hudson, "I think you were mistaken. A few people handed me some small contributions, but I must say that a good opportunity has been lost."

Next morning at breakfast a letter arrived at Colonel Puget's house addressed to Hudson Taylor. It brought good news. A ship called the *Lammermuir* had come into the Port of

London, and would be sailing for China soon after May 20. Accommodation was right for his band of missionaries and he could have the whole of it. Would he like to inspect it at once?

Colonel Puget came down late, looking tired.

"I haven't had a good night," he admitted.

After breakfast, he invited Hudson to his study.

"Here are the contributions to your work which I was handed last night," he said. "I thought last night, Mr Taylor, you were in the wrong about a collection. I am now convinced you were quite right. As I thought in the night of the streams of souls in China ever passing into the dark, I could only cry as you suggested, 'Lord, what wilt Thou have *me* to do?' I think I have obtained the guidance I sought, and here it is."

Colonel Puget handed Hudson Taylor a cheque for five hundred pounds. "If there had been a collection," he added, "I would have given a few pounds to it!"

Five hundred pounds would be worth well over ten thousand pounds at today's values.

KEEPING A COOL HEAD 25

Despite those who said the whole idea was madness, Hudson Taylor booked the *Lammermuir* to take him, his family and the team of CIM missionaries to China. They even took the harmonium from Coborn Street and carried it below deck.

May 26, 1866, dawned a lovely day. From all directions, young men and women, their friends and families, converged on the East India dock in London and climbed aboard the smart two-year-old clipper. In addition to Hudson and Maria and their four children, sixteen others would be travelling. From Scotland came blacksmith Lewis Nicol and his wife Eliza, carpenter James Williamson, stonemason George Duncan, and Jane McLean, product of William Pennefather's training school and known as the "Biblewoman." Londoners included Emily Blatchley, a college graduate and secretary, Jennie Faulding who had graduated with her, teacher Mary Bowyer also from Pennefather's school, carpenter and draper Josiah Jackson, and John Sell. In addition were an Irish teacher, Susan Barnes; blacksmith and farm mechanic William Rudland; Mary the daughter of Mrs Bausum; Mary Bell to be nurse to the Taylor children and a Swiss governess named Louise Desgraz. James Meadows' fiancee Elizabeth Rose, a bright girl with little formal education, completed the party.

They all looked forward to joining James Meadows, Stephan Barchet, George Crombie an Aberdeen farmer, John Stevenson son of a Scottish laird, and and Jean Notman who were already working as CIM missionaries in China. God had more than answered the prayers for five!

Only Hudson and Maria had been to China before. No one in England would guarantee to support them in China; there were no unmarried European women anywhere in China away from the ports, and yet this party held nine unmarried women, all destined for the interior of a country which despised foreigners.

The *Lammermuir* was an up-to-date square-rigged sailing ship with an iron frame and three masts, not unlike the *Cutty Sark*. Captain Bell had been converted to Christ just two years previously and was very sympathetic to his passengers. Those who had come to see them off included the Bergers, the Howards of Tottenham, the Fauldings, Hudson's mother, Amelia and Benjamin. All these and more gathered with the missionaries in the saloon and stern cabin for a prayer meeting. Then, as the *Lammermuir* was towed through the dock gates, they began to sing, "Yes, we part, but not for ever."

"Here's a pretty go!" Mr Brunton, the first mate, moaned. "We're going to have a whole shipload of missionaries psalm-singing all day long. I wish I was out of it!"

Many of the wellwishers stayed on board as far as Gravesend and then returned to London.

"See that ye fall not out by the way," said William Berger quoting Scripture, as he disembarked.

Maria recorded that Hudson was feeling as well as he ever had in his life. He was anxious that everyone had plenty to do and quickly gave the missionaries their first Chinese lesson of the voyage. Many more followed. He fixed up bookshelves and encouraged everyone to work to make their cabins homelike. He installed his harmonium in the stern cabin. In spare moments, Hudson settled down to read Winer's *Greek Grammar of the New Testament* and Bishop Wordsworth on Leviticus. William Rudland described him as "young and active, quite one with the young men of the party." Rudland thought of Maria as "quieter, in some ways perhaps more mature — and such rare judgment; calm sweetness about her face; most restful ... she gave a good deal of time to the children."

Captain Bell had a crew of 34 men and boys, at least two of whom besides himself were committed Christians. A menagerie of dogs, sheep, pigs, geese, ducks and chickens went with them. Captain Bell gave the missionaries virtual freedom of the ship, but they learned to make themselves scarce when the officers barked their orders and the crew sprang into action handling the sails. At times the missionaries too could make themselves useful. Lewis Nicol, the blacksmith, forged some parts for the ship; when the pumps gave trouble, Rudland the mechanic with Nicol and Williamson, the carpenter, put them right.

They were served magnificent meals and Hudson Taylor worried that they were being spoilt. Early in the voyage, one dinner began with a choice of hare or chicken soup. This was followed by preserved mutton, minced hare, chicken and ham with potatoes and turnips. Next a choice of plum pudding, apple pie, damson pie, blackcurrant tart or rhubarb tart. Then biscuits and cheese with nuts, almonds, malaya raisins and figs. All this took an hour and three-quarters to get through.

Buxom Mary Bell was a great hit with the sailors and had no intention of spending all her time childminding. She offered to hold a Bible class for the admiring sailors who fell over each other to join. By June she reported "one or two anxious men to be rejoicing in Jesus."

"We almost live on deck," Jennie Faulding wrote as they neared the equator. "Oh, I have enjoyed today! The sea is so lovely and the air so beautiful ... the captain makes great pets of the children. The sunsets are so lovely and I never saw the moon so bright. I threaded a very small needle and read quite small print on deck (in the moonlight) ... I never thought it would be so enjoyable. I can't work very hard, I lose so much time watching the waves ... There is no unpleasantness with anyone on board ... and the young men don't trouble me in the least ... Emily and I have nice walks and talks together ... Mr Taylor has a tin bath and an apparatus by means of which we can get the water in at our cabin windows so I enjoy a sea-bath sometimes ..."

There was some unpleasantness though. In July, Josiah Jackson invited Hudson Taylor into the stern cabin to talk with George Duncan, Lewis Nicol and himself.

"Have we got all our outfits?" Jackson asked.

"Yes, as far as I know," replied Hudson Taylor, "except for the socks. There has been some mistake with those, I'm afraid."

Due to a misunderstanding in London, fewer socks than intended had been packed.

"We have not been supplied as Mr and Mrs Berger said we would be," said George Duncan.

"You had better each give me a list of the items in which you think you are deficient," said Taylor.

The three men agreed to do this.

"I saw a list of articles supplied to the Presbyterian missionaries," said Jackson. "It amounted to a very different outfit from ours."

"We have never intended to take them as our pattern," said Hudson Taylor. "They are persons of different position in society and will in any case wear those things in China, which we shall not do. We've done what we can to get you comfortable outfits. I'm sorry that I was unable to get you some light clothes, and about the mistake over the socks. But you do have good useful outfits for which I think you should be thankful."

❋ ❋ ❋ ❋ ❋

All through the voyage, Hudson Taylor and his colleagues held meetings. They noticed a change in the attitude
of the crew as card-playing gave way to Bible-reading and
silly songs to hymns. At one meeting in the forecastle,
passengers and crew sat on sea-chests, planks, chairs, or various parts of the ship's fittings. A few, who were half-ashamed
to be there, hid behind the capstan or stood near the doors.

The sailors were wary of Mr Brunton, the first mate. He
was violent, he swore, and was a bully. William Rudland
thought at times that he was demon-possessed. Then suddenly
in July he seemed to soften. He begged John Sell to pray
with him; he allowed Hudson Taylor to read the first chapters
of Romans to him and seemed to understand them, but couldn't
apply them to himself.

In early August they ran into strong gales and Brunton
went about swearing terribly. The missionaries and converted
crew met to pray for him. Then, in the early hours of one
August morning, Brunton allowed Hudson Taylor to read
him the story of the passover in Exodus, and explain the
meaning of God's message, "When I see the blood I will
pass over you."

Suddenly Brunton shouted, "I see, I see, how blind I've
been!"

His conversion was dramatic. "Soon," wrote a delighted
Hudson Taylor, "he began thanking God and praying not
only for himself but for the crew and Captain Bell, for his
wife and children and for the mission."

Next day, Brunton's face seemed to have changed. He
"called out his watch," Rudland recalled, "confessed to them
his unreasonableness, saying he had been on the wrong side
— and completely confessed Christ." Brunton was not alone.
As a result of the services held on board, and the Bible
classes arranged by Mary Bell and others, the number of
Christians in the crew grew to 24.

✳ ✳ ✳ ✳ ✳

By Monday, September 10, they were within a few days'

sailing of Shanghai. The weather was squally, but the crew were busy cleaning and painting the poop so that it would look its best on arrival in China. All the time, the barometer was steadily falling and the sea becoming rougher.

By Tuesday, a typhoon was blowing. The wind was so fierce that all the sails had to be rolled down. Objects were washed about the deck and the rain and sea drenched the dogs, sheep, geese and chickens. The sea came over the poop deck into the saloon. No one slept for two nights; the lifeboats were washed away.

On Wednesday, the wind dropped and they could see Taiwan, then known as Formosa.

By the end of the following week, though, they knew they were heading for another typhoon. To make matters worse, Captain Bell was seriously ill with half his face paralyzed.

They never forgot the night of Friday September 21. The *Lammermuir's* starboard bulwarks were washed away, leaving a wide opening for the waves which surged on to the main deck.

Early on the Saturday morning, the jib and fore staysails broke away from their supports. The sea was so rough that the crew refused to go out and secure them. Captain Bell, though so ill, and Mr Brunton went on to the forecastle. Brunton himself crawled out on to the jib booms and some others followed. But they had to be called back when the ship began to nosedive into the sea.

Next the lee upper bulwarks gave away and the water was washing over that side too. Then two more booms gave way, followed by three masts including the main mast. All were hanging by their wire ropes, swinging wildly as the ship rolled. At any moment they might crash on to the decks. The decks themselves were full of water, in which floating timbers, tubs, buckets and casks crashed about, threatening to injure passengers and crew.

It seemed impossible that they could survive. The sailors were petrified and gave up trying to save the vessel. The missionaries prayed. Hudson Taylor kissed each of his children.

William Rudland noticed that Taylor kept perfectly calm.

The captain came into the saloon.

"Put on your lifebelts," he shouted. "She can scarcely hold together two hours more!"

The missionaries sang *Rock of Ages*.

Captain Bell began to grope his way towards the forecastle where the crew were crouching in despair. He was carrying his club and looking grim.

Hudson Taylor ran up to him.

"Don't use force till everything else is tried."

Taylor himself went into the forecastle and talked quietly to the men.

"I believe God even now will bring us through this all right. But of course our safety also depends on the greatest care in navigating the ship — that is up to you. We will all help. Our lives are in jeopardy just as much as yours."

Then, as the crew watched unmoving, Hudson Taylor and the male members of the CIM began to secure the floating objects. As they worked, the sea often washed over them and all the time they were knee deep in water. But they managed to haul ropes, lash timbers and man those pumps which were still working. At last they were able to persuade some of the sailors to help them. Slowly and painfully they secured the swinging masts. The noise was deafening: the roar of the water on the decks, the clang of the chains, the tearing of the sails as the masts crashed into them and the sharp smacking of the torn sails in the gale made it almost impossible to hear shouted orders.

The water casks had been washed away. Cooking was out of the question. From time to time they grabbed a biscuit with cheese or butter to keep up their strength.

By now the worst of the typhoon had moved away and the barometer was rising again, but the wind and waves took many hours to die down.

On Tuesday, September 25, the sun shone brightly and the sea was quieter. The crew were able to tighten the fixed rigging of the main mast, which had been swaying dangerously.

They opened the hold and hauled out new sails, all wet and holding water in their folds. They repaired the last of the pumps and reduced the level of water on board. The *Lammermuir* made good progress towards Shanghai, sailing on into a fine moonlit night.

On the Wednesday evening they took a pilot on board, and on the Sunday a tug steamer towed them up to Shanghai where the broken and battered boat became an object of intense interest. They thanked God that, though many passengers and crew were badly bruised, not a single life had been lost nor a single bone broken.

In a letter to Mary Berger, Maria reflected that "in all human probability had not we and our party been on board, the *Lammermuir* would not have reached port." Hudson Taylor had kept his head while more experienced men around him had panicked.

BY THE SHORES OF WEST LAKE 26

"There is so much English mixed with what is foreign," Jennie Faulding wrote, describing her first impressions of Shanghai. Chinese houses looked like prisons to Jennie, with their high walls enclosing a courtyard. The shops were "large and fine", open to the very narrow streets.

George Duncan was impressed with the courtesy of the Chinese. "They are very quiet and polite to us; far more than any of our countrymen would be with them." Louise Desgraz watched a Chinese funeral. Firecrackers "to frighten away the evil spirits", counterfeit money being burned for the dead man's use in the other world, lanterns to light his way; "what with the noise and the glare of the fire, it was an awful sight ... I was glad to get away." It seemed to her a vivid demonstration of the enslavement of the Chinese to Satan.

The *Lammermuir* party had brought with them printing presses with spare parts, a large supply of medicines, and apparatus to set up a hospital and dispensary. But where were these things to be stored till they could establish a base inland? During the voyage they had prayed about this, and the answer came on the very evening they arrived.

William Gamble of the American Presbyterian Mission Press visited the party aboard the *Lammermuir*, and offered them the use of a large warehouse for as long as they wanted, as well as accommodation for the whole party during their stay in Shanghai. Hudson went ashore with Gamble that same evening and saw the warehouse and living accommodation. Both were ideal.

Next month, Jennie wrote, "I'm glad we're not going to stay in Shanghai — the Chinese here are so money-loving ... and the English so worldly and stylish, everyone knows everyone's business. I suppose we are pretty well talked about." She was right of course, and what set the tongues wagging as much as anything was their dress. The men had had the front part of their heads shaved and false *bianzi* attached to the back, and were wearing full Chinese dress. Maria dressed like a Chinese lady but the girls' outfits were not yet ready. The Shanghai papers began to poke fun at the "pigtail mission."

William Rudland recalled later, "I did not like the Chinese dress much at first, but I like it better now." Josiah Jackson said, "It was not a little trial to us, especially the shaving of the head ... At first I could not see the necessity of wearing the costume; but I can quite see it now."

They would have left Shanghai sooner, but for the British consul's hesitation about the wisdom of their plan to move inland to Hangzhou and the difficulty in getting the Chinese authorities to sign the necessary permits. But by November they were ready to move.

Hangzhou had stood on the shores of the beautiful West Lake for over two thousand years. Not far from the South Gate in the turreted walls, the Qiantang river flowed into a magnificent estuary two or three miles wide, and then to Hangzhou Bay. The lake stood amid forested hills with pagodas, temples and ancient tombs dotted among the trees. The surface of the lake was interspersed with little islands and the water rang with the sound of thousands of ducks, geese and swans.

Everywhere magnolia, azaleas and camellias grew and for centuries the mulberry groves had supported a thriving silk industry. More than a million people lived in Hangzhou including poets and painters, and the rich in their mansions.

When the *Lammermuir* party made their first exploratory visits, they could still see the debris left over from the Taiping Rebellion. A Manchu garrison was stationed near the West Gate; the provincial governor and his mandarins lived in restored palaces. Although a handful of missionaries were already there, Hangzhou was larger than Ningbo and there was work for many missions to do.

Hudson Taylor and Mr Tsiu, who had been converted under Hudson's preaching some years earlier in Ningbo, found just the place to establish a CIM base in Hangzhou. No 1 New Lane was on the edge of the residential sector, among old houses which had suffered too much damage during Taiping fighting to be wanted by merchants or mandarins. It was an old mansion with whitewashed walls which before the rebellion had belonged to a wealthy family of mandarins. Its thirty or so large rooms could easily be further partitioned.

Even on their first visit, Hudson Taylor and Tsiu's minds raced with the possibilities. The main entrance led into a large pavilion, which would make a marvellous chapel; round a partly-roofed large courtyard stood a dozen rooms some of which could be made into a clinic close ·to the chapel — patients could listen to the gospel while waiting for treatment. The two men could see where reception and dining rooms, office and printing rooms, servants' rooms and storage rooms would go. Upstairs were two sections reached by different staircases, ideal as separate quarters for the single men and women. A sheltered and secluded rock-garden would offer peace and relaxation.

Of course the house would need a lot of attention and, as Emily Blatchley delightfully put it when she saw it, "there is a great superabundance of both dust and ventilation, and it comes far short of its full complement of doors and windows."

Taylor secured the property at a reasonable rent, and the

team moved in and began the repairs and alterations. They bought timber, nails and a large quantity of stout grass-paper. The carpenters and handymen in the team set about making frames and partitions of larch planking for outer walls and strong paper for inner walls and ceilings. Hudson closed a hole six feet by nine in his own bedroom wall with a sheet. They got hold of pictures to hang on the walls, and covered the floors with reed mats; they bought some furniture and constructed some themselves, keeping warm as they worked by burning charcoal in brass pans. Fortunately it was a mild winter.

At the turn of the year, plasterers came to replace the sheets and paper with thick lath and plaster.

Gradually the team became a familiar sight in that part of Hangzhou, and William Rudland wrote, "I attribute a great deal of the quiet we have had to our wearing Chinese dress; we go about and are taken but little notice of."

When James Meadows and George Crombie travelled from Ningbo to Hangzhou towards the end of 1866, they passed through the large and important town of Xiaoshan, ten miles from Hangzhou and fifty from Shaoxing where John and Anne Stevenson, two other CIM missionaries, were working. Meadows and Crombie argued the strategic importance of establishing a base in Xiaoshan, and the two men went there with Hudson Taylor to spy out the land. After preaching to city audiences they managed to rent a small house. The landlord agreed to let it to foreigners on condition that they would wear Chinese clothes. It was agreed that Lewis and Eliza Nicol would be pioneers of the work in Xiaoshan.

✳ ✳ ✳ ✳ ✳

George Moule was a CMS missionary of about Hudson Taylor's age who had begun to work in Ningbo in 1858 and had come to Hangzhou in 1864. His family's name is well known in church history. In London Hudson Taylor had corresponded with his father, the Rev Henry Moule, about the romanized

Ningbo vernacular New Testament. Henry's sons all went to Cambridge and George, Arthur and Handley followed him into the Anglican ministry. Arthur also worked in China. Handley wrote hymns and later became Bishop of Durham. George Moule had warmly welcomed the *Lammermuir* party to China — but now the relationship was turning sour.

The style of missionary work favoured by Moule contrasted strongly with that favoured by Hudson Taylor. The CMS had built a Gothic-style church in Ningbo, and dressed and lived largely as westerners. On arrival in Hangzhou, the Moules had continued their western style of living and looked with disapproving eyes at the young CIM missionaries walking about the town in Chinese dress.

George and Adelaide Moule began to invite members of the CIM team for meals, and Lewis Nicol got into the habit of grumbling about various things which he thought were wrong at New Lane. He distorted the truth about the way Hudson Taylor conducted affairs until at last his imagination ran almost total riot. The Moules were ready listeners. When Lewis Nicol, John Sell and Josiah Jackson visited his home, Moule held forth about his objections to Europeans wearing Chinese clothes. He also thought it was dangerous for so many unmarried men and women to live together at New Lane, and that Hudson Taylor was too familiar and intimate with the young ladies in the party. Moule became convinced that the responsibility for avoiding damage to the missionary cause rested on his own shoulders.

On January 2, Stephan Barchet and Lewis Nicol travelled the ten miles to Xiaoshan and clinched the deal on the house there. Not long afterwards Lewis's wife, Eliza, and a Chinese companion joined them. James Williamson helped Nicol convert a ground-floor room of the Xiaoshan property into a chapel and guest hall. Nicol returned to Hangzhou on the 25th to ask whether Tsiu might come and open the new accommodation.

Everyone at New Lane was astonished when they saw Nicol. He was wearing European clothes — and had been for a week. This was despite the fact that the CIM had promised the landlord in Xiaoshan that the occupants would dress as Chinese; it also disregarded the agreement that all prospective missionaries had made with Hudson Taylor in London.

Hudson Taylor decided not to challenge Nicol immediately, recognizing that in the heat of the moment he might make the wrong move. Next day, Nicol returned to Xiaoshan with Tsiu.

On Sunday, many came to hear the gospel preached at the Xiaoshan chapel. The following day Nicol and Tsiu went out into the streets, Nicol dressed in his English clothes.

On Monday evening at about 8.30, Lewis, Eliza and James Williamson were upstairs writing and Tsiu and a servant were downstairs. Suddenly Tsiu saw that the street outside the house was full of men with lanterns; the magistrate's sedan chair was outside the door. Tsiu ran upstairs to tell Nicol, who came down to find the magistrate standing at the bottom of the stairs; about fifty of the magistrate's men were in the chapel. Nicol bowed to the magistrate who promptly gripped him by the shoulders and began to handle him roughly.

After a while the magistrate became more polite, sat down and motioned to Nicol to do the same. One of his staff whispered that the reason for this erratic behaviour was that the magistrate was drunk. Nicol ordered some tea.

"I don't want it!" said the magistrate. "D'you think I'll drink foreign devil's tea? Fetch the other English occupant of the house!"

James Williamson appeared, carrying his passport; the magistrate refused to look either at his or Nicol's passport. He then demanded to see Eliza, leered at her and made suggestive remarks. Next he insisted on being shown every room in the house, and had to be assisted by his staff as he toured. Upstairs he sat down and asked a torrent of questions about England, announcing that Christianity was a depraved and prohibited religion.

Then the alarmed landlord arrived and handed the

magistrate a note. The gentleman declined to read it and virtually ignored the landlord.

Eventually he came downstairs and turned to Tsiu.

"Beat him!" he ordered. No charge was brought.

The Nicols and James Williamson looked on in helpless horror as two men took hold of Tsiu. One held him by the *bianzi* and the other by his feet. Two other men began to beat him on the thighs, giving him six hundred lashes to his bare skin, then a hundred lashes on the sides of his face.

The magistrate turned to Nicol and Williamson. "Will you leave the house tomorrow?"

Nicol nodded agreement. Hudson Taylor had previously instructed him, in case of trouble, not to enter into a dispute with local authorities but to refer any disputes to the British consul. The magistrate then left with a final comment to the Nicols, James Williamson, Tsiu and their servant.

"If any of you remain tomorrow, you will be beheaded."

At daybreak, Tsiu went ahead with a servant and reached New Lane first. Only able to speak with difficulty, he described what had happened. Nicol arrived next, leaving Eliza and James Williamson in the boat with those belongings they had been able to bring with them.

It was a tense meeting. Nicol's tone suggested that he saw the incident as his own affair. But then he asked: "Should I go to Ningbo and lay the matter before the consul?"

"The matter should certainly be reported to the consul at once," Taylor replied. "But it's for me as superintendent of the mission to write. However, before I involve myself in this capacity, I must ask whether you are prepared to acknowledge me as your leader and director. Do you consider yourself a member of the mission, a fundamental principle of which is that I should be, in all matters not affecting the conscience, the guide and director? Why did you discard your Chinese clothes without consulting me, in disregard of the agreement made when the property was rented?

"The incident has involved such serious complications for

the mission that, although at this moment I should prefer to show you only sympathy, I must have your answer before I report to the consul. Who are the victims of the outrage, individuals or the mission?"

"I acknowledge your right to direct the mission," replied Nicol. "But I have had a great deal on my mind and used my own judgment in this matter. If I had been fluent in Chinese I would have stayed in Chinese clothes. I will wear them again when I can speak Chinese freely. At the moment I feel insecure, and foreign clothes give me protection and respect."

Events in Xiaoshan had surely demonstrated that foreign clothes gave no such protection.

They brought Eliza and the baggage up to the house and Hudson Taylor waited for what he described as Nicol's "own good feeling" to lead him to change back into Chinese clothes.

When he was satisfied that he fully understood what had happened, Taylor wrote to British Consul Forrest in Ningbo. He described the events in detail, adding, "I would fain hope that you may see it right to vindicate the honour of our country, and our rights under the Treaty of Tientsin, by requiring such a proclamation to be put out as shall cause our persons and our passports to be respected, and shall give the natives confidence in rendering us their legitimate services."

With more experience of working with well-meaning consular authorities and mandarins in the best interests of the mission, Taylor later stopped bothering about the vindication of his country's honour.

NEW LANE 27
COMES ALIVE

W hen news of Tsiu's flogging reached England, CIM supporters wrote letters of sympathy and encouragement. Tsiu replied by describing his thoughts as he was being beaten: "This truly is not real disgrace: though deeply painful, there is joy in it. When your younger brother ... was punished with beating ... he remembered the words of the Holy Writ spoken by Jesus, 'Blessed are those who are persecuted for righteousness sake, for theirs is the Kingdom of Heaven'; and likewise the Scripture, 'Behold happy is the man whom God correcteth; therefore, despise not thou the chastening of the Almighty: for He maketh sore, and bindeth up; He woundeth, and his hands make whole.'"

Early in February 1867, Taylor asked Nicol to change back into Chinese clothes. He refrained from pointing out that James Williamson had been dressed as a Chinese in Xiaoshan and had been left alone.

"The reasons you gave for wearing English clothes in Xiaoshan do not apply in Hangzhou," Taylor told him.

"No, I won't wear Chinese clothes," Nicol replied. "I will not be bound neck and heel to any man."

"If you persist in wearing English clothes, it is likely to prove injurious and possibly dangerous to the mission."

"Then I suppose I had better make my way at once to one of the free ports."

"I'm not sure but what that may prove to be the best course," said Hudson Taylor. But Nicol continued to move about Hangzhou dressed in English clothes.

Also in February, a new group of missionaries arrived in Hangzhou. John McCarthy's first sight of the scene in New Lane engraved a picture on his mind which never left him. It was the Chinese New Year holiday and the crowd outside the CIM clinic was even larger than usual. Hudson Taylor was standing on a table preaching to the people. As the McCarthy family were shown into the house, Taylor waved his hand and acknowledged them with a brief word of welcome, then carried on preaching.

New Lane had come alive. Taylor was seeing more than two hundred patients daily. Succesful operations for cataracts seemed like miracles to the Chinese. Sedan-chairs would queue up outside the house dropping patients and waiting to be hired for the return journey. Food and drink sellers moved in and did a good trade. Tsiu would preach to those who waited or, to give him a break, Hudson Taylor would appear from time to time and speak or sing himself. He had taken to playing his harmonium, much to the crowd's delight.

One   day, Maria said to a Chinese helper, "I think so many coming to be cured proves the ordinary people don't believe that foreigners want to take out their eyes."

"Yes, but a woman who came to the clinic was so frightened when she saw Mr Nicol that she went away without being attended to," replied the helper.

The issue wouldn't go away. John Sell had now sided with Nicol and was wearing English clothes. Jane McLean sympathized with them.

A letter from William Berger revealed that Nicol had been writing disloyal and complaining letters to him. Berger wrote to Taylor: "Should you decide to send him home you are at liberty to do so at my expense."

Midst all these tensions, one happy event: Maria Hudson Taylor was born on February 3, and mother and baby did well.

❋ ❋ ❋ ❋ ❋

John McCarthy fitted in well at New Lane. At thirty, he was more mature than some of the *Lammermuir* party. He cheerfully agreed to wear Chinese clothes from the start and quickly made good progress with the language. He took no notice of Lewis Nicol's attempts to influence him towards his negative way of thinking. Taylor began to feel less isolated; he called his team together and reminded them of what he had said in London about his principles and strategy, and the terms on which they had agreed to become members of the CIM. Turning to each of them in turn he asked, "What did you understand to be the agreement you came to with Mr Berger and myself?"

"That until we mastered the language, we would wear English clothes for our protection," replied Nicol.

"I disagree," said James Williamson. "I understood according to the views you have expressed about financial arrangements and dress."

"I agree with that," said William Rudland. "You would be the director of the mission and have the direction of funds."

George Duncan said, "I have always had some darkness in my mind about this, but I understood that when I came to China I was unintelligent and in these things was under your direction."

By the end of the discussion, everyone except Nicol and Sell was supporting Taylor.

In March, George Moule came to New Lane and delivered a letter to Taylor. "My main objection," he had written, "is ... that by domiciling in your own house so many unmarried females you are doing that which if I am not mistaken would be viewed with mistrust and disapproval even in England; and which among the Chinese gives a reasonable handle to the worst of imputations upon the morality of European Christians ...

"Living as you do in very confined premises, having some of the restraints of social etiquette relaxed by your relation to these ladies as their physician, and some by the position you have assumed as their spiritual pastor, having them, further, to so large an extent dependent upon you as their only easily accessible friend and adviser of experience in China, since you have removed them from the neighbourhood of the bulk of missionary society — you would be more than human if you were not capable of being tempted to lay aside in some measure the reserve with which for their sakes and your own they ought to be treated.

"You are conscious that you are not more than human and therefore as one who has known something during more than twenty years of the 'single plague of his own heart'; and something of the infirmities of other Christians, and who is, in respect of age and missionary experience, not younger than yourself, I have taken upon myself most solemnly to urge you ... to consult, in all reasonable self-diffidence, with those of the other missionaries who you can trust for their piety and wisdom, as to the best method of putting a speedy end to the present organization of your mission, so that imminent perils (as I conceive them to be) may be averted ..."

Moule was reported to have called the CIM establishment at New Lane "scandalous", and "worse than a Romish convent". A year later, Moule expanded his criticisms and accusations about goings-on at New Lane to include references to kissing and "nocturnal visits". Group photographs of the CIM at this time often show the people at Hudson's side with a hand on his shoulder: in the photograph of the *Lammermuir* party issued openly to supporters, Emily Blatchley has a hand on Hudson's shoulder and Jennie Faulding appears to be holding his arm. A goodnight kiss from them would have been only natural. Affection was vital to Emily particularly, as her own family had all died.

After reading Moule's letter, Hudson Taylor insisted on a meeting with him to clarify the issues and asked James Williamson to go with him. Each of the ladies was asked to give James a statement about Hudson's behaviour towards them.

When they arrived at Moule's home, Moule asked, "Have you come on business?"

"Yes," replied Hudson Taylor, "I have come to discuss your letter to me."

"I have nothing to add to my letter," said Moule.

"I have," said Hudson Taylor. "I want an explanation of your impeachment of my private moral character!"

"I have not impeached your private moral character."

"Your behaviour has been the most consummate piece of priestly presumption I have ever heard of," said Hudson Taylor.

It was a nasty emotional scene — but it achieved nothing.

✳ ✳ ✳ ✳ ✳

Towards the end of February, Lewis Nicol wrote Hudson Taylor a note complaining that he was misunderstood. Taylor replied with a note which began "My dear Brother", saying that he very much wanted to see the breaches healed, and this would come about only if they were definite and open with each other. He suggested that Nicol wrote again telling him exactly what he was complaining about. Nicol replied with a letter which rambled on for three foolscap pages, mostly about clothes.

All the ladies of the *Lammermuir* party except Nicol's wife, Eliza, and Jane McLean then drew up a declaration which said, "Our household arrangements (in Hangzhou) are far more strict, and 'the restraint of social etiquette' more rigidly observed than they would be at home; and in Mrs Taylor (whose presence among us seems to have been ignored) the lady members of our mission have one to whom they can at all times look for sympathy and counsel ... we have no sympathy with any movements made to assail Mr Taylor's character, which has been, throughout our intercourse with him, that of a gentleman, a Christian, and preeminently a Christian missionary ..."

In March, Nicol wrote another note. He complained that his wife had received five dollars less than the other women when they reached China! He also asked Hudson Taylor what his complaint was against him.

To this Taylor replied: "It is a task which gives me no pleasure ... I have to complain of your want of truthfulness — often I believe unintentional ... but yet, untruthfulness ... persisted in after you have been corrected. I have to complain of your want of honest, open, straightforwardness — of your jealous, proud self-confident spirit, which makes you a torment to yourself, and a source of sorrow to those around you; of your perpetual fault-finding and grumbling about almost everyone and everything ... And finally of that spirit of insubordination which leads you to persist in your own way ... Your difficulties are in yourself and not in your surroundings. These traits of character have caused troubles in Scotland, in England, on the *Lammermuir*, and here ... I told you expressly and explicitly, in the presence of Mr Berger ... that I should only feel bound to assist you so far as you acted in accordance with my directions ... if you still wish me to feel myself responsible for affording you all assistance of every kind, I must in view of all that has passed request you to give me in writing a statement of your intention to recognize me placed by God at the head of this mission and to submit to my direction in its affairs ..."

By May, Hudson Taylor had received no reply to this request. When challenged about this, Nicol said, "It would take more time than I have to spare to answer the letter ..." and he asked Taylor to come to Xiaoshan to discuss things.

Hudson Taylor and Maria decided that only a meeting in the presence of others could solve the problem. They put the New Lane team in the picture and everyone agreed to fast and pray about it the next morning, May 10. Then unexpectedly Nicol himself arrived from Xiaoshan, and Taylor took this as an answer from God. Nicol proceeded to air his latest grievances and make a number of statements which were shown to be untrue. Finally he was persuaded to sign a statement which set out the real facts of the situation.

In June, Nicol turned up again with the news that Eliza was ill. Hudson Taylor returned to Xiaoshan with him and supervised her pregnancy, making many journeys between Hangzhou and Xiaoshan and behaving as if nothing had happened to come between the two men. The Nicols also had to leave their first house in Xiaoshan, but Hudson Taylor found them another. He saw this as a step of faith, hoping that Nicol would mend his ways.

By this time news of Nicol's complaints and allegations, and George Moule's championship of them, were beginning to reach London. Until detailed statements of the facts reached them, the Bergers had to rely on their faith in Hudson and Maria. Fortunately the Goughs, William Pennefather, George Muller, the Howards and Lord Radstock and his family were unshaken by accusations of dark goings-on in New Lane. However Henry Venn, General Secretary of the CMS, unfortunately believed the reports, much to Berger's annoyance.

Berger took the precaution of writing to Hudson Taylor, saying, "You will I am sure be extra careful to put it out of the power of Mr Moule to establish any lack of prudence or undue intimacy."

And telling Nicol to mend his ways, Berger wrote, "I believe God has put honour upon dear Mr Taylor as He has upon Mr Muller of Bristol."

THE GARDENER PLUCKED A ROSE 28

In June 1867, Taylor went with John McCarthy, George Duncan, Tsiu and two servants to explore the region southwest of Hangzhou. The boat in which they set off up the Qiantang river was, like so many in China, flat-bottomed and covered with a semi-circular roof made of bamboo matting — surprisingly efficient in keeping off the rain.

McCarthy looked at their fellow-passengers. "Some were lying, some sitting, some eating, and some smoking — almost all chattering, the foreigners in *their* dress forming the staple subject of conversation." They settled down for their first night aboard, enjoying a beautiful moonlight, a brisk wind in their favour and no mosquitoes.

They awoke to find that the wind had dropped and that five or six men were pulling them along with ropes. They washed in hot water which the boatmen provided for a few coins, and then held a short service. When Taylor read a passage from the Bible and preached the gospel, his audience listened well.

They tied up in the evening at a boat-station which served the town of Fuyang, about forty miles from Hangzhou, and walked to the city up a winding path and stone steps which had been carved out of the city walls.

John McCarthy vividly described the following night's scene on board: "Next to Mr Duncan lay a poor unfortunate with chains around his legs ... it appears he had been an accomplice in a murder, and his sentence of capital punishment had been commuted to banishment. Opposite him were a couple of opium smokers, who, as soon as everyone else had settled down for the night, had their lamps out, and, after settling themselves in a comfortable position, indulged their depraved appetite. At the other side, and packed very closely, were five or six mandarin's servants who, with a few soldiers and other people, along with our party, made the boat quite full enough."

Next day, at Tonglu, Hudson Taylor and his companions visited a temple and pagoda on a hill above the river. One of the priests seemed persuaded by their arguments for worshipping the one living and true God.

"But if we gave up the false we would not be able to repair our temple," he said.

Next day, they came to a village where Taiping fighting had reduced the number of houses fit to live in to three. The villagers gave them plums and tea and refused any payment. The missionaries explained the Christian message and presented them with a Chinese gospel.

Moving on to a village up in the hills, they bought some provisions. McCarthy wished their friends at home could have seen them as they returned to their boat. George Duncan led the way, his shaved head protected by an enormous straw hat with a brim as wide as his shoulders. In one hand he carried a palm-leaf fan, and in the other a live cockerel hanging by its legs and complaining noisily. It ended up as dinner just the same. Taylor came next, wearing an equally gigantic hat, his arms full of other shopping. McCarthy followed with a thousand cash — the change from a dollar — slung around his neck. Their clothes had once been white, but after a week in a boat they now looked distinctly grubby.

Back at the boat they enjoyed hot tea and a hot wash.

Taylor, Duncan and Tsiu then left McCarthy with a servant and travelled to Lanxi with their elderly cook. Their lodgings at Lanxi were not luxurious: the roof leaked, the floor was dirty. A few pieces of matting lay folded up on the floor, waiting to be nailed across cracks in the wall when the rain blew in. There was no chimney, so when the cook prepared meals their eyes smarted. Their beds were made of bamboo frames and deal boards; each man spread a railway rug and a pillow on his bed for softness and covered it with a mat to keep him cool. A mosquito-curtain provided the finishing touch. The room also boasted a table, a stool, a plank supported on two trestles, and a stove which they carried in and out at meal-times. In an act of sheer self-indulgence, George Duncan had spent six pence on a chair!

They hired an excellent Chinese teacher for Duncan, who began rapidly to improve his knowledge of local expressions. When Hudson Taylor left for Hangzhou, Duncan was going out each afternoon into the temples and tea-shops selling portions of Scripture and tracts and talking to the people.

On his return journey, Hudson Taylor found himself in a boat lashed to another travelling to the same destination. When the boats tied up late in the evening, it seemed too good an opportunity to miss. He preached to the passengers in both boats until he was worn out and assumed that they would be weary with listening. He said a short prayer and indicated that the proceedings had come to an end. But no one moved, and his audience made it clear that they wanted to hear more. So Hudson began again, and talked for a long time. Again he stopped; no one moved. Then people began asking questions, which Taylor answered at length. By this time he felt utterly exhausted and very cold. "It was I," he recalled, "who had, after urging on them the immediate importance of turning to Christ, to remind them of the lateness of the hour, and to suggest that it was time to retire."

Next morning he called on Lewis and Eliza Nicol in their

new home before returning to Hangzhou and finding things going well.

"All the way," John McCarthy wrote, recalling this trip down the Qiantang river, "either on boat or on shore, in the teashops — in the street or in temples, wherever people congregated, they heard the story of redeeming love ... It was evident that the real motive power of the life of the Lord's servant was that the love of God had been shed abroad in his heart, and that there was a real love for the Chinese people and a true appreciation of the many sterling qualities in the Chinese character, which raised them so entirely above the other heathen nations ..."

❋ ❋ ❋ ❋ ❋

Like her lawyer father, Maria had a good mind. She reflected carefully on the pros and cons of donning Chinese dress and of the role of women in the work of the mission, and put her thoughts on paper in a letter to Mary Berger. They are clear, concise and elegantly expressed. "I am satisfied that our Chinese dress gives us a decided advantage. I had misgivings before leaving England about the *ladies* wearing Chinese dress on this ground: the Chinese despise their own families, while they respect foreign ladies; will they treat us with as much respect, and shall we have as much weight with them, if we change our dress? But I have found no ground for retaining this misgiving; on the contrary I am satisfied that the force of character, education, and Christian principle give us weight with Chinese of both sexes, which neither wearing our own dress could give, nor adopting the Chinese costume could take away. I, for one, have been treated with quite as much respect in the latter as in the former. I know that those who prefer the foreign dress think it commands respect. I very strongly disbelieve this ...

"I have not heard from the Chinese the slightest aspersions on the character or position of our dear sisters. A great deal that we do must appear strange to the Chinese. Our coming out here at all is strange. That so many grown-up ladies should be *unmarried* is certainly strange; for an unmarried woman of twenty would be hard to find among them ... Miss Faulding was saying to me this afternoon that she wished she could make herself into a dozen persons and yet keep one, for then all the time might be well spent."

Hudson Taylor's own understanding of the case for wearing Chinese clothes was rooted in his deep respect for Chinese culture and his sensitive perception of the role of the missionary, in which he was far ahead of his time:

"We have to deal with a people whose prejudices in favour of their own customs and habits are the growth of centuries and millenniums. Nor are their preferences ill-founded. Those who know them most intimately respect them most, and see the necessity for many of their habits and customs — this being found in the climate, productions, and conformation of the people.

"There is perhaps no country in the world where religious tolerance is carried to so great an extent as in China; the only objection that prince or people have to Christianity is that it is a foreign religion, and that its tendencies are to approximate believers to foreign nations.

"I am not peculiar in holding the opinion that the foreign dress and carriage of missionaries — to a certain extent affected by some of their converts and pupils — the foreign appearance of the chapels, and, indeed, the foreign air given to everything connected with religion, have very largely hindered the rapid dissemination of the truth among the Chinese. But why need such a foreign aspect be given to Christianity? The word of God does not require it; nor I conceive would reason justify it. It is not their denationalization but their Christianization that we seek.

"We wish to see Christian Chinese — true Christians, but withal *Chinese* in every sense of the word. We wish to see churches and Christian Chinese presided over by pastors and officers of their own countrymen, worshipping their true God in the land of their fathers, in the costume of their fathers, in their own tongue wherein they were born, and in edifices of a thoroughly Chinese style of architecture ...

"Let us in everything unsinful become Chinese, that by all means we may save some. Let us adopt their costume, acquire their language, study to imitate their habits, and approximate to their diet as far as health and constitution will allow. Let us live in their houses, making no unnecessary alterations to external appearance, and only so far modifying internal arrangements as attention to health and efficiency for work absolutely require.

"Our present experience is proving the advantage of this course. We do find that we are influencing the Chinese around us in a way which we could not otherwise have done. We are daily coming into contact with them, not in one point, but in many; and we see the people becoming more or less influenced by the spirit, piety and earnestness of some of those labouring among them. But this cannot be attained without some temporary inconvenience, such as the sacrifice of some articles of diet. Knives and forks, plates and dishes, cups and saucers, must give place to chopsticks, native spoons and basins (and food) ...

"In Chinese dress, the foreigner, though recognized as such, escapes the mobbing and crowding to which, in many places, his own costume would subject him. In preaching, while his dress attracts less notice his words attract more. He can purchase articles of dress and also get them washed and repaired without difficulty and at a trifling expense in any part of the country."

These were the ideas, and this was the vision, that inspired Hudson and Maria in their work. In directing the mission, Hudson shied away from drawing up lists of rules and regulations. But he passionately believed that the Chinese would only be won for Christ if those from the west who brought them the gospel understood and respected their ancient culture. He expected the cheerful cooperation of his fellow workers in the task. These were the terms under which all of them — including Nicol — had agreed to serve. If they did so, constrained by the love of Jesus, the reward would be great.

The cost would be great, too.

✳ ✳ ✳ ✳ ✳

Taylor had longed "to have a little miniature of my precious Maria." So it had been a happy day in Ningbo, back in 1859, when he had first set eyes on baby Grace. Aboard the *Lammermuir*, she had simply put her trust in Jesus. Now a happy child of eight, she had a favourite spot in New Lane where she loved to play — a paved rock-garden with a pool among the shrubs and two or three shady trees.

In August, when they were on a hilltop holiday to escape the great heat, Grace went off her food and began to lose weight; she complained of a headache and on the eighth a high fever set in. Next day, as she lay in the fresh air on William Rudland's camp bed, she became incoherent. Hudson Taylor was away and George Duncan carried her to Maria's bed. Jennie Faulding wrote, "I will never forget seeing her ... in his arms with her beautiful hair hanging carelessly about her shoulder and looking so pretty."

Hudson Taylor rushed back and quickly saw how ill she was. It was meningitis.

"Cut off all her hair and apply cold compresses."

Maria carefully followed his instructions.

"May she be spared to grow it again," she said.

Mary Bell helped with the nursing and reported that Taylor "was so brokenhearted he cried most of the day." To talk privately to Maria, he took her out to a secluded rock-pool in a gully where they sometimes bathed.

"There's no hope of Gracie recovering," he told Maria.

They commended her to God and pleaded with Him to do the best for her and for them.

Back at her bedside, he said to Grace, "I think Jesus is going to take you to Himself. You are not afraid to trust yourself with Him, are you?"

"No, papa," came the reply.

Next day, Hudson wrote to William Berger. "Beloved brother — I know not how to write to you, nor how to refrain. I seem to be writing almost from the inner chamber of the King of kings — surely this is holy ground. I am striving to write a few lines from the side of a couch on which my darling little Gracie lies dying ... Dear brother, our heart and flesh fail, but God is the strength of our heart, and our portion for ever. It was no vain nor unintelligent act, when knowing the land, its people and climate, I laid my dear wife and the darling children with myself on the altar for this service."

Four days later, Grace showed signs of pneumonia.

On Friday evening, August 23, the Taylor family and those closest to them gathered round Grace's bed. Hudson began one hymn after another, though at times his voice failed. Maria sat bent over Grace, now unconscious. At twenty to nine her breathing stopped.

"I never saw anything look so lovely as dear little Gracie did the evening following her death," Mary Bowyer wrote, "the sweetest expression of countance one could behold on earth."

"Our dear little Gracie!" wrote Hudson. "How I miss her sweet voice in the morning, one of the first sounds to greet us when we woke — and through the day and at eventide! As I take the walks I used to take with her tripping at my side, the thought comes anew like a throb of agony, 'Is it possible that I shall nevermore feel the pressure of that little hand, nevermore hear the sweet prattle of those dear lips, nevermore see the sparkle of those bright eyes?' And yet she is not *lost*. I would not have her back again ... The Gardener came and plucked a rose."

WHO SPOKE OF REST? 29

G reat celebrations at New Lane on Christmas morning, 1867: William Rudland married Mary Bell. After a blissful honeymoon in a houseboat, they returned — William to supervise the printing presses and workmen, and Mary to continue for the time being to care for the Taylor children.

By the end of 1867, the CIM had taken over the next-door house. Now No 1 housed most of the married couples and the single girls; No 2 housed the McCarthys and the single men. Propriety would now not only be observed, it would be clearly *seen* to be observed.

Hudson Taylor, approaching his late thirties, had put on some weight and was now more capable of prolonged physical exertion. Early in 1868, he set off on foot to walk over the hills to Taizhou where Josiah Jackson was working; *All the way,* he mused, *one comes to a town or village every two or three miles — many of them towns of considerable size, where multitudes are born and live, and die, never leaving their native place. The thought forces itself upon one with painful intensity; and as you pass through town after town seeing others in the distance it becomes more and more oppressive. When and how are these poor souls to be reached with the gospel message?*

Although he was physically stronger, Hudson Taylor was showing every sign of suffering from stress. His "neuralgic headaches" were so bad that Maria tried to handle all she could of his day-to-day work. Jennie Faulding reckoned his neuralgia was brought on entirely by anxiety and overwork. The CIM was now virtually as large as the LMS, until then the largest Protestant mission in China.

Back home, Berger was weighed down with the problem of interviewing and trying to select new candidates for the mission. Hudson Taylor wrote to him: "We, as a mission, differ from all the other missions. As soon as some persons arrive here they find a sufficient answer to every question in, 'the American missionaries do this, or the Church missionaries do that; why can't we?' ... The missionaries of almost all the societies have better houses, finer furniture, more European fare than we have or are likely to have. But there is not one of them settled in the interior among the people. Unless persons are prepared to stand alone — separate from these societies and those who imitate them — they should never join our mission at all ... Let them know, too, beforehand, that if they are hearty, loyal members of this mission, they may expect the sneers and even opposition of good, godly men."

He went on to give quite clear and unambiguous advice to William Berger. "I only desire the help of such persons as are fully prepared to work in the interior, in the native costume, and living, as far as possible, in the native style. I do not contemplate assisting, in future, any who may cease to labour in this way. China is open to all; but my time and strength are too short, and the work too great to allow of my attempting to work with any who do not agree with me in the main on my plans of action ...

"China is not to be won for Christ by quiet ease-loving men and women ... The stamp of men and women we need is such as will put Jesus, China, souls, first and foremost in everything and at every time — even life itself must be secondary ... Of such men, and such women, do not fear to send us too many. They are more precious than rubies."

✳ ✳ ✳ ✳ ✳

The time had come to reduce the numbers of CIM missionaries stationed at Hangzhou and move further inland. In Zhejiang, the region to the south of the city now had a nucleus of missionaries and Christians hard at work. Anglicans, Presbyterians and Baptists were all beavering away at Ningbo. The most likely strategy would be for the McCarthys and Jennie Faulding, who had built up the strongest links with Hangzhou Christians, to stay while the rest moved on. George Duncan had already begun to break new ground in unoccupied provinces and it was time for others to support him.

Not everyone agreed with this strategy. William Berger pleaded with Taylor to consolidate what had already been achieved, but most of the team in China agreed with his vision of expansion. Hudson expressed his thought well in a poem.

Who spoke of rest? There is rest above.
No rest on earth for me. On, onto do
My Father's business. He, who sent me here,
Appointed me my time on earth to bide,
And set me all my work to do for Him,
He will supply me with sufficient grace —
Grace to be doing, to be suffering,
Not to be resting. There is rest above.

Tensions on other matters — particularly the issue of dress — rumbled on, with one or two of the women tending to support Lewis Nicol. Berger told Taylor that he had grave doubts whether it was right for Nicol, who now said he had no confidence in either of them, to be allowed to continue as a member of the mission. The pain of possibly having to dismiss him gnawed away at Hudson Taylor while he continued to hope that Nicol might mend his ways.

June 1 1868 was a key date in the CIM's expansion strategy. A houseboat travelled north-west up the Grand Canal, crossed the three-mile-wide Yangzi river, carried on up the Canal for twelve miles and tied up at the major city of Yangzhou. Aboard were Hudson Taylor and Maria, their four children, Hudson's secretary Emily Blatchley, the children's nurse Mary Rudland, four Chinese Christians from Hangzhou, as well as Tianxi, a young man Hudson had adopted eleven years earlier, and Ensing, a Chinese lady engaged to marry Li Lanfeng, the CIM's head printer.

Back in the thirteenth century Marco Polo had been governor of Yangzhou in the service of Kublai Khan. The Grand Canal wound its way through the south and east of the city and was spanned by many beautiful arched bridges. Famous for its wealth and the beauty of its women, Yangzhou also boasted an octagonal pagoda, graceful temples and magnificent gardens. But it was also notorious for the unruly behaviour of some of its citizens.

The city had hardly been touched by passing missionaries and even the Catholic church had only an orphanage, looked after by a Chinese director.

Aware of the reputation of Yangzhou mobs, Hudson Taylor and his family adopted a cautious approach during their first week in the city, not venturing out of their houseboat at times when they might attract undue attention. They left it to their Chinese companions to do the house hunting. But after some days it began to rain heavily, and they found that the roof of the boat leaked at every join. So they decided to move into what Maria described as "a first-rate Chinese hotel" in Yangzhou.

It was not until July 20 that they were able to take possession of the rambling building which was to become their home in Yangzhou. The house shared an entrance lane about a hundred yards long with several neighbouring houses. Two gates at the north end of the lane opened into an area of courtyards, gardens, rockeries and passageways between scattered buildings, each with only a few rooms and ideal for a mixed party. The main house consisted of a guest hall open to a courtyard, and a stairway with two living rooms on each side. At the top of the stairs a trapdoor could be lowered to isolate the bedrooms from the ground floor of the house. Taylor called carpenters in, and they stayed for a month repairing the property and adapting it for the party's needs.

✳ ✳ ✳ ✳ ✳

As Hudson Taylor and the CIM missionaries moved away from the coast to areas where westerners were hardly known, so they were to experience more opposition, often stirred up and encouraged by the scholar-gentry.

These scholars were the elite of Chinese society and the best of them were genuine intellectuals, men of culture. They honestly sought to practise Confucian principles and understood the richness of Chinese history and civilization. They appreciated and enjoyed the glories of their country's art and decorative printing, its priceless jades and porcelain, silks and lacquer, sculpture and carving. The sincere Confucian was often a dignified, self-disciplined gentleman, considerate of others including even uncultured "barbarians" from across the seas.

At the same time belonging to this elite, from which the top mandarins were drawn, carried an obligation to defend the ancient Chinese institutions. They saw Confucianism as preserving stability. While some of them recognized and welcomed what was good in western knowledge and culture, many rejected and opposed it.

The Christian gospel's emphasis on the individual was at odds with the Chinese ethic that the family was above the individual. Might not personal conversion undermine the very fabric of society? The act of preaching was often seen as an insult, for the preacher assumed the position of a teacher, and who could teach the scholars? And didn't Christian preachers challenge Chinese ancestral practices and deny the truth and validity of Buddhism, Daoism and Confucianism?

Unknown to the CIM party, the Yangzhou scholars and some military figures in the town held a meeting. They decided to stir the people up by circulating rumours about the missionaries, and force them to leave Yangzhou.

From that time on stones began to be thrown at the missionaries' windows. Anonymous posters made absurd accusations against them. The missionaries were called "Brigands of the Religion of Jesus" and the posters announced that they were in the habit of scooping out the eyes of the dying, eating children in their hospitals, and cutting open pregnant women to make medicine.

Soon an angry crowd gathered outside the house. The missionaries spent nearly a whole day arguing with the people. and denying the charges against them. Hudson Taylor wrote to Prefect Sun, the top official in the city, enclosing a copy of one of the offending posters and asking him to suppress this sort of behaviour. He received an evasive reply.

The same day, Saturday August 15, the party heard rumours that a riot was likely, and built barricades at strategic points to block the entrances. Before long a crowd of one to two hundred people gathered outside. That evening George Duncan arrived on what was meant to be a short visit, and had to force his way through the crowd. He decided to stay to help if he could. By force of circumstances the house now held four missionary men (Taylor, Duncan, Reid and Rudland), five women and four children, as well as nineteen Chinese.

Taylor wanted to send the women and children away to safety, but the women begged him not to do so. On Sunday the mob made several unsuccesful attempts to break into the house, and a horrible poster was circulated threatening that the house and its occupants would be burnt down.

On Monday things were a little quieter. The missionaries circulated some notices of their own, stating how foolish the slanders against them were and explaining that as soon as the repairs were completed, people would be invited to visit the premises for themselves. These tactics worked for a while.

On Wednesday, Taylor wrote again to Prefect Sun, reminding him of the treaty which stated that "British subjects are permitted to buy ground and build chapels in the interior and furthermore are allowed at every place at their own convenience to travel without detention, molestation or hindrance and that in case of need they may with confidence look for protection and aid at any time."

Prefect Sun replied, "As persons who get up this kind of report and placard generally do it in the dark and without either name or surname, it is not easy for me in a short time to lay hold of them."

On Saturday, August 22, the American chargé d'affaires at nearby Zhenjiang, Captain Sands, visited Yangzhou briefly with another foreigner to see the temples and pagodas. Both were wearing foreign clothes. They found the city quiet. But someone began to circulate a rumour in the tea-houses and along the streets that more foreigners had come and that 24 children were missing. A crowd soon gathered at the CIM premises and burst open two of the gates into the courtyard and garden area. Hudson Taylor stationed guards at the entrance on to the main street and instructed carpenters to repair the damage to the gates. But the crowd was in a very ugly mood.

"FIRST QUIET THE PEOPLE!" 30

Saturday evening, August 22: the crowd outside the CIM's house in Yangzhou had grown to eight to ten thousand. Some were armed with knives, spears and clubs and were throwing chunks of brick. Those in front were hammering on the main door trying to break in.

"The foreign devils have eaten 24 children!" they shouted.

Duncan and Taylor sent messengers to the Prefect but received no reply. They decided they would have to leave the others and go to the Prefect themselves. First they boarded up a window whose shutter had given way after someone had thrown a brick at it.

"Dear God," they prayed, "protect those we are leaving behind and go with us as we face the mob."

They left via a neighbour's house and managed to elude the rioters. But they were quickly spotted.

"The foreign devils are fleeing!" someone shouted, and a chase began.

Fortunately Hudson Taylor knew a route through some fields and it was now getting dark. But they had eventually to go through the main street, and were at this point pelted with stones and bricks. As they approached the Prefect's house, the *yamen*, the gatekeepers were just closing the gates, but hadn't yet bolted them. As the crowd caught up with Taylor and Duncan, the gates gave way and the two men were propelled into the entrance hall, falling flat on their faces. They picked themselves up and rushed in to the judgment hall, shouting over and over again the two words which Chinese mandarins are bound to pay attention to at any time of day or night.

"Save life! Save life!"

They were shown into the secretary's office and left to wait. Hudson could hear the yells of the mob at his house more than a mile away. Were they destroying his home — and perhaps his family? It was three-quarters of an hour before they were ushered in for an audience with Prefect Sun.

"Tell me what you really did with the babies?" he asked. "Is it true that you bought them from our people? What really is the cause of all this rioting?"

"I'll tell you the real cause of all this trouble," said Hudson Taylor, exploding. "It's your neglect in not taking appropriate measures when the problem was small and manageable. I must now ask you to take steps to repress the riot and save any of our family and friends who may still be alive. After that you can make any inquiries you wish. Otherwise I cannot answer for the result."

"Ah!" said the Prefect. "Very true, very true! First quiet the people, and then inquire. Sit still, and I will go to see what can be done. You must stay here. I will have no chance of achieving anything unless you keep out of sight."

Hudson Taylor and Duncan waited while the Prefect went to the scene of the riot. After two hours, he returned.

"All is now quiet. The city's military governor, the captain of the soldiers and two magistrates have been to the scene and have arrested several people who were plundering the premises. They will be punished. I will send for sedan chairs so that you may return under escort."

"All the foreigners left in the house have been killed!" Taylor and Duncan were told as they were carried back. Sickened and horrified, they asked God to support them, hoping desperately that this report was at least exaggerated. But as they drew nearer, a strange smell seemed to confirm it.

A pile of half-burnt reeds showed an attempt had been made to burn the house down. One wall had collapsed. The remains of boxes and furniture were scattered all over the place. They saw papers, letters, broken work-boxes, writing desks, dressing-cases, medical instruments and smouldering remains of books. But no sign of Taylor's family or the other missionaries. What had happened to them? The report they had received must be true.

* * * * *

After Taylor and Duncan had gone to the *yamen*, Henry Reid and William Rudland guarded the doors and entrances to the house as long as possible. But the mob broke in. The women and children shut themselves in Maria's room, pleading with God to protect them.

Eventually Rudland entered the room. He was so exhausted that he could hardly stand, and his clothes were stained with mud. At any moment they expected the rioters to come up the stairs and into the room. Then they heard Reid's voice from the courtyard below. It sounded hollow and hoarse.

"Mrs Taylor! Come down if you can. They're setting the house on fire, and I can't help you."

Their only hope of getting out was through the window. Someone had the presence of mind to throw mattresses and pillows out first to soften any falls. William Rudland climbed out on the sloping roof under the window. He let his wife down, followed by Ensing.

Freddie[1] was to go next, but as they were passing him

[1]Howard Taylor, the future biographer

through the window he said:

"Let Bertie go first, he's so frightened!"

So Herbert went down next, followed by Freddie.

Henry Reid then hurried these four away and hid them in a well-house. At that point rioters began to come up the stairs. A tall, bare-chested man came into Maria's bedroom. As he opened the door they could see other men carrying boxes out of other bedrooms. Maria spoke first.

"You see we are all women and children. Aren't you ashamed to molest us?"

The man made no reply.

Maria kept talking for a few minutes. The man began to carry out body-searches, feeling all over their thin summer dresses. Emily Blatchley had previously tied a small bag with seven or eight dollars inside her dress. The man discovered it and snatched it from her.

"You have more somewhere," he snarled. "Give it to me or I'll cut off your head!"

Then he tore off Louise Desgraz's pocket and took away a brooch from her hair. Catching sight of Maria's wedding ring sparkling in the light of a candle, he snatched it from her finger. Next he started searching the boxes and drawers, and Annie Bohannan quickly took the opportunity to run downstairs with baby Maria behind a man who was carrying off a large box. This shielded the baby from flying stones. She rushed through the fire and arrived safely in the well-house with the baby.

Henry Reid had returned and was shouting for the rest to hurry down. The smoke was beginning to choke them; walls were collapsing and the mob was screaming. Just after they had let Louise Desgraz down by a rope made of sheets, the men below threw a heap of burning objects under the window and cut off any further chance of escape by that route.

Three now remained upstairs: Maria, Rudland and Emily. The man who had entered the room turned to Rudland, caught him by the hair and dragged him down on to the projecting roof. He struggled to remove Rudland's watch. Rudland managed to throw it out into the darkness, hoping that the man might leave them to search for it. Enraged, the man tried to throw Rudland off the roof, but Maria and Emily dragged him back into the room. The man then picked up a large brick from the wall and raised his arm to crash it down on Rudland's head. Maria quickly put out her arm to stop the blow and the man turned to hit her instead.

"Would you strike a defenceless woman?" Maria asked him.

The man looked startled and dropped the brick. He climbed out on to the roof and shouted to the rioters below.

"Come up, come up!"

Henry Reid had now managed to drag the fire in the yard away from the window.

"There's not a moment to lose," he shouted up. "You must jump. I'll catch you."

Maria went to the edge of the roof, which was twelve to fifteen feet from the ground. She was six months pregnant. There was a great risk of injury but nothing else to be done. She jumped. Reid didn't manage to catch her but was able to break her fall. She landed on her side, her right leg twisted under her, and managed to get to her feet.

Maria watched as Emily prepared to jump. To her horror, just as she jumped a flying brick hit Reid on the side of his face. The blow blinded him and all but knocked him unconscious. With no one to break her fall Emily landed heavily on her back; she was stunned, but wearing her hair in the Chinese style protected the back of her head.

Rudland had lowered himself from the roof without injury and was helping Maria. He had been attacked by a man with a club but escaped with only a bruise, although a hernia later developed. Emily led Reid away, semi-conscious and in agony from the blow. Maria was bleeding freely from one injury, but the severe twist her leg had received gave her more pain.

Rudland rounded everyone up and led the party through

a doorway into a neighbour's house. They were taken quickly to a room far inside the house where they sat and waited, anxiously wondering what had happened to Taylor and Duncan. Reid lay groaning with pain; Maria was almost fainting from loss of blood; Emily found that her left arm was bleeding and she couldn't move it — she discovered later that she had suffered a compound fracture of her elbow.

"Mamma, where shall we sleep tonight, as they have burned our bed?" one of the children asked Maria.

"God will give us somewhere to sleep."

One of the Chinese teachers gleaned the latest news. "The Prefect has come with his soldiers and is driving away the rioters. The magistrate is personally guarding this house to protect us. But there's no news of Mr Taylor and Mr Duncan."

✳ ✳ ✳ ✳ ✳

At last, they heard a familiar voice outside the room. The door opened and in walked Taylor! His only injury was from a stone which had struck him on the knee on the way to the *yamen* and left him with a limp. Now that they were all together again they thanked God that they were alive. Taylor called the magistrate in to see Reid's condition.

They returned to their own house just after midnight. It had not been burnt down: their neighbours had managed to put the fires out. Hudson and Maria went into their own room and found clothes and belongings scattered everywhere, after the rioters had searched desperately for money and valuables. The pages of Maria's Bible were lying about all over the house. When they were all collected up, not a page was missing.

The rioters had ransacked every room except, curiously, Emily's. And it was there that the most important papers and the bulk of the money had been kept. None of it was touched.

That night, as the missionaries slept, a guard of soldiers and some of the mandarin's men kept watch outside the house. A crowd began to gather again. Reid was still in very bad shape and everyone was stiff and sore. They prayed together. The crowd grew larger. Taylor sent a Chinese servant to Zhenjiang to inform the British consul, Clement Allen, what had happened. With the help of carpenters he then nailed together some doors and boards and temporarily closed up the holes in the walls.

It was still quite early in the morning when Taylor set off to ask the Prefect for more help. No one attempted to harm him.

"His Excellency has sent for the magistrate who will return with you to the house."

Taylor, the magistrate and some soldiers returned to the house; the soldiers dispersed the large crowd which had now gathered.

"It is not safe for any member of your party to leave the city now," the magistrate told Hudson Taylor. "I want you to write a letter to the Prefect at once. Be careful to describe what has happened as a 'disturbance' not a 'riot', or the people will be more incensed than ever. Ask the Prefect to punish those who have been arrested and to quiet the people by proclamations. Thus we may restore peace before night, and you will not have to leave the city."

Taylor wrote a letter describing what had happened as mildly as he could. But the letter was intercepted and opened. The magistrate returned it to him saying it could not be sent.

"The truth has to be told," Taylor said.

"If you persist in sending that letter to the Prefect," replied the magistrate, "I will go back and have nothing more to do with the matter. You may protect yourself as best you can. But I warn you that the lives of all your party will probably be lost."

The magistrate was clearly anxious to obtain a letter which could be used as evidence that there had been no riot. Taylor had no alternative but to sit down and write almost at the magistrate's dictation, making no mention of the fire or the robbery.

"The only safe plan," said the magistrate when the letter was finished, "will be for me to remove you for the present to Zhenjiang."

In the afternoon, the magistrate hired sedan-chairs and coolies and escorted the party of CIM missionaries to the South Gate. The same day, Sunday August 23, 1868, Prefect Sun and the magistrate issued a proclamation.

A Prohibitory Proclamation

The Prefect and Magistrate of Yangzhou have received the following communication from the English missionary Mr Taylor. "The people have been disseminating false reports that the missionaries keep children in their house and secretly boil and eat them, but the people know nothing of the matter and there really is nothing of the sort done. Last night there was a countless crowd of people (round the house) creating a disturbance and I beg that they may be punished and a proclamation be issued to quiet the populace."

The Prefect and magistrate therefore declare that the disorderly proceedings of the populace in the missionaries' house were exceedingly rude and ill-mannered and they accordingly issue this prohibitory proclamation for the information of the people forbidding them hereafter to create any disturbance at Mr Taylor's house. If anything of that sort occurs the offenders will be severely punished. Disobey not! The proclamation to be posted in every street.

On their journey to Zhenjiang, still under an escort of troops, Hudson Taylor and his colleagues met the British, American and French vice-consuls on their way to investigate. Allen and the other consuls saw for themselves the debris which the rioters had left. The CIM party were sympathetically received in Zhenjiang.

"CHRISTIANITY WITH GUNBOATS" 31

The British authorities were determined not to accept the incident in Yangzhou without vigorous protest and appropriate action. Consul Walter Medhurst decided to go to Yangzhou and bring Prefect Sun to Nanjing to explain in person to the imperial viceroy why he hadn't responded more quickly.

On Tuesday September 8, Medhurst set off in a small steamer with an escort of marines, accompanied by vice-consul Allen and the French consul. A French frigate guarded the mouth of the Grand Canal until the return of the expedition. Hudson Taylor was unable to go with Medhurst due to an infection, so George Duncan and Josiah Jackson represented him.

Someone warned Prefect Sun of Medhurst's visit and he waited with his retinue at a minor gate of the city, intending to conduct the delegation as inconspicuously as possible through back streets to his *yamen*. The party entered through a main gate, however, and marched through busy streets as conspicuously as they could. They arrived at the *yamen*, took possession of it, stationed guards at the doors, and demanded an interview with the Prefect.

When Prefect Sun arrived back to find British marines at his doors, he was terrified. He attempted to argue that what had happened on the night of the 22nd was nothing more than a little excitement and unruliness. Medhurst had not the least intention of accepting this and set out a series of demands which Sun said were not in his power to grant. Medhurst insisted on taking the prefect to Nanjing so that his demands might be put before the viceroy; this Sun agreed to, provided he could go in his own boat and not as a prisoner.

Medhurst and his retinue then went with Prefect Sun to the CIM's devastated premises. Although cunning mandarins had carried out emergency repairs, there was enough debris to indicate the extent of the damage which the mob had inflicted.

Medhurst met with Hudson Taylor to receive details of the precise injuries suffered by the missionaries, and then went on to Nanjing. Viceroy Zeng Guofan received him with elaborate ceremony and some signs of friendliness, but did not treat Medhurst's complaints seriously. It seemed he was stalling until he had received more details from his officials.

When Sun eventually arrived, Medhurst continued to press the demands he had made at Yangzhou and Zeng continued to stall.

Then the commander of Medhurst's marine escort was taken seriously ill with dysentery and had to be rushed in his own ship to Shanghai, leaving Medhurst with only his own small boat. Without the trappings of power added by the gunboat, he was no longer treated with respect by the Chinese. The viceroy changed his tone and refused even to consider Medhurst's demands. He would only order Prefect Sun to issue a proclamation dealing with the incident.

Medhurst dismissed this response as totally inadequate, demanded to inspect any proclamation before it was issued and said that all relevant papers on the Yangzhou incident would be forwarded to the British minister in Beijing.

✳ ✳ ✳ ✳ ✳

In September, 1868, Hudson Taylor dismissed Lewis Nicol from the CIM. In his letter he told Nicol that he was acting after "conference with and with the concurrence of all the brethren of the *Lammermuir* party and as many of the other brethren of the mission as I have had the opportunity of meeting." He went on, "I do not dismiss you because of your denominational views ... nor yet for your preference for the English costume; nor indeed on any other ground in whole or in part than that of habitual and deliberate falsehood." Over a long period, Nicol had been telling lies about the mission to members of the CIM and othe missions.

Hudson Taylor asked John McCarthy to vet the contents of the letter and then deliver it by hand to Nicol. McCarthy told Taylor, "We hardly knew how much we valued your love, till it was nearly lost to us (in the riot). May we be bound closer and closer together — for the Lord's sake ... for the sake of this needy land ... Thank God, dear brother, and take courage, for if ever you were helped in writing a letter, I believe you were in the one I have just handed to Nicol. What pain it cost you to write that letter I can guess." McCarthy also wrote to William Berger, praising Hudson Taylor's qualities and defending him against all accusations. His only crime, he said, was that of trying to do ten men's work instead of one.

William Berger sent Nicol a gift of twenty pounds for his current needs and offered to book and pay for a passage back to England for him and his wife Eliza. However, Nicol chose to stay in Xiaoshan, and then helped briefly in the hospital in Ningbo. After that nothing is known of him.

In October, Susan Barnes and Margaret and Jane McLean, who had always sympathized with the Nicols, resigned from the mission. Jane McLean continued on very friendly terms with Hudson Taylor; Susan Barnes and Margaret McLean worked with the LMS for a while.

All this played on Taylor's health and Maria hoped

desperately that they would be able to get away for a few days' rest and change.

✳ ✳ ✳ ✳ ✳

Since the Yangzhou riots, the CIM had come in for a lot of criticism in the British press, even among Christians. Donations declined. Many people believed, wrongly, that Hudson Taylor had appealed for help from the British consul, who had come to his aid with a gunboat against the Chinese authorities. In fact, of course, he had appealed to the Chinese authorities when the riot began, and merely *informed* the British consul after the incident had occurred. The consul had then acted on his own initiative.

Taylor and his family were formally reinstated in their Yangzhou home on November 18, 1868. A Catholic priest described how, shortly before the reinstatement, "Mr Medhurst (the British consul) ... and Mr Taylor are taken solemnly through the streets to a large pagoda to accommodate 400 men. Scholars with buttons precede the retinue of mandarins. The two ringleaders had been arrested; the others, by joining the procession, gave the necessary satisfaction to foreigners. Two heralds at the head announced to people in the streets, *People — take care not to hurt the foreigners, or to call them 'foreign devils'; but give them the titles of great men.* Mr Taylor is taken back to his house, perfectly repaired at the expense of the mandarins." And it was at the Yangzhou house that Maria gave birth to a boy on November 29, 1868. They called him Charles Edward.

In March, 1869, the House of Lords debated the Yangzhou incident and its aftermath. The Duke of Somerset, plainly antagonistic, said that when he had heard the mission's name was the China Inland Mission he was not surprised at what had followed. "Now, what I want to ask is — what right have we to be sending inland missions to China — what right have we to be trying to convert the Chinese in the middle of their country? ... I have a decided objection to this system of supporting missionaries in the interior of China ... The fact is, we are propagating Christianity with gunboats; for the authorities of inland towns know perfectly well that if they get into trouble with a missionary a gunboat will come up ... We ought, I contend, to recall these inland missionaries ... A missionary, indeed, must be an enthusiast; if he is not an enthusiast, he is probably a rogue. No man would go up and live up one of those rivers and preach Christianity unless he were an enthusiast, and being an enthusiast he is more dangerous ..."

The Foreign Secretary, however, pointed out to his noble friend that "with regard to reducing the number of missionaries ... the Government is not precisely responsible in that matter, and that if missionaries choose to go or stay there our power of evicting them from China is small." But he did suggest that the missionaries would do better "to follow in the wake of trade when people have learned to see in it material advantage to themselves, rather than to seek to lead the way in opening up new locations."

All this was too much for the new Bishop of Peterborough, Dr Magee. In a maiden speech, he delivered a defence of missionaries which established his reputation as one of the best debaters of the day. He began by arguing that the Duke of Somerset had given a piece of advice which no missionary would accept — "namely, to leave some particular parts of the world unconverted, or flee from attempts to convert them, because, forsooth, these attempts might prejudice the interests of British trade. The youngest and least zealous of missionaries would probably reply that, important as were the interests of British trade, there was something in his eyes more sacred even than that sacred opium trade for which Great Britain once thought it worth while to wage war — namely, obedience to the command of His Master to go forth and seek to convey the gospel to every living soul, at whatever risk to himself or others ... It was surely unworthy of a Christian nation to say that if its subjects engaged in any trade, however demoralizing, they should be protected from the least infraction of their rights, or from the least insult, by all the might of Great Britain; but that, if they became missionaries and happened to displease the susceptibilities of the Chinese, they should be left to their fate, or saved from the mob by a forcible expatriation."

Dr Magee said that the Duke of Somerset had advocated stringent measures towards troublesome missionaries, but pointed out that had such a course been always and successfully pursued, then neither the noble Duke nor himself would have become Christians at all. Furthermore, "the noble Earl, the Foreign Secretary, has advised the missionaries to 'follow in the wake of trade'. Perhaps the noble Earl would mention the kind of trade in whose wake they were to follow? ... Were they to 'follow in the wake' of the opium trade ..., or were they to wait until British traders had inoculated them (the Chinese) with all their vices before they commenced teaching them the gospel? Instead of waiting for this the missionary felt that he had a higher duty imposed on him by a higher Master to go forth and preach the gospel ..."

The Lords debated the matter at length and with animation; and the Duke of Somerset was finally unsuccessful in his demand for missionaries to be recalled from inland China.

Notable among those who stood loyally by the CIM in the face of so much criticism was George Muller. He had been sending money direct to individual CIM missionaries, with the result that sharing funds out equally became difficult. Berger took this up with Muller who immediately accepted the point. Some time after the Yangzhou incident, with bad publicity still raging, Taylor received a letter from Berger.

> Mr Muller, after due consideration, has requested the names of all the brethren and sisters connected with the CIM, as he thinks it well to send help as he is able to each one, unless we know of anything to hinder ... Surely the Lord knew our funds were sinking, and thus put it into the heart of His honoured servant to help.

Muller's cheques to each of the missionaries arrived by the same post; and with the cheques a letter "for all the dear brethren and sisters connected with the China Inland Mission", part of which read:

My chief object is to tell you that I love you in the Lord; that I feel deeply interested about the Lord's work in China, and that I pray daily for you. I thought it might be a little encouragement to you in your difficulties, trials, hardships and disappointments to hear of one more who felt for you and who remembered you before the Lord ...

During the 1870s, Muller sent CIM missionaries approximately £2,000 annually — a massive amount in those days.

William Pennefather spoke up for Taylor and the CIM at the popular Mildmay Conference in London Lord Radstock, Sir Thomas and Lady Beauchamp, and the Goughs were among others whose confidence in Hudson Taylor remained unshaken throughout this difficult time.

In late May and early June, 1869, the Taylor family managed to get the break Maria had been so desperately hoping for. They travelled with Emily Blatchley to the beautiful island of Putuo in Hangzhou Bay; here was a peaceful setting with a mass of rhododendrons, long sandy beaches and tranquil temples — a popular resort enjoyed by the citizens of Ningbo and Shanghai.

The break came to an end all too quickly, and Taylor returned to a mountain of work. He was responsible now for eighteen missionaries and their families and six Chinese Christian workers. "Almost daily," he wrote, "I had letters from some group of workers asking for guidance, and wondering whether to stay or leave the station, as work for the time being was impossible. I knew not what to advise, but in each case, like Hezekiah, I spread the letters before the Lord, and trusted Him to teach me how to reply to them."

THE WAY TO HAPPINESS AND POWER 32

Throughout the summer of 1869 Hudson Taylor's morale was low. Irritability was his "daily hourly failure", and sometimes he even wondered whether someone so dogged by failure could be a Christian at all. Long periods of separation from Maria added to his inner tension and a bout of severe illness in August, probably pneumonia, didn't help.

With all this went a sense of need. He saw that both he himself and the CIM needed more holiness, life and power. He believed the personal need was greater: "I felt the ingratitude, the danger, the sin of not living nearer to God."

He prayed, he agonized, he fasted, he tried to do better, he made resolutions. He read the Bible more carefully, he ordered his life to give more time for rest and meditation. But all this had little effect. "Every day, almost every hour, the consciousness of sin oppressed me. I knew that if only I could abide in Christ all would be well, but I *could not*. I began the day with prayer, determined not to take my mind off Him for a moment; but pressure of duties, sometimes very trying, constant interruptions apt to be so wearing, often caused me to forget Him. Then one's nerves get so fretted in this climate that temptations to irritability, hard thoughts, and sometimes unkind words are all the more difficult to control. Each day brought its register of sin and failure, of lack of power. To will was indeed present with me, but how to perform I found not."

He began to ask himself a series of questions: *Is there no rescue? Must it be thus to the end — constant conflict and, instead of victory, too often defeat? How can I preach with sincerity that to those who receive Jesus, "to them gave He power to become the sons of God" (ie Godlike) when it is not in my own experience?*

Instead of growing spiritually stronger, he seemed to be growing weaker and giving in more to sin. He hated himself, he hated his sin. "I felt I was a child of God: His Spirit in my heart would cry, in spite of all, 'Abba, Father': but to rise to my privileges as a child I was utterly powerless ... I began to think that, perhaps to make heaven the sweeter, God would not give it down here. I do not think I was striving to achieve it in my own strength. I knew I was powerless. I told the Lord so, and asked Him to give me help and strength; and sometimes I almost believed He would keep and uphold me. But on looking back in the evening, alas! there was but sin and failure to confess and mourn before God."

This wasn't his state of mind and spirit every minute or even every day of those summer months. Rather, he said, it was a "too frequent state of soul; that toward which I was tending, and which almost ended in despair. And yet never did Christ seem more precious — a Saviour who *could* and *would* save such a sinner! ... And sometimes there were seasons not only of peace but of joy in the Lord. But they were transitory, and at best there was a sad lack of power."

Throughout the period, he recalled, "I felt assured that there was in Christ all I needed, but the practical question was how to get it out." With the biblical picture of Christ as the vine (John 15) on his mind, he wrote, "He was rich, truly, but I was poor; He strong, but I weak. I knew full well that there was in the root, the stem, abundant fatness; but how to get it into my puny little branch was the question."

Gradually he began to gain insights which were to bring him through this period. First, he saw that *faith* was the precondition for gaining what he wanted — it was "the hand to lay hold on His fulness and make it my own." But he didn't have this faith. He struggled for it, but it wouldn't come. He tried to exercise it, but in vain. "Seeing more and more the wondrous supply of grace laid up in Jesus, the fulness of our precious Saviour — my helplessness and guilt seemed to increase. Sins committed appeared but as trifles compared with the sin of unbelief which was their cause, which could not or would not take God at His word, but rather made Him a liar! Unbelief was, I felt, *the* damning sin of the world — yet I indulged in it. I prayed for faith, but it came not. What was I to do?"

The second insight came in the shape of a letter from John McCarthy. Hudson had shared with McCarthy something of the turmoils through which he was passing and they had often discussed the pursuit of holiness together. Taylor was working in Zhenjiang when McCarthy's letter arrived. McCarthy's struggles had echoed those of his leader.

I do wish I could have a talk with you now, about the way of holiness. At the time you were speaking to me about it, it was the subject of all others occupying my thoughts — not from anything I had read, not from what my brother had written even, so much as from a consciousness of failure; a constant falling short of that which I felt should be aimed at; an unrest; a perpetual striving to find some way by which I might continuously enjoy that communion, that fellowship at times so real, but more often so visionary, so far off! ...

Do you know, dear brother, I now think that this striving, effort, longing, hoping for better days to come, is not the true way to happiness, holiness or usefulness; better, no doubt far better, than being satisfied with our poor attainments, but not the best way after all. I have been struck with a passage from a book of yours left here, entitled *Christ is All*. It says:

"The Lord Jesus received is holiness begun; the Lord Jesus cherished is holiness advancing; the Lord Jesus counted upon as never absent would be holiness complete.

"This (grace of faith) is the chain which binds the soul to Christ, and makes the Saviour and the sinner one ... A channel is now formed by which Christ's fulness plenteously flows down. The barren branch becomes a portion of the fruitful stem ... One life reigns throughout the whole.

"They who most deeply feel that they have died in Christ, and paid in Him sin's penalties, ascend to highest heights of godly life. He is most holy who has most of Christ within, and joys most fully in the finished work. It is defective faith which clogs the feet, and causes many a fall."

This last sentence I think I now fully endorse. To let my loving Saviour work in me His will, my sanctification is what I would live for by His grace. Abiding, not striving nor struggling; looking off unto Him; trusting Him for present power; trusting Him to subdue all inward corruption; resting in the love of an almighty Saviour, in the conscious joy of a complete salvation 'from all sin' (this is His Word); willing that His will should truly be supreme — this is not new, and yet 'tis new to me. I feel as if the first dawning of a glorious day had risen upon me. I hail it with trembling, yet with trust. I seem to have got to the edge only, but of a sea which is boundless; to have sipped only but of that which fully satisfies. Christ literally all seems to me now the power, the only power for service; the only ground for unchanging joy. May He lead us into the realization of His unfathomable fulness.

How then to have our faith increased? Only by thinking of all that Jesus is, and all He is for us: His life, His

death, His work, He Himself as revealed to us in the
Word, to be the subject of our constant thoughts. Not
a striving to have faith, or to increase our faith, but
a looking off to the Faithful One seems all we need;
a resting in the Loved One entirely, for time and for
eternity.

Hudson Taylor put McCarthy's letter down and later
recalled, "As I read I saw it all! 'If we believe not, He abideth
faithful'. I looked to Jesus and saw (and when I saw, oh,
how joy flowed!) that He had said, 'I will never leave you'.
Ah, there is rest! I thought, *I have striven in vain to rest
in Him. I'll strive no more. For has He not promised to abide
with me — never to leave me, never to fail me?*
That day, Taylor shared McCarthy's letter with the others
who were staying in the CIM house in Zhenjiang. Emily
Blatchley wrote in her journal, "He too has now received
the rest of soul that Jesus gave me some little time ago."
In the next few days, Hudson Taylor continued to reflect
on the subject. God gave him new insights and clarified
his thinking. "As I thought of the vine and the branches,
what light the blessed Spirit poured into my soul! How great
seemed my mistake in having wished to get the sap, the
fulness *out* of Him. I saw not only that Jesus would never
leave me, but that I was a member of His body, of His
flesh and of His bones. The vine now I see, is not the root
merely, but all — root, stem, branches, twigs, leaves, flowers,
fruit: and Jesus is not only that: He is oil and sunshine,
air and showers, and ten thousand times more than we have
ever dreamed, wished for or needed. Oh, the joy of seeing
this truth!
"... It is a wonderful thing to be really one with a risen
and exalted Saviour; to be a member of Christ! Think what
it involves ...
"The sweetest part, if one may speak of one part being
sweeter than another, is the *rest* which full identification
with Christ brings. I am no longer anxious about anything,

as I realize this; for He, I know, is able to carry out *His will*, and His will is mine.

"... I cannot say (I am sorry to have to confess it) that since I have seen this light I have not sinned; but I do feel there was no need to have done so. And further — walking more in the light, my conscience has been more tender; sin has been instantly seen, confessed, pardoned; and peace and joy (with humility) instantly restored ...

"Faith, I now see, is 'the *substance* of things hoped for', and not mere shadow. It is not *less* than sight, but *more*. Sight only shows the outward forms of things; faith gives the substance. You can *rest* on substance, *feed* on substance. Christ dwelling in the heart by faith (ie His Word of Promise credited) is *power* indeed, is *life* indeed. And Christ and sin will not dwell together; nor can we have His presence with love of the world, or carefulness about 'many things'."

When he visited Yangzhou, one of the first people Hudson Taylor spoke to was Charles Judd. Judd, who had joined the CIM the previous year through the influence of Dr Barnardo, was recovering from an illness.

"Oh, Mr Judd," Taylor said, walking up and down the room as he so often did with his hands behind his back, "God has made me a new man! God has made me a new man! I have not got to *make* myself a branch, the Lord Jesus tells me I *am* a branch. I am *part of Him*, and have just to believe it. If I go to Shanghai, having an account, and ask for fifty dollars, the clerk cannot refuse it to my outstretched hand and say that it belongs to Mr Taylor. What belongs to Mr Taylor my hand may take. It is a member of my body. And I am a member of Christ, and may take all I need of His fulness. I have seen it long enough in the Bible, but I *believe* it now as a living reality."

"He was a joyous man now," Judd wrote, "a bright happy Christian. He had been a toiling, burdened one before, with latterly not much rest of soul. It was resting in Jesus now, and letting Him do the work — which makes all the difference! Whenever he spoke in meetings after that a new power seemed to flow from him, and in the practical things of life a new peace possessed him. Troubles did not worry him as before."

Since 1868, *The Revival* magazine in Britain had been publishing a series of articles on holiness by R Pearsall Smith, whose thinking was one of the main influences giving rise to the Keswick Convention meetings. Copies of the magazine reached every CIM station in China during 1869; this almost certainly explains Emily Blatchley's comment that Taylor had "received the same rest of soul that Jesus gave me some little time ago." "The exchanged life" and "union with Christ" came to sum up the CIM thinking.

The Bergers, who were familiar with *The Revival* articles, expressed reservations about overstressing the passive, receptive aspect of holiness; they underlined the need for active resistance to evil and of effort to obey God. In his books a few years later, Bishop Ryle was also to correct what he considered the imbalance of the Keswick teaching. But there is no evidence that Hudson Taylor and his colleagues in China were deficient in effort or active service.

PEOPLING HEAVEN WITH THOSE WE LOVE 33

Ever since March 1869 five-year-old Samuel Taylor had been suffering from tuberculous enteritis. Hudson and Maria kept Samuel with them, even on their travels, leaving Herbert, Howard, Maria and Charles with Emily and their nurse and coming back to them whenever possible. But this unsettled way of life upset the children and they were all prone to the ailments to which life in China exposed them.

With great reluctance and after agonized thought and prayer, Hudson and Maria decided to send the four oldest home to England, leaving one-year-old Charles with his mother and father in China. Emily Blatchley, with TB already far advanced in her own lungs, agreed to escort them on the journey. She would have died but for the change of climate. Hudson Taylor described the prospect of parting with the children as "the dark cloud which lies before us". But Samuel never left China. His condition worsened and he died in February, 1870, when he was nearly six.

✳ ✳ ✳ ✳ ✳

Maria herself, still only 33, was suffering from the same condition which took Samuel from them. And she was pregnant again. Her baby was born on July 7, 1870 in Zhenjiang. Maria chose the name Noel: to her it meant "Peace". Shortly after Noel had been born, Hudson felt Maria's pulse. He didn't like what he felt; and as Mary Rudland brought a candle into the room Hudson watched the colour drain from Maria's lips and face. She was suffering from severe internal bleeding.

Hudson Taylor stayed up all night with Maria and Noel. For a week Maria grew weaker but Noel seemed to be doing well. Then he developed a severe infection of the mouth, with diarrhoea, and died on July 20, only thirteen days old. Maria chose two hymns for the funeral.

A letter came with news that Emily and the children had arrived safely in England, and Maria was glad to think of the fun they would have there, living at first with Hudson's parents. They buried Noel on a cool evening beside his brother Samuel in the little walled cemetery not far from the river bank at Zhenjiang. Maria wasn't well enough to be there.

"I trust I may not have to trouble you again soon," Hudson Taylor said to the gravedigger after the service.

"I think she is needed for the Lord's work," he told Charles Fishe, who had joined the CIM team in China the previous year. "That's a comfort to me and leads me to hope for her."

After the funeral, at about eight o'clock, Hudson Taylor returned home and said to Maria, "I think it would be good for you to move for a while to the other house in the cooler suburb on higher ground."

"Could I have my bath there as often as I like?"

He nodded, and soon fell asleep.

Maria asked Louise Desgraz to cover him over to keep him warm.

He awoke after an hour or so and asked Maria, "Is there anything I can get you?"

"No, you must go and get some tea. Mrs Rudland has some waiting for you."

Hudson went into the next room and was chatting to the Rudlands when they heard a faint cry of "Hudson!" Taylor ran to Maria and found her standing beside her bed, very faint and unable to speak or move. He lifted her back into bed and arranged the pillows and bolster around her. He administered some stimulants, but feared the worst.

"Ask God to keep my heart quiet and guide my judgment," he said to the Rudlands.

Rapid palpitations began. Hudson Taylor didn't think that Maria's lungs would be able to stand the work which was now required of them. He gave her food and medicine. At 12.30, he persuaded William and Mary Rudland and Henry Reid to go to bed.

"My head is so hot," Maria complained as she regained the strength to speak.

"I will thin out your hair for you."

Hudson found Maria's head so "congested" that he had to cut off all her hair.

When he had finished, Maria felt the top of her head. She smiled. "That's what you call thinning out, is it? Well, I shall have all the comfort and you all the responsibility as to looks!"

She threw her thin arms around him and kissed him.

Then she dozed off to sleep. Hudson left and Louise Desgraz sat with her. In another room, Taylor prayed with the Rudlands and Reid. Neither he nor they could pray unreservedly for Maria's recovery.

At 2 am he gave Maria some more food and medicine and sat with her till three. Louise refused to leave Maria so he asked her to wake him at four. As the sun rose he could see that Maria was dying. It was July 23.

"My darling," Hudson said, "do you know that you are dying?"

"Dying!" said Maria. "Do you think so? What makes you think so?"

"I can see it, darling. Your strength is giving way."

"Can it be so? I feel no pain, only weariness."

"Yes, you are going home. You will soon be with Jesus."

"I am so sorry, dear."

Then she paused, as if correcting herself for feeling sorry.

"You are not sorry to go to be with Jesus, dear?" Hudson asked.

He never forgot the look she gave him. Looking right into his eyes, she said, "Oh no, it's not that. You know, darling, there hasn't been a cloud between my soul and the Saviour for ten years past. I cannot be sorry to go to Him. But I am sorry to leave you alone at this time. Yet He will be with you and meet all your need."

Everyone in the house, and Thomas Harvey and Robert White from the other CIM house in Zhenjiang, gathered round her bed.

The Chinese servants and teachers loved her. They came into the room and she had something to say to each of them.

"Come to Jesus so that you will meet me in heaven," she said to those who weren't Christians.

She gave Hudson a kiss each for Herbert, Howard, and Maria in England and had a message for them all. Then she could speak no more. She put one arm around Hudson's neck and one on his head, indicating that he should look up to heaven. Her face, he noticed, had a look of "unutterable love and trust". Her lips moved but no sound came.

Then she fell asleep. As the others watched, they saw her sleep become lighter and lighter. It wasn't easy for them to tell when she died. She had felt no pain.

Hudson knelt down beside the bed and prayed:

"Dear God, thank you for giving my darling Maria to me. Thank you for the twelve and a half years of happiness we have had together. Thank you for taking her to your own blessed presence. I dedicate myself anew to your service. Amen."

He scribbled a note (which still exists) to the American

Presbyterians in Hangzhou. It read:

> Would Mr Dodd gently break these tidings to Miss
> Faulding and Mr and Mrs McCarthy? Excuse the request
> and brevity. Mrs Taylor died of consumption of the
> bowels; baby also of diarrhoea. They are truly blessed!
> And I too. My heart wells up with joy and gratitude
> for their unutterable bliss, tho' nigh breaking. "Our
> Jesus hath done all things well". Yours in Jesus, J Hudson
> Taylor.

He sent a lock of Maria's fine, light brown, almost blonde,
hair to his parents and to each of the children. He wrote
on the envelope, "One half: I dare not risk all by one ship.
Take great care of it. JHT."

On Thursday, July 28, Charles Fishe and Thomas Harvey
in white gowns, the Chinese dress of mourning, walked ahead
of Maria's coffin which was carried by eight Chinese men.
Hudson Taylor and the other missionaries walked behind,
also dressed in white. Behind them came the British and
American consuls, the foreign officers of the Imperial Maritime
Customs, and nearly all the English and American residents
in that part of China. The Western community wanted to
erect a tombstone for her, but Hudson asked to be allowed
to provide it himself.

At the graveside, Hudson Taylor himself read the burial
service and a paper describing Maria's family, her conversion,
life in Ningbo, in the Yangzhou riot and subsequently.

Three days later, he wrote a moving letter to his three
children in England. He said: "Noel had soft, sweet little
eyes, and long silky eyelashes, and a dear little mouth just
like Grace's used to be." He told them about Maria's last
messages for each of them. Then he said: "It may be that
God will take away your dear Papa too before very long.
But God will always be a Father to you." He was suffering
from dysentery, frequently fatal at that time, which may explain
why he struck such a morbid note in a letter which would

in any case have come as a shattering blow for the children.

Reflecting on Maria's death, William Berger wrote, "Hers was indeed a useful life. To us its prolongation appeared necessary, for her dear husband's sake, the children's, and the work's. But the Lord saw differently. Her knowledge of the Chinese customs, their language, and modes of thought was at once comprehensive and intimate; and at the very time of her last illness she was engaged in writing and correcting important works for the press. She is gone; she has ceased from her labours; she sleeps in Jesus. Her sun went down while yet in its meridian, and the place on earth which knew her, which she so efficiently and untiringly filled, will know her again no more. It remains for us to imitate so bright an example."

In Robert White's home high above Zhenjiang with a grand view of the Yangzi, Hudson Taylor sat alone with his thoughts. He wrote: "A few months ago, my house was full, now so silent and lonely — Samuel, Noel, my precious wife with Jesus; the elder children far, far away, and even little Charles in Yangzhou. Often, of late years, has duty called me from my loved ones, but I have returned, and so warm has been the welcome. Now I am alone. Can it be that there is no return from this journey, no home-gathering to look forward to! Is it real, and not a sorrowful dream, that those dearest to me lie beneath the cold sod? Ah, it is indeed true. But not more so than that there is a homecoming awaiting me which no parting shall break into ... 'I go to prepare a place for you'. Is not one part of the preparation the peopling it with those we love?"

He wrote to Jennie Faulding, thanking her for her letter of sympathy: "The more I feel how utterly I am bereaved, and how helpless and useless I am rendered, the more I joy in her joy, and in the fact of her being beyond the reach of sorrow. But I cannot help sometimes feeling, oh! so weary ... My poor heart would have been overwhelmed and broken, had I not been taught more of His fulness and indwelling ... I am not far from her whom I have loved so long and so well; and she is not far from me. Soon we shall be together ... Goodnight." And then he seems to have remembered that Jennie was single for he added, "Jesus is your portion ... Yours affectionately in Him, J Hudson Taylor."

"From my inmost soul," Hudson wrote to his mother ten days after Maria's death, "I delight in the knowledge that God does or deliberately permits *all* things, and causes all things to work together for good to those who love Him.

"He, and He only, knew what my dear wife was to me. He knew how the light of my eyes and the joy of my heart were in her ... But He saw that it was good to take her; good indeed for her, and in His love He took her painlessly; and not less good for me who must henceforth toil and suffer alone — yet not alone, for God is nearer to me than ever."

A LOVE THAT WAS NOT JEALOUS 34

The CIM's work was going well. At Hangzhou, the church at New Lane grew to 67 as fifteen more Chinese were baptized. Wang Lae-djun had opened four country outposts with regular services and was supervising seven full-time Chinese evangelists and Bible distributors. John McCarthy held continuous Bible teaching and evangelism training classes which prepared large numbers of Chinese for fruitful Christian work. Sometimes with and sometimes without McCarthy, they visited people in their homes and preached and talked in teashops.

Also in Hangzhou, Jennie Faulding was successfully and imaginatively running several schools. When Hudson Taylor visited one of these, Jennie showed him into a long bedroom with seven windows and a row of six double beds for the boys, with one for their teacher in the opposite corner. Each boy had two little shelves of his own, and a nail on which to hang his things.

"The boys clean their own rooms," she told Hudson, "and help to wash their own clothes. I keep an old woman almost fully employed making, mending, and washing for the boys.

She is a nice old body called Granny Yang. She finds her food, and I give her four pence half penny a day. She stays till about five in the evening. One of the boys came to me last night to ask for baptism, and there are several more among them wishing to profess themselves Christians."

Wang Lae-djun reckoned that at least fifty of his Hangzhou congregation had become Christians through Jennie's influence. In addition to her thriving school work, Jennie had been visiting house to house in the city ever since her arrival in Hangzhou.

In the early months of 1871, Hudson Taylor was beginning to think seriously of making a short visit to Britain. The Bergers were urging him to return, and he could see the need to have face to face discussions with them, build up his links with the mission's supporters and see his "three strong, rompy children" in England.

Other members of the team were also due for a trip home. Jennie Faulding's parents had been reminding her for some time that she had initially gone to China for a five-year spell. It was understood that when Hudson returned she would travel with him. James and Elizabeth Meadows also needed a time in England. James was in poor health and another summer in China might have killed him.[1]

Among the responsibilities which delayed Taylor's return was delivering babies. In May he officiated for the wife of the American consul; and in July Charles and Elizabeth Judd became the proud parents of Frederick, who later became a leading member of the CIM.

Hudson wrote to his own children, "I have sold the harmonium to help me complete the building of the school, in remembrance of dear Mama ... I have played on it today, for the last time, some of her favourite tunes."

John McCarthy and Jennie Faulding travelled from Hangzhou to Zhenjiang and arrived at a plan of campaign with their leader. McCarthy would take over Jennie's

---

[1] In fact he recovered, and died in China over forty years later.

responsibilities in Hangzhou; Jennie would join the Meadows family in Shanghai and sail with them. Charles Fishe would act as official secretary to the mission in China. At first the plan was for Taylor to leave as soon as he was free, but as it turned out they all travelled together, plus Li Lanfeng, the printer, who was to live with Hudson in London and receive personal tuition from him.

Hudson and little Charlie (now two and a half) steamed down the Yangzi with Pere Sechinger, a Catholic priest who had been involved in the aftermath of the Yangzhou riots. He struck Hudson as "earnest and devout" and, he recorded, "he spoke of converts in a way that greatly pleased me." Roman Catholic missionaries had of course been working in China for much longer than Protestants. Their method was to travel far into the interior of the country, to dissociate themselves entirely from the merchant community, and to dress in Chinese clothes.

On the voyage, James Meadows' health was poor and Elizabeth's time was taken up with looking after their children. The result was that Hudson Taylor and Jennie spent many hours in each other's company. They had much in common — they talked and prayed, and enjoyed the complete relaxation from the pressures of life in China. Hudson also discovered he loved Jennie and wanted to marry her. It was little more than a year since Maria's death, but by the standards of the time it would not be seen as indecent haste for Hudson to express his feelings. In those days of high mortality, early remarriage was normal, especially where there were children to be provided for. Hudson was 39 and Jennie 28.

Sailing through the Red Sea, Hudson wrote to Jennie's parents. "I do not so much ... ask you to give up a daughter ... as ask you ... to make room in your hearts ... for me also." He spoke of his joy at finding his "love and feelings so fully reciprocated."

Hudson and Jennie talked freely about Maria, the first love whom he could never forget. Jennie loved Maria too.

They would always be able to talk happily about her without embarrassment.

"The last wish Maria expressed to me," Hudson wrote, "was that if she were removed, I would marry again ... Seeing the love I have for her is not likely to undergo any change or diminution, I do not want one or two years, or five, to forget her in. You do not know how I love her, nor how seldom for one hour she is absent from my waking thoughts ... And my dear Jennie would not wish it otherwise. She has her own place in my heart, which Jesus has given her, a place all the larger because her love is not jealous."

On September 21, 1871, they arrived in Marseilles and caught a train to Paris, reaching London four days later.

"We can agree to your marriage only after Jennie has been home for a year," Mr and Mrs Faulding told them.

There was of course no legal reason why they should obey this demand, but they didn't want to act against her parents' wishes. Jennie pleaded with them in tears; Hudson tried to persuade them.

"Neither of you is physically fit," said Mrs Faulding. "That is my objection to an early marriage."

Jennie's mother eventually backed down and Joseph Faulding, whose objections had never been as vehement as his wife's, helped make the arrangements for the wedding. The knot was tied on Tuesday November 28 in Regent's Park Chapel. There was no honeymoon, and they joined the children at 64 Mildmay Park, London.

✳ ✳ ✳ ✳ ✳

Neither William nor Mary Berger was in good health. And William had another preoccupation. He had for some time been attracted by the idea that those who died as non-Christians would not be punished eternally. Some Anglican, Baptist and Brethren churches had expelled members who taught this and if it became widely known that Berger was sympathetic to it, support for the CIM among orthodox believers would almost certainly fall dramatically.

Berger had worked tirelessly for the CIM but he had never been good at public relations. He had edited the *Occasional Papers*, which shared news with the CIM's supporters, in a methodical but rather ponderous style. He knew he wasn't the right person to keep interest in the mission high, and requested Taylor to find successors for him and Mary.

Early in January, 1872, Hudson Taylor rented a new house, 6 Pyrland Road, on the edge of fields near the village green and duck-pond at Newington Green. The family moved in on January 15, and Hudson used the house as a base for a busy schedule of activities. He took Lanfeng with him to meetings and showed him the sights of London, interviewed and advised candidates, and as far as possible acknowledged every donation personally.

He made another journey through the West Country, meeting Robert Chapman again in Barnstaple, staying with George Muller and preaching at Bethesda Chapel in Bristol.

Back in London for the Mildmay Conference, Hudson Taylor shared the platform with America's most famous evangelist, D L Moody. Lustily the huge congregation sang *Waft, waft ye winds His story* and resumed their seats expectantly. Hudson Taylor stood up with a twinkle in his eye but a serious point to make.

"My dear friends," he said, "the wind will never waft it! If the blessed story of His love is to be taken to the dark places of the earth, it must be taken by men and women like ourselves ... who wish to obey the great missionary command."

During the conference, Henrietta and Lucy Soltau, daughters of a Devonshire barrister, stayed with the Taylors at 6 Pyrland Road. One day after lunch Hudson Taylor led the Soltau sisters plus Jennie and Emily Blatchley into the sitting room, and they all stood looking at a map of China showing the nine provinces where no CIM missionaries were working.

"Now," Hudson asked them, "have you the faith to join

with me in laying hold of God for eighteen new men, to go two by two to the unoccupied provinces?"

Henrietta and Lucy entered into a covenant with Taylor to pray every day until it happened; then they all joined hands while Hudson prayed the first of many prayers for the eighteen vital new men.

✳ ✳ ✳ ✳ ✳

On Hudson's birthday, five-year-old Maria brought him a present she had made herself. He took her on his knee and examined what she had given him: a small piece of wood in which she had inserted a peg with half a cockleshell hung on the top. Without admitting that he had no idea what it was, he talked to her about the gift. Soon she put him out of his embarrassment.

"I thought you would like best a ship to take you to China."

Her father was delighted. "Probably no gift I ever received gave more pleasure, or was more carefully treasured and as often thought of."

Maria was right. It was time for Hudson and Jennie to make the arrangements for their return to China, and this time they left behind a much more comprehensive team to look after "home affairs". Emily Blatchley would do much of the work the Bergers had done. Henry Soltau (brother of Henrietta and Lucy) and Richard Hill, an architect and civil engineer, would act as honorary secretaries of a new Council of Management of the CIM (in time to become known simply as the "London Council"). Other members of the Council were its treasurer, John Challice, a company director; William Hall, a deacon from Bryanston Hall; Theodore Howard; Joseph Weatherley; and George Soltau (another brother) who was responsible for the training of candidates.

Hudson Taylor had managed to persuade a long list of people to act as a Council of Reference for the CIM, including Thomas Barnardo, Robert Chapman of Barnstaple,

Grattan Guinness, George Muller, William Pennefather and Lord Radstock.

❋ ❋ ❋ ❋ ❋

In October, 1872, Hudson and Jennie Taylor arrived back in China, at first making their home in Hangzhou. Jennie took John McCarthy's place as the overseer of the church there and Hudson made plans to visit the cities south of Hangzhou after Christmas.

In April, 1873, Jennie gave birth to stillborn twins. It was typical of her resilience that she wrote to her mother, "It was a very anxious time for Hudson." She now looked forward to moving to Yangzhou in mid-May and making it their base in China.

Taylor's plan was that much of the work in Hangzhou should now be done by Chinese Christians. This was typical of his overall strategy: he wanted to make the CIM's work more and more, as he put it, *native and interior* with as few foreign workers as possible. His eventual aim was to have one superintendent and two assistant foreign missionaries in a province, with Chinese helpers in each important city, and colporteurs (Bible distributors) in the less important places. He hoped that before the end of 1873 he would be able to open a college to train Chinese workers.

He was delighted to find that Chinese Christians were growing more and more efficient in the work of evangelism and church building, and had no doubt that the future of the church in China lay with them. "I look on all us foreign missionaries as a platform work round a rising building," he wrote. "The sooner it can be dispensed with the better; or rather, the sooner it can be transferred to other places, to serve the same temporary purpose, the better for the work sufficiently forward to dispense with it, and the better for the places yet to be evangelized." This approach remains a keystone of missionary strategy today.

The most encouraging area of growth, not just for the

CIM but for other missionary societies, was Zhejiang, the province to the south of and including Hangzhou. In the decade since the defeat of the Taiping Rebellion in 1864, the number of Chinese preachers in Zhejiang had grown from fifteen or twenty to one hundred, and the number of Christians from four hundred to over fourteen hundred. Over a hundred of these were educated men with high academic qualifications. The Chinese church was growing strong, and beginning to be equipped to tackle the evangelization of the whole Empire.

UPS AND DOWNS 35

Hudson Taylor longed for the CIM to have an admin-istrator in China who would free him for pioneering work, evangelism and church planting. In May, 1873, he sat down and wrote a letter to Henry Soltau.

Had I here the cooperation of one able, thoroughly reliable, fellow worker, of faith in God, tact and influence with our missionaries, I should say that in three years' time our work might be doubled in extent and increased manifold in usefulness. But here I have no one who is sufficiently superior, educationally and mentally and spiritually, to the others to take the position I propose.

Now, my dear Brother, will you not come out and go into the work with me? ...

Is it not a worthy object, can any sacrifice be too great to hasten its realization? Is not He whom we serve deserving of all our time, our strength, our power? ...

I do not write in any hasty excitement. I know as much, perhaps, of the difficulty of obtaining what I propose, as most do. I know, too, something of the sacrifice which this step would involve to you. But in view of eternity how can we weigh these things? Each of these provinces is as large as an European kingdom. Can we seriously contemplate their populations of 15, 20, 25 millions each, and be willing to leave them to perish?

"I do wish Mr Soltau had faith to cast himself upon God," Hudson Taylor wrote to Emily Blatchley. "I wish you could find time to talk and pray with him about it." But Taylor didn't realize how ill with tuberculosis Emily was. Letters on their way to him described her condition as "precarious" and "going home".

While Soltau was making up his mind, Taylor was rarely without a tricky problem. After a spell of success in Taizhou, William and Mary Rudland were getting conceited. Printing Rudland's accounts of his success in the *Occasional Papers* seemed to aggravate his tendency to pride. Then there was an outbreak of anti-foreign and anti-Christian feeling in Taizhou and Rudland changed into foreign clothes, to indicate that he had the power of the consuls and gunboats behind him. Mary Rudland thought she saw a young Chinese missionary kissing the wife of another Chinese Christian. She spoke out and both men left the work in Taizhou in a huff. Rudland offered to resign from the CIM.

At Ninghai Chinese workers began to demand higher wages for their Christian service. "Oh for a baptism of the Holy Ghost ... the only remedy for our troubles," Hudson said in a note to Jennie.

✳ ✳ ✳ ✳ ✳

In November, 1873, Charles and Elizabeth Judd arrived back in China after a spell in England. With them came Mary Bowyer, Henry Taylor (no relation) and a colourful new CIM missionary, Fred Baller. Baller had a sharp and perceptive eye and vividly recorded his first impressions of Hudson Taylor. He had no idea of the problems which were facing the mission's leader. Seeing him in wadded winter clothing he thought him "the oddest figure I have ever seen." But he soon found that Hudson Taylor combined light-hearted humour with saintliness.

On November 7, Hudson Taylor took Henry Taylor and Baller to Nanjing and gave them his total attention for ten days, introducing them to the delights and perplexities of Chinese customs. One thing that particularly impressed Baller was Taylor's ability to make a bargain. The Chinese themselves were always loud in Hudson Taylor's praises when he was hiring boats, drawing up contracts, buying land or houses. He would raise points calmly and deliberately, and thoroughly go into those raised by the other party. His apparent lack of hurry was a great strength in negotiations. He well understood the rather circuitous Chinese way of thinking — slowly focussing in on a point in greater and greater detail.

Baller had no doubt that Taylor's business skills saved the mission large sums of money. "His abilities would easily have placed him in the front rank had he taken up any line of business."

✳ ✳ ✳ ✳ ✳

Towards the end of a gruelling tour of CIM stations in October, 1873, Taylor headed back towards Taizhou, longing to see Jennie again. For her part, Jennie was worried stiff, not having heard from him for several days and imagining that he was ill, alone and needing her. So, escorted by William Rudland, she set off to try to find him.

"Mrs Taylor left this morning for Ninghai," they told Hudson, when he arrived at Taizhou.

"Imagine my dismay," he wrote to her, "that you had left this morning. I have been kissing you, darling, in my mind all last night, nearly, and all today." Eventually they were reunited at Ninghai, and the following month they spent Christmas alone together in Taizhou.

In the opening months of 1874 money was short. Hudson

Taylor wrote to the Honorary Secretary Richard Hill, "I never was happier in the work, or freer from care, tho' I have no funds ... PS. Let me beg that no *appeal* be made for funds." There was no need. A letter arrived from George Muller, containing more than £300 (a very substantial sum at that time).

"Oh! my dear brother," Taylor wrote to treasurer John Challice, "the joy of *knowing* the *Living* God, of resting on the *Living* God ...I am but His agent; He will look after His own honour, provide for His own servants, supply all our need according to His own riches, you helping by your prayers and work of faith and labour of love."

But even substantial donations like this didn't last long. The CIM's work cost about one hundred pounds a week. More than fifty buildings — houses, chapels and schools — had to be kept in repair, and on four-fifths of them rent had to be paid. The work now stretched over five provinces and travelling expenses were growing.

Though the administrative burden of running a large mission took up much of his time, Hudson Taylor was still happiest out and about with the Chinese. On a boat at Taiping, he got into conversation with an old man of 72.

"What is your name?"

"My name is Dzing. The thing which troubles me is this: the world is all vanity, and what is to be done about our wrong doing?"

"Yes, that is *the* question, and it is to reply to it that we missionaries have come to China."

"Our scholars say that there is no hereafter, that the several elements of the soul are scattered at death — but I cannot think it is so."

His natural Chinese scepticism was leading him towards the truth.

❋ ❋ ❋ ❋ ❋

For his first birthday after their marriage, Jennie presented Hudson with a new Baxter polyglot Bible. He began, as usual, to note the dates as he read it through. On a blank page at the end, he wrote in pencil:

January 27th, 1874. Asked God for 50 or 100 additional native evangelists and as many foreign superintendents as may be needed to open up the 4 *fu* (prefectures) and 48 *xian* (counties) still unoccupied in Zhejiang. Also for the men to break into the 9 unoccupied provinces.

At the end of May, Hudson Taylor and Charles Judd made plans to travel five hundred miles up the Yangzi to Wuhan. They left on June 1st on a little river steamer, the *Hanyang*, for a three-day journey.

After leaving Jiujiang, Taylor began to climb down a steep ladder, but on the second or third step from the top his foot slipped and he fell feet first to the bottom, landing very heavily on his heels. The pain in his spine and ankles was intense. For a while, he found it almost impossible to breathe or to move. At Wuhan, he was taken to an inn and helped on to a bed and over the next few hours his breathing grew easier.

Josiah Cox, a Wesleyan missionary in Wuhan, insisted that Hudson Taylor move into his home. After a period of rest the pain in Hudson's back eased, and although he needed crutches he assumed that the injury was not serious.

Hudson and Jennie began to think of returning to England to see the children and attend to various pressing matters. They set off at the end of August. Bad news was waiting for them in Marseilles: Emily Blatchley had died of TB in July. And during the voyage, the condition of Taylor's back deteriorated. By the time he reached London he could hardly get about even on crutches.

By December, 1874, Hudson Taylor lay on his back in a four poster bed at 6 Pyrland Road, almost completely paralyzed in his back and lower limbs. A rope fixed above his head allowed him to lift himself just enough to turn from side to side. At this crucial stage in the history of the CIM, he would have to direct affairs from his bed. The room became the mission's central office. John Stevenson and other volunteers spent hours at Hudson's bedside writing to his dictation. The CIM Council began to meet there. Jennie wrote a note to William Rudland, himself lying ill in Reading, which said, "It seems very unlikely that either we or you will ever see China again." The tone was quite unlike Jennie — but it shows how ill Hudson must have been at this time.

Then Taylor went down with severe dysentery. He wrote a new will, leaving everything to Jennie. She was pregnant again, and the children were being looked after by the Howards, the Grattan Guinness family and Amelia — who now had nine of her own, with another on the way.

By Christmas, however, Hudson was beginning to recover. At the bottom of his bed hung a map of China, so that he could look at the nine provinces and think of "the eighteen" for whom a number of people were now regularly praying. He dictated an "Appeal for Prayer on behalf of more than 150 million of Chinese" which was published in several magazines. It ended, "Will each of your Christian readers at once raise his heart to God, and wait one minute in earnest prayer that God will raise up this year eighteen suitable men to devote themselves to this work. Warmhearted young men, who have a good knowledge of business, clerks, or assistants in shops who have come in contact with the public and have learned to cover the wants and suit the wishes of purchasers, are well fitted for this work. They should possess strong faith, devoted piety, and burning zeal; be men who will gladly live, labour, suffer, and if need be, die for Christ's sake."

After breakfast on January 7, 1875, everyone at Pyrland Road met at Hudson's bedside for prayer. Everyone except Jennie. She was in a nearby room preparing for her baby to be born, and had not told anyone she was in labour. One of the children popped in to see her and returned to the prayer meeting with a message.

"Would Louise please come at once?"

When Louise Desgraz reached Jennie her baby had already been born. She ran back to Hudson's room and wheeled a small sofa to the side of his bed. He rolled himself on to it. They rushed this makeshift hospital trolley with Hudson Taylor MRCS, LM (RCS) FRGS aboard into Jennie's room. With great difficulty he sat up and did what was immediately necessary, and then collapsed back on to the sofa exhausted. They called the baby Ernest: another future missionary to China.

✳ ✳ ✳ ✳ ✳

In March, 1875, Henry Soltau at last responded to Hudson Taylor's invitation and agreed to become the CIM's administrator in China. He sailed with John Stevenson at the end of the month. The two men would be particularly looking into the possibilities of entering Western China via Burma.

There was more good news. Twenty young men had presented themselves in response to the widely publicized appeal for "the eighteen", and several of them looked promising. Hudson Taylor's replies to their enquiries usually included this passage: "If you want hard work, and little appreciation of it; value God's approbation more than you fear man's disapprobation; are prepared, if need be, to seal your testimony with your blood, and perhaps oftentimes to take joyfully the spoiling of your goods ... you may count on a harvest of souls here, and a crown of glory that fadeth not away, and the Master's 'well done'."

Seven years had passed since all the bad publicity for the CIM following the Yangzhou riots, and by 1875 the mission was back in favour. The good news and better publicity were a tonic to Hudson Taylor and he continued to improve. By April he was able to get up and down the stairs and into the garden. Might he, after all, be able to return to the land he loved?

NO ONE HAS EVER LACKED **36**

The CIM's *Occasional Papers* were pocketsized pamphlets of ten to thirty pages. Hudson wanted to give the publication a catchier title and change its format. Jennie suggested "China's millions and our work among them". The phrase went to the heart of the CIM's task and was used until the end of 1875. Then simply *China's millions* was enough. The publication turned into an eye-catching and topical magazine which has continued to the present day.[1]

In May, 1875, Taylor added up his receipts for the month to date. They came to only £68, nearly £235 less than the cost of running the mission in China for three weeks. The household at 6 Pyrland Road met every day to pray for China. Hudon told them of the deficit and said,"Let us remind the Lord of it."

That evening the postman brought a letter with a cheque for just over £235. Surely this meant that God approved of what Taylor was doing!

---

[1] The magazine is now called *East Asia Millions*. See epilogue

In June, having exchanged his crutches for sticks, he addressed a holiness convention in Brighton under the heading "Trusting God". When leaving Brighton he found himself on the station platform with Count Bobrinsky, who had been at the meeting. Bobrinsky was a former Russian government minister.

"We must travel together," said the Count.

"But I am travelling third class," Hudson Taylor answered.

"My ticket admits of my doing the same."

On the way, Bobrinsky took from his pocket-book a banknote which he handed to Taylor. It was for fifty pounds, the equivalent of between £1,500 and £2,000 today.

"Haven't you made a mistake?" Hudson Taylor asked.

"It was five pounds I meant to give, but God must have intended you to have fifty."

Back at Pyrland Road, Hudson Taylor found the household had met together to pray about an amount which was needed in China. Funds in hand were just over £49 short of what they needed. Bobrinsky's gift was received with delight; incidents like this strengthened the faith of the household.

A lecturer in theology, C G Moore, often visited Hudson Taylor at Pyrland Road. He recalled that Taylor's study was full of packing cases and that the walls were lined with rough bookshelves. Near the window a writing table was littered with letters and papers. In front of the fireplace, a rug neatly covered a low, narrow, iron bedstead. There was scarcely a scrap of carpet on the floor.

Hudson Taylor lay down on the iron bedstead and began a conversation which Moore later described as "one of life's golden hours". Hudson Taylor didn't come across at all like the great man he had expected. There were no "high and imposing airs" — it was the sort of greatness of which Christ spoke when He said the meek would inherit the earth.

Another visitor to Pyrland Road remembered six-and-a-half-year-old Charlie Taylor putting most difficult questions to his father while Herbert (14) and Howard (13) enjoyed a tussle under the table.

One donor to the mission, appropriately named Mrs Rich, wrote to say she had heard CIM missionaries were frequently so poor that they had to give up the work and take secular employment.

Hudson Taylor replied swiftly, asking Mrs Rich to show her informant his reply. "He has been entirely misled ... I do not believe that any child or member of the family of anyone connected with our mission has ever lacked food or raiment for a single hour, though in many cases the supply may not have come *before* it was needed.

"*No one* has been hindered in work by lack of funds; *no one* has ever suffered in health from this cause; *no one* has ever left the mission on this ground, or has remained dissatisfied on this score, to my knowledge ..." He conceded that there had been "periods of stringency" but argued that these had stirred up the Chinese to give their own money to spread the gospel, rather than thinking that rich societies could do it all. He explained why various members of the mission had left or been dismissed — in no case for financial reasons. Mrs Rich resumed her support.

❋ ❋ ❋ ❋ ❋

Taylor now thought he would be well enough to return to China at some stage. But who would interview new candidates, produce *China's Millions*, and arrange for funds to be sent out? He had been trying to persuade his sister Amelia and her husband Benjamin to join him, or another society, in China. He visited them at Godalming.

"Would you at least think of joining me for a while at Pyrland Road as an experiment? I need help producing and distributing *China's Millions* as well as entertaining candidates." He offered to provide them with a house and income from a big legacy from Jennie's uncle in Australia.

Benjamin and Amelia finally agreed, and moved to 2 Pyrland Road in August. They remained there for forty years — the home becoming immensely popular with CIM people. Hudson and Jennie lived in No 6, while No 4 in the middle was used for offices and by candidates.

Applicants were flooding in in response to the appeal for the eighteen. Six experienced men had volunteered from the mission itself. In August, fifteen hundred people packed the Metropolitan Tabernacle, Spurgeon's church, to give a good send-off to three more. After another nine joined the mission by February 1876, Jennie wrote, "This makes up the Eighteen." She didn't draw up a precise list of who she meant, but there appear to have been twenty at this stage — and more followed. At least six women also went out during 1876.

Hudson Taylor would have to leave soon to instruct all these novices in the delights and idiosyncrasies of Chinese life. But first he needed to appoint a fulltime administrator to replace Richard Hill, who had resigned, and proposed William Soltau as his successor. Hudson Taylor began to train William and give more responsibility to Benjamin.

Taylor's longstanding friend Miss Stacey died in Tottenham in May 1876. For a week, this blow made him ill and he found it difficult to apply himself to his work and public engagements. But he recovered from his grief and sailed in September, intending to be away for only forty weeks. Jennie stayed at home to look after the six Taylor children, including her own two, and play a full part in the administrative work at Pyrland Road.

In Paris Hudson's document box containing all the work he intended to do on the voyage got left behind. So apart from writing frequent, and sometimes very intimate, letters to Jennie he had something of an enforced holiday.

* * * * *

After arriving in Shanghai at the end of October, Hudson Taylor travelled to Zhenjiang and went down with dysentery — an illness which recurred all through his life. But news of the signing of the Chefoo Convention on September 14, 1876, a week after he had left England, filled him with excitement for the future.

Foreigners were now guaranteed safe travel throughout China, providing they held a passport. Within four months of the signing of the Convention, CIM missionaries had entered six new provinces, travelling to parts of China never before reached by foreigners. The young missionaries met a mixture of friendliness and hostility. "The women," recorded Henry Taylor, on a journey to Honan, "go in, heart and soul, for idolatry, as you know, but still find their hearts unsatisfied and their minds in a maze."

Within a month Taylor's box of documents turned up in Zhenjiang and from then on he was fully stretched. "I have four times the amount of work I can do," he complained. Charles Fishe had gone home on furlough and there was no one else to take his place as secretary to the CIM in China. Then there was the work of editing *China's Millions*.

At the end of the day — or sometimes at two or three am — Hudson would sit down at his harmonium and play his favourite hymns, usually getting round to:

Jesus, I am resting, resting, in the joy of what Thou art;
I am finding out the greatness of Thy loving heart.

On one occasion, George Nicol was with him when a pile of letters brought news of dangers and problems facing a number of missionaries. Taylor leaned against his desk to read them and began to whistle *Jesus, I am resting, resting*.

"How can you whistle, when our friends are in such danger?" Nicol asked.

"Suppose I were to sit down here and burden my heart with all these things; that wouldn't help them, and it would unfit me for the work I have to do. I have just to roll the burden on the Lord."

✳ ✳ ✳ ✳ ✳

A General Conference of Missions was to be held in Shanghai in May, 1877. It looked as if it might be controversial. Missions had multiplied since Robert Morrison arrived in China seventy years earlier, and the five hundred missionaries from various societies didn't all see their task in the same light. Some, like the CIM, stressed the importance of direct evangelism and church planting; others thought more in terms of educating and "elevating" the Chinese people. The CIM was criticized for sending young and inexperienced missionaries on long journeys deep into China. The "Term Question" might also generate a good deal of heat — the issue of what Chinese term was the best equivalent for the Scriptural idea of God.

Taylor was afraid of problems unless there was an outpouring of God's Holy Spirit at the conference. So he arranged for a group of thirty or so missionaries from four societies to meet at Wuhan for prayer and spiritual preparation. At the close of the session, Griffith John of the LMS said, "I thank God for Mr Taylor; I thank God for the CIM; I thank God for my younger brethren" — the pioneers who were penetrating deep into west China.

About 140 men and women from eighteen missions and three Bible Societies met at the main Shanghai Conference three weeks later. The controversial "Term Question" was avoided, although the issue nearly caused a row during one address. Hudson Taylor defended the CIM's policy of travelling long distances with the gospel as a way of preparing for the more settled work of church building. Most people did not support the two speakers who argued that secular literature and the teaching of Western science was more likely to get rid of superstition than religion was. They preferred the line taken by Griffith John and Hudson Taylor who, while recognizing the value of literature and science, argued that the missionary's first aim should be to proclaim the knowledge of God, sin and salvation.

Altogether there was far more agreement than disagreement, and on the whole the CIM came out of it well. Hudson Taylor's verdict was that the conference was the most important step missions to China had yet taken.

After the Shanghai Conference, and suffering from neuralgia, Hudson Taylor set off on a tour of the Zhejiang mission centres. With him for most of the way went Elizabeth Wilson, fulfilling in her middle age a lifelong ambition to give herself to missionary work. Prematurely grey, she was well received and respected by the Chinese. More than once the travellers were entertained in village temples which had been cleared of their idols and given over to Christian worship.

Elizabeth Wilson never forgot the little white skin box which held Hudson Taylor's papers, or his habit of praying for the mission three times a day, mentioning each of his colleagues by name.

Taylor had now exceeded his originally planned forty weeks in China, but he wanted to carry out one more ambition before he returned to England. He arranged a conference in Ningbo for Chinese pastors and evangelists related to English and American societies, was thrilled by their contributions, and looked forward to the day when such meetings could be held in every province of China.

And then it was time to return to England. Jennie's two toddlers, Ernest and Amy, didn't recognize the man who turned up for Christmas, and Hudson enjoyed getting to know them. With Herbert at sixteen, Howard fifteen, Maria ten and Charles nine, plus Millie Duncan, the doubly-orphaned child of George Duncan who also lived with them, it was a noisy Christmas.

A DREAM COMES TRUE 37

T he northern provinces of China, especially Shanxi, were experiencing one of the worst famines the world had known, brought on by a prolonged drought and a failure of the wheat and other crops. Both the Wuhan and Ningbo conferences had contributed funds, at Hudson Taylor's suggestion.

Back in England, Taylor publicized the situation in meetings and in the press, and donations came in for famine relief rather than mission purposes. He authorized missionaries in famine and refugee areas to take in two hundred destitute children, giving priority to orphans. But he wanted to do more. Only four months after the long separation from Jennie, he made a painful suggestion.

"You know that I can't leave Britain yet. Would you consider going with a party of new missionaries, and supervising the orphanage scheme in China until I can come to join you?"

Jennie was 35, with two children of her own aged three and two as well as Maria's surviving four to care for. She prayed about Hudson's suggestion for two weeks and decided to go.

When Amelia, who had ten children of her own, heard her sister-in-law's decision she said, "If Jennie is called to China, I am called to care for her children."

Hearing this news, a friend called on Jennie. "I think it's wrong of you to leave your children and husband even for a cause like this."

Jennie went to her bedroom. She was only too aware of the cost.

"Dear God," she prayed, "please confirm that it's right for me to go. Fifty pounds now would be worth more to me than a fortune at any other time. It would be a guarantee that my other needs would be met."

Needing her own faith strengthened and an answer to those left behind, she put out two "fleeces" like Gideon. One prayer for enough money for the journey, and another for the sizeable sum at that time of fifty pounds for herself and Hudson. The answers would be a promise from God that He would bless those she was leaving behind more than if she stayed with them, and that He would stand by her and help her.

"I want you to pray with me for two things without knowing what they are. I'll tell you the answers when they are given," she said to the children at family prayers next morning.

That afternoon, a Mr Harris called at Pyrland Road.

"Is it true that you are going out to China?"

"Yes, I'm getting ready to go."

Mr Harris handed her a cheque for ten pounds — the exact amount the mission allowed for outfitting.

Four days later, a letter arrived from Hudson's parents addressed to Jennie. It contained fifty pounds. She took it to show him, but finding he had someone with him, left it without speaking.

When she returned, Hudson said, "I'm considering how the Lord would have me use this money."

"Oh, that money's mine," said Jennie. "I have a claim on it that you don't know about."

Ten days later, Jennie left home, escorting a party of seven young men and women to China. A new member of the

London Council saw the Taylors' parting and later told Hudson: "I felt just as if I were parting from my own wife, and the thought was altogether more than I could bear ... and yet I suppose that if God called us to part, He would enable us to do so with the same calmness that you enjoyed yesterday."

After her arrival in Shanghai, Jennie travelled to Shanxi with two younger women missionaries, escorted by linguist Frederick Baller. They were the first western women to go deep into inland China. Jennie began work among children orphaned in the famine, an initiative continued by a CIM team after she had returned to Shanghai.

In his loneliness, Hudson asked seventeen-year-old Herbert to come and share his study and bedroom. Later, he took three-year-old Ernest to the Fauldings' home in Barnet to help him convalesce from whooping cough. "He enjoyed himself famously," he recalled, "and I am somewhat better for it too. I enjoyed the quiet and the hayfield, and putting him to bed at night, and praying with him and dressing him. He clung to me so tenderly."

✳ ✳ ✳ ✳ ✳

After Jennie had left, Taylor was able to concentrate on the continued reorganization of the CIM in England, following William Berger's resignation. He visited each of the members of the London Council in their own homes. But as the year went on, the problems got worse. George Soltau resigned due to pressure of work, and the Council suggested that Benjamin Broomhall and William Soltau should be joint "assistant secretaries". Taylor didn't feel this was an ideal solution as William Soltau's heart didn't really seem to be in the work, and his brother-in-law Benjamin was bad at meeting deadlines and economizing. He'd been unable to find the right editor for China's Millions.

In the summer of 1878, after an acute attack of malaria, Taylor accepted an invitation to take a holiday in Switzerland.

At Pontresina the glaciers intrigued him, and he spent three days exploring the mountains, taking a few biscuits in his pocket, his Bible to read, and his umbrella as a sunshade. He thought the air was helping to heal his system.

"I have been thinking, darling," he told Jennie, "that all this refreshment, all this kindness, is the answer of God to *your prayers* for me; and the thought has given added pleasure to all I have enjoyed." He returned to England feeling "wonderfully well" but with the mission's problems still to solve.

Part of the solution to the problem of editing *China's Millions* seemed to be to give more work to Benjamin — but someone to take overall responsibility was still needed. In the new year Taylor approached Theodore Howard from a Tottenham family of chemical manufacturers, who were old friends and supporters of the mission. He agreed to take over as Director of the mission in the event of Taylor's death, and to act as Director in Britain during his absences abroad. Benjamin Broomhall was appointed General Secretary of the CIM's home affairs, with John McCarthy and William Soltau acting under his direction.

On December 31, 1878, the CIM's day of prayer was observed at Pyrland Road, at a time when many small children were dying of "spasmodic croup". During the evening prayer meeting, a nurse appeared at the door with a child she thought had died. They called Taylor, who rushed to the back of the room. As he ran, a woman suggested that he should pray for the child. "Yes, pray," he shouted back, "while I work."

Taylor found that the small girl was blue and limp. His first efforts to revive her failed. Then he tried the kiss of life. After several minutes, the child's colour changed and she began to breathe. In the night she had occasional convulsions but survived without harm, and grew up to become a CIM missionary. His son Howard commented some years later, "He prayed about things as if everything depended upon the praying ... but he worked also, as if everything depended on the working."

✳ ✳ ✳ ✳ ✳

In February 1879, Hudson Taylor left England to return to China and be reunited with Jennie. On the way, he visited George Muller and Charles Spurgeon in Mentone: Muller was on a preaching tour and Spurgeon was taking a break from the demands of the London Metropolitan Tabernacle. Spurgeon recorded that Taylor didn't look like a man who would be selected as the leader of a large organization; he was lame and short. His character seemed to Spurgeon to be a combination of meekness with strength — there was no self-assertion about him, but a firm trust in God. He was too certain of the presence and help of God to turn aside from a chosen course of action. After Hudson left, Spurgeon said that the word *China, China, China* rang in his ears in the special musical way in which Hudson said it. He noticed, too, that Hudson was already growing a *bianzi*.

In the Indian Ocean, Taylor grew so ill that a Singapore doctor doubted whether he would reach Hong Kong alive. A pile of letters waiting for him in Singapore included one from Jennie. "I have been spreading before the Lord some of the numerous difficulties that await you, and thinking of them with something of rejoicing. What a platform there will be for our God to work and triumph on! And how clearly we shall see His hand! ... In the Master's presence the servant's only responsibility, and his sweetest joy, is to obey. Our faith must gain the victory for our brethren and sisters."

Jennie thought him very run down when he arrived in Shanghai, and his dysentery returned before he had managed to deal with his correspondence. An LMS missionary advised them to go to the northern port of Chefoo before the hottest weeks of the summer arrived. There Hudson and Jennie stayed with Frederick Ballard, a young customs officer married to a missionary, whose house stood on the shore of a bay surrounded by hills. As he recovered, Hudson sat on a verandah breathing in the sea air, watching the junks and steamers, and enjoying the smell of the seaweed. In a neighbouring building lived Charles and Elizabeth Judd, also convalescing, with their family.

So the dream of a CIM sanatorium on this ideal stretch of coast emerged. And walking in the rising ground above the bay, Hudson Taylor and Charles Judd came across a bean-field which seemed the ideal spot on which to build. It had a gully with a fresh water stream running down beside it. But could they afford it?

"Do you want to buy land?" a farmer asked them.

Taylor and Judd knew well how the price of Chinese soil rocketed as soon as anyone showed interest in it, and therefore expressed only mild concern.

"Then will you buy mine?"

The farmer offered them the bean-field at a surprisingly fair price, and neighbouring farmers did the same. Taylor drew plans for a ten-roomed house with a verandah. The two men employed a team of builders, brickmakers, stone-masons and carpenters who lived on the site in tents; some were converted to Christ during the construction period. Timber and fittings came from two wrecks in the bay — oak beams, Norwegian pine, and teak planking for the floors.

"I don't say that the house was well built," Charles Judd reported when the work was done, "but it was wonderfully good considering our lack of experience ... It was marvellously cheap; and the Europeans in the Settlement were amazed at the rapidity with which it was put up. They could hardly believe their eyes when they saw it finished!" In fact the building lasted until 1915, when a more modern hospital took its place.

After this first sanatorium, or "Judd's house", as it was known for a while, the CIM built a convalescent home, a school for the mission children, a hospital, and a dispensary. The later buildings were built to higher standards with more thought for comfort and convenience.

✳ ✳ ✳ ✳ ✳

Timothy Richard was an able and influential young Welsh Baptist. Originally he had applied to join the CIM but was advised to go out with the Baptist Missionary Society, and arrived in China in 1870 at the age of 25. Richard began to attach great importance to the idea of establishing the Kingdom of God on earth, and protecting the poor and needy from tyranny. Living in the northern province of Shandong, he had been moved by the great famine of 1877-79, at its worst in Shanxi. He longed to see China so transformed by contact with the best features and techniques of the west that such a disaster would never occur again. Richard argued that God had worked through other religions such as Confucianism, Buddhism and Daoism. If the aspects of them which were similar to Christianity could be pointed out, their followers could be won over to faith in Christ, and in time the whole life of China would undergo a thorough Christian transformation. He greatly admired the best features of Chinese civilization and spent a lot of time studying the Chinese classics and religious writings. He made special efforts to reach educated people, and later used his influence to establish a university in Shanxi where western ideas were taught alongside Chinese history and culture.

Hudson Taylor thought he was "driving a good theory to death" by his reluctance to preach and his preference for moral tracts which spoke about God but not Christ in order gently to prepare the way for the gospel.

But Timothy Richard was persuasive, and began to win over some members of the CIM, particularly those who lived in the Shanxi area. The phrase "Shanxi spirit" was sometimes used to describe the loss of evangelical fervour resulting from Richard's thinking. The faith of one CIM member broke down completely and he had to be recalled; another talked of leaving the CIM to work instead with a society which provided a regular salary. Three or four missionaries did resign from the CIM as a result of Richard's influence, though some later returned to their previous convictions. Richard himself resigned from the Baptist Missionary So-ciety as he became more liberal in his thinking, but he continued to work in China for nearly fifty years.

Taylor didn't see the defections from his mission as necessarily Richard's fault — rather it was the "inevitable result of a strong and attractive character over weaker minds."

Eastern China

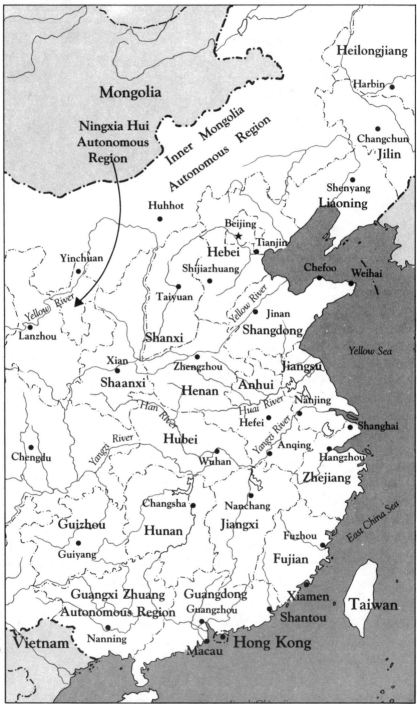

A HOUSEHOLD NAME 38

Hudson Taylor believed that Chinese women played a bigger part than men in influencing the growing generation morally and in their attitude to religion. And the best people to reach Chinese women with the gospel were Christians of their own sex. In 1879 he wrote in *China's Millions*, "The Lord increase the number of lady workers in China tenfold!" In the same year, Jennie had been among the first western women to go deep into north China, taking the love of Christ to those suffering the effects of famine in Shanxi.

The city of Wuhan stands where the Han River meets the Yangzi. For years Taylor had it in mind to use this area as a base from which to advance deeper into China. In February 1880 he arrived there to prepare a group of women, including some unmarried ones, for pioneering journeys to western provinces. Other societies didn't agree that it was sensible to use unmarried women in missionary work, so he kept his plans secret for the moment.

Two unmarried women seemed especially suited to what he had in mind. The first was Jane Kidd who was, in his words, as "playful as a kitten". After a year in China, she could conduct an animated conversation in Chinese and they decided that she should go with the widow, Ellen McCarthy, to join George Clarke and his wife in Guiyang, in the province of Guizhou. They would be escorted by Frederick Baller. The second, Miss Fausset, was to go up the Han River to join George and Emily King in Hanzhong. Taylor spent a week with the travellers preparing them for what lay ahead with daily Bible studies, times of prayer, and practical hints on conducting business with the Chinese.

"You have only the great God to take care of you!" he told them.

Jane Kidd, Ellen McCarthy and Fred Baller set off in a houseboat captained by a Christian. When they anchored at the mouth of the Dongting Lake people came aboard, and the Chinese women stroked Jane and Ellen's hands and cheeks.

"You're beautiful," they said.

The captain and his wife told them about Jesus.

After a journey of eight weeks, they arrived at Guiyang in April 1880. Jane Kidd had made history by becoming almost certainly the first single western girl to enter one of China's far western provinces.

Back at Wuhan, Taylor had to consider who should escort Miss Fausset. Elizabeth Wilson, a fifty-year old with four years experience in China, was game to be one companion. Her greying hair meant that she was respected by the Chinese. But Taylor believed a male Christian escort was also essential and all available missionaries and Chinese Christians were busy doing other things — except Huang Kezhong, a man in an advanced stage of leprosy who had been converted under Charles Judd's preaching.

Huang and Taylor went off to hire a boat. They slept in the same compartment aboard the boat for the night, and in the morning Hudson packed food baskets for the journey. When the ladies joined them, Miss Fausset had two complaints.

"Poor Huang's bedding smells," she said, "and this vegetable oil has spoiled the flavour of the meat."

Hudson arranged for Huang's bedding to be exchanged for a new wadded *pugai*. He travelled with the party for several hours and then went ashore for a while.

When he returned to the boat, he was carrying a basket full of sweet potatoes, eggs — and some lard to replace the sub-standard vegetable oil. They prayed together, and Taylor slipped away in his little boat to return to Wuhan.

Miss Fausset, Elizabeth Wilson and Huang travelled a thousand miles up the Han River, through its rapids, and arrived in Hanzhong after a journey lasting nearly three months. Huang had proved a superb escort and, as well as bringing women and girls to hear the gospel from the two ladies, had been an energetic witness for Christ himself.

Apart from a few fairly minor incidents, Jane Kidd, Ellen McCarthy, Elizabeth Wilson and Miss Fausset made these remarkable pioneering journeys deep into China without coming to harm. Nothing can detract from their massive courage, but their experiences say something, too, about the character of the Chinese people. Indeed, some claimed that women were far safer in China than in New York or London.

✳ ✳ ✳ ✳ ✳

In July 1881 Hudson's mother died, and in August Jennie's. Jennie had to go home to see to family affairs, and while she was on the way Hudson's father also died. The couple began a long and painful period of separation, keeping in touch only by detailed, loving letters.

In November Taylor joined a small band of CIM missionaries in Wuhan for prayer, Bible study and a discussion of the progress of the mission's work in China. He and A G Parrott, who was soon to become Hudson's corresponding secretary, were walking together on a hill outside the town, talking of the need for expansion. The mission already had 96 missionaries (including wives) working with about one hundred

Chinese colleagues in seventy stations, and was responsible for feeding over one hundred Chinese children in the mission's schools. Taylor believed that the size of the task still remaining meant expansion was essential.

Taylor and Parrott considered how many more people were needed. Perhaps fifty or sixty could be placed but that wouldn't be enough, taking losses into account. Then the words of Luke 10:1 (AV) came into Taylor's mind, "After these things the Lord appointed other seventy also ..." Surely this was too much to ask — it had not been a good year for funds. As they walked, Parrott caught his foot on something in the grass.

"Look," he said, picking up a string of one hundred coins, "do you see this? If we have to come to the hills for it, God will be able to give us all the money needed!"

On Sunday, they took tea with two other missionaries and all four promised to pray for seventy more until they came. On the Monday evening, during prayer with all the missionaries who had assembled at Wuhan, Taylor prayed specifically for the seventy. "I quite believe he prayed the prayer of faith tonight," recorded Parrott. "There was a great spirit of expectancy." Taylor worked out in detail on paper how 42 men and 28 women would be situated, province by province and city by city.

"Couldn't we meet again," someone suggested, "and have a united praise meeting when the last of the seventy has reached China?"

"We shall be scattered then. Why not have the praise meeting now and give thanks for the seventy in advance?"

After the praise meeting, the missionaries made their ways back to their stations with a message to send throughout the mission. At meetings early in December, all members of the mission present agreed to pray every day for the seventy until they were given. Taylor promised to telegraph Pyrland Road and ask them to receive and send out this number of new recruits if his colleagues in China would continue praying.

In January 1882, Taylor drafted an appeal to the home churches which was signed by 77 members of the mission in China. "Souls on every hand are perishing for lack of knowledge; more than a thousand every hour are passing away into death and darkness ... Can we leave matters thus without incurring the sin of blood-guiltiness?"

The appeal referred to the needs of all Protestant missionary societies, and then set out the needs of the CIM in detail. There would be no need to worry about funds, providing the mission put God's kingdom first; but the appeal added a word of caution to prospective candidates. "Mere romantic feeling will soon die out amid the toilsome labour and constant discomforts and trials of inland work, and will not be worth much when severe illness arises and perhaps all the money is gone. Faith in God alone gives joy and rest in such circumstances." Then came the word of encouragement. "We ourselves have proved God's faithfulness and the blessedness of our dependence on Him. He is supplying and ever has supplied all our need ... He makes us very happy in His service, and those of us who have children desire nothing better for them, should the Lord tarry, than that they may be called to similar work and similar joys."

The year 1882 gave no particular encouragement that the prayers for seventy new missionaries would be quickly answered. Donations didn't increase and only eleven missionaries, eight women and three men, went out to China. Some workers retired from the mission, and in some stations the work seemed to be slipping back rather than flourishing. All this deeply depressed Taylor in the early months of the year, but he was able to report to Jennie in the summer that he had never been in better health; he asked her to join him in praying for men of spiritual power with leadership qualities.

In June, Taylor preached at a CIM conference in Anqing on the north shore of the Yangzi. His subject was the Song of Solomon[1] — an Old Testament book he had fallen in

---

[1]Hudson Taylor's booklet *Union and Communion* (now out of print) is on the same theme.

love with a quarter of a century earlier in the difficult period
before his marriage to Maria. Few who attended the Anqing
conference ever forgot his talks, and the result was an
outpouring of the Holy Spirit. Some delegates spent several
nights in prayer and everyone devoted a day to fasting and
prayer. "The Holy Spirit seemed so to fill us this morning,"
Taylor recorded, "that several of us felt as if we could not
bear any more."

By December 1882, he and Jennie had been separated
for fourteen months. He wrote to say he hoped it wouldn't
be long before they were reunited, and that they would never
again have to endure such a long period apart. From Shanghai
he told her that many enjoyed the meetings at which he
preached — but he wondered if they realized what it cost
him and Jennie. "Is anything of value in Christ's service
which costs little?" he asked.

* * * * *

Funds in the closing months of 1882 had been no more
than adequate to meet the awesome needs of the mission.

"Dear Father, we know that you love to please your children,"
someone prayed on about February 1, 1883, at one of the
daily Chefoo prayer meetings. "Will you lead one of your
wealthy stewards to give liberally to encourage timid ones
at home?"

A few days later Taylor sailed for England and at Aden
learned the answer to the prayer. On February 2, at Pyrland
Road, Benjamin Broomhall had received a donation of three
thousand pounds for work in China.

* * * * *

Nearly seventeen months after they parted, Jennie travelled
to Paris to meet her returning husband at Easter 1883. In
this splendid springtime setting, Hudson recorded, "as we
sat side by side in the cab, though she had so much to

say and I had too, I could only take her hand and be silent
— the joy was too deep for words!"

In England, Taylor found that the mission was now held
in high regard. This was partly due to Benjamin Broomhall's
skills at public relations, but the CIM's achievements also
told their own story: heroic pioneers, including women, had
settled in nearly all China's inland provinces and were
apparently supported by faith in God without appeals for
funds. John McCarthy had walked across China from Wuhan
in the east to Burma in the west. John Stevenson and Henry
Soltau had walked in the opposite direction from Bhamo
to the Yangzi and then on by boat to Shanghai — 1,900
miles in 86 days — becoming the first westerners to cross
China from west to east.

These remarkable walks marked the beginning of a thorough
survey of China by the CIM. As the years went by, missionaries
visited every important city and town systematically, gathering
and recording information essential to future work. On the
way they distributed Scripture portions and tracts and preached
to impromptu audiences.

From all over the British Isles, Taylor received invitations
to speak about the mission he led and its pioneering adventures.
Hudson Taylor had become something of a household name.

"If you are not dead yet," a child wrote to him, "I want
to send you the money I have saved up to help the little
boys and girls of China to love Jesus."

"Will you do me the kindness," wrote Canon Wilberforce
from Southampton, "to give a Bible reading in my house
to about sixty people ... and spend the night with us? *Please*
do us the favour in the Master's name."

"Do preach for me at the Tabernacle," wrote Spurgeon.

"My heart is still in the glorious work," wrote William
Berger from the south of France, enclosing a cheque for five
hundred pounds. "Most heartily do I join you in praying
for seventy more labourers — but do not stop at seventy!"

On a warm evening in June 1883, twelve young men
gathered round Taylor in a Gloucester schoolroom. He began

to tell them simply of his days as a medical student and of his preparations for work in China. "I felt as though I had never yet given up anything for Christ," one of them later recorded, "never yet learned to trust the Lord ... I was so moved that I had to ask Mr Taylor to stop: my heart was broken." Three of the twelve went to China.

At Salisbury, the wife of a conference convener went out of a sense of duty to hear Taylor speak, expecting it to be a dreary affair. "As Mr Taylor began to speak, a great calm and stillness came over me — a fresh revelation of God's coming to meet human need. The fountains of my inmost being were broken up ... I saw a little of what consecration really meant; and as I began to yield myself to God, fresh hope, light and gladness came into my life — streams that have been flowing ever since."

When Taylor spoke, people noticed not only that he never hinted at an appeal for funds but that he loved to speak well of other missions. At the conference in Salisbury, a Canon Thwaites was impressed by the unique combination of humility and power which marked Taylor's addresses: "a power of the Holy Spirit which was intense, almost awful." The conference ended with a praise meeting at which, although the CIM was never mentioned, people consecrated their lives to work for China. There was no collection but "people emptied their purses, stripped themselves of their jewels, handed over their watches, chains, rings and the like."

In parallel with a gruelling schedule of speaking engagements, Taylor dealt with at least 2,600 letters over a period of ten months in 1883/84. Two large manuscript books list them: when received, when answered, a line about their contents. No doubt other less formal letters went unrecorded. He would soon employ a private secretary but that wouldn't be enough.

The administration of the mission in China needed attention. Taylor therefore devoted his energy to praying about and discussing possible options with members of the London Council. The result was a carefully drafted letter sent to every member of the mission in August 1883. It suggested that just as the organization of the mission in England was through the London Council assisting the Director, so a China Council should be introduced to assist him or his successor in China. The members of the council would be the Superintendents of districts, who would in turn be assisted by district councils of the missionaries. Taylor believed that this would provide a mechanism for local matters to be dealt with quickly, bring him into regular contact with his most experienced missionaries, and secure more effective supervision and expansion of the work. The letter ended, "I shall be glad to hear from you how these suggestions strike you, and how far they commend themselves to your mind."

* * * * *

During 1883 twenty new missionaries left for China, and in 1884 the number rose to 46. The prayers for the seventy were not only answered but exceeded.

SOMETHING BETTER THAN CRICKET 39

Hudson and Jennie dreaded another parting, but in January 1885 it had to come: he was needed in China. Jennie and the children said their farewells, and Hudson slipped away from Pyrland Road in a cab. Back in the house, Amelia Broomhall comforted Jennie for a minute or two and then it was back to work, making the final arrangements for a group of talented and privileged young men to go to China.

The "Cambridge Seven" had already spoken at a series of meetings in England and Scotland. On February 2, they were to speak in Cambridge itself. Students of the University and citizens of Cambridge squeezed into the Guildhall. First to tell his tale was a handsome Cambridge graduate and former captain of Trinity College boats, Stanley Smith.

"The love of Christ constrains us," he said, "to go out to the world. Unless we spread abroad the light, we will find in England that we cannot hold our own with the powers of darkness."

Then came another tall and powerfully built oarsman, Montagu Beauchamp, son of a baronet. Two soldiers spoke next: Dixon Hoste, from the Royal Military Academy and the son of a General; and Lieutenant Cecil Polhill-Turner, from Eton College and the second Dragoon Guards. Another old Etonian followed. C T Studd, the most famous name of them all, was England's best all-round cricketer and had returned from Australia with the Ashes in 1883.

"I want to recommend to you my Master," said Studd. "I have had many pleasures in my time, and have tasted most of the delights this world can give; but I can tell you that these pleasures are as nothing compared with my present joy. I had formerly as much love for cricket as any man could have; but when the Lord Jesus came into my heart I found that I had something infinitely better. My heart was no longer set on the game: I wanted to win souls to serve and please Him."

Arthur Polhill-Turner, Cecil's brother, had been converted, like Studd's father, under the preaching of the American evangelist D L Moody. Arthur had probably been the first of the seven to speak of going to China back in 1882. The seventh, William Cassels, had been ordained and planned to join the CMS. But when he discovered it had no plans to move into inland China he applied to join the CIM. Then his mother intervened.

"His six brothers have all gone overseas," she told Taylor. "Please don't take William as well."

"I hold a parent's wishes sacred," Taylor replied, "and I will certainly not encourage William if you oppose it."

But later she changed her mind and wrote to Taylor that she didn't wish to prove "a bad mother to one of the best of sons."

All of the seven were from Cambridge except Dixon Hoste. A correspondent in *The Record* reflected on why the CIM had attracted to it such a remarkable group of men who had so much to leave. He put it down to "the uncompromising spirituality and unworldliness of the programme of the mission responded to by hearts which have truly laid all at the Lord's feet."

Other meetings arranged to say farewell to the Cambridge Seven, including a crowded one in London, attracted a good deal of publicity for the CIM. The mission's standing was now as high as it had been low following the Yangzhou riots.

The seven men left London on February 5, 1885, and arrived in Shanghai on March 18 to be met by a Chinese-looking gentleman they didn't immediately recognize as Hudson Taylor. Their main task was to make progress with the study of Chinese, and they were soon on their way inland dressed in Chinese clothes. They began the slow journey up the Han River to Hanzhong in the south west corner of Shaanxi.

C T Studd and the Polhill brothers decided that learning Chinese was a hard and tedious business, and therefore prayed for a Pentecostal gift of Chinese speech. When they arrived at Hanzhong, they persuaded two young missionary women to do the same. Taylor didn't approve: "How many and subtle are the devices of Satan," he wrote, "to keep the Chinese ignorant of the gospel." He began to tell new missionaries, "If I could put the Chinese language into your brains by one wave of the hand I would not do it." Going through the slow process of submitting to a Chinese scholar, and watching and listening to evangelists and experienced missionaries, taught wisdom as well as language.

❋ ❋ ❋ ❋ ❋

Hudson Taylor hoped to be able to return to England before the end of 1885, as there was much to be done at home. But first he needed to move forward the establishment of a China Council and the appointment of superintendents, to press ahead with the appointment of a deputy director and to introduce training centres for the study of Chinese. Finally he wanted to see something of the work in the interior, especially in the province of Shanxi.

One difficulty after another, which he saw as attacks of Satan, made it obvious that an early return to England wouldn't after all be possible. His proposed changes in organization were not well received by all. In the early days the system of all missionaries dealing with Taylor direct had led to a family feeling about the mission, and his plans to delegate responsibility to superintendents in charge of districts were only introduced in the face of initial opposition and misunderstanding.

But Taylor made some progress. He appointed William Cooper superintendent of Anqing and pastor of the church there; and he put gifted linguist Frederick Baller in charge of a missionary training centre also based in Anqing. James Meadows, Taylor's first-ever recruit 23 years earlier, became superintendent of Zhejiang, the coastal province south of Shanghai. And, most important of all, he made John Stevenson his own deputy.

John Whiteford Stevenson, son of the laird of Thriepwood, Renfrewshire, sailed for China some months earlier than the Lammermuir party, and arrived in Ningbo in February 1866. An impressive looking Scotsman, tall, broad-shouldered, and somewhat reserved when he first joined the mission, he believed in "work and unwasted days". He had toiled in Ningbo, Shaoxing and Burma; in 1880 he had undertaken that incredible walk across the breadth of China. Taylor now wrote to all members of the mission and told them that Stevenson would help him by visiting many places he couldn't reach, represent him in his absences from China, and deal with questions raised by the superintendents which needed immediate decisions. He was to remain deputy director until 1916.

Taylor and his team had been thinking about new CIM premises in Shanghai, and a site on Wusong Road seemed eminently suitable. Taylor prayed at a noon prayer meeting in the summer of 1886 that the required sum would be given in time for them to take up the option to buy. That very afternoon 28-year-old Glasgow businessman Archibald Orr Ewing, a friend of Stevenson, arrived from Britain and offered £1,500 towards the total purchase price. Taylor signed the contract for about two acres of land at just under £2,500. The CIM in China so impressed Orr Ewing that he formally joined the mission, wound up his business affairs in Scotland, and paid the full cost not only of the site but also of the extensive buildings later put up.

✳ ✳ ✳ ✳ ✳

Taylor had never yet visited the northerly province of Shanxi which had suffered so cruelly in the great famine of 1876, although Jennie had pioneered CIM's magnificent work there with orphans. The province was nearly as large as England and Wales and, despite the famine, had an estimated population of nine million. Among those now serving God there were the Rev William Cassels of the Cambridge Seven. Taylor hoped he would eventually establish a Church of England district in the huge western province of Sichuan.

In the intense heat of June 1886 Taylor finally set out to visit Shanxi, with his oldest son Herbert, now 25, and a Dr Edwards. Food was difficult to find and the younger men got used to Taylor's cheerful invitations to join him late at night — sometimes after they had fallen asleep from exhaustion — and tuck into "midnight chicken". Most of the Shanxi missionaries, including five of the Cambridge Seven, were assembled at the provincial capital, Taiyuan, to meet Taylor. A week of meetings followed, and Montagu Beauchamp called the book of Taylor's messages he edited, *Days of Blessing.*

"When God's grace is triumphant in my soul," Taylor said at the Shanxi meetings, "and I can look a Chinaman in the face and say, 'God is able to save *you*, where and as you are', that is when I have power. How else are you going to deal with a man under the craving for opium? The cause of want of success is very often that we are only half saved ourselves. If we are fully saved and confess it, we shall see results ...

"Let us feel that everything that is human, everything

outside the sufficiency of Christ, is only helpful in the measure in which it enables us to bring the soul to Him. If our medical missions draw people to us, and we can present to them the Christ of God, medical missions are a blessing; but to substitute medicine for the preaching of the gospel would be a profound mistake. If we put schools or education in the place of spiritual power to change the heart, it will be a profound mistake. If we get the idea that people are going to be converted by some educational *process*, instead of by a regenerative recreation, it will be a profound mistake. Let all our auxiliaries be auxiliaries — means of bringing Christ and the soul into contact — then we may be truly thankful for them all ... Let us exalt the glorious gospel in our hearts, and believe that *it* is the power of God unto salvation. Let everything else *sit at its feet* ... We shall never be discouraged if we realize that in Christ is our Sufficiency."

Taylor's next destination was Hongtong, for a bigger conference involving three hundred Chinese Christians and missionaries. John Stevenson had arrived before Taylor and had a chance to spend some time with a remarkable Chinese Christian whose name was to become famous in the history of the CIM.

An ex-Confucian scholar, Hsi had been converted in 1879 through the witness of David Hill, of the Wesleyan Methodist Missionary Society. Previously an opium addict, he had cured himself of his habit through his faith in Christ, and set up refuges where other addicts could be cured through faith and prayer as well as medicine.

For five or six weeks Stevenson travelled with Hsi, visited his home and refuges, listened to his preaching, and saw him shepherding Chinese Christians. "I was profoundly impressed," Stevenson recalled. "His spirituality and earnestness; his prayer and fastings; the intensity of purpose — nothing in the world but the *one thing* — and his ability as a practical leader were most remarkable. I have never seen such influence over others! He was so strong that all seemed to yield to him, and yet humble too. I was especially struck by the way

people came to consult him. He had everybody's burdens
to bear, and was always ready to advise and pray with those
who needed help.

"His knowledge and use of the Scripture also impressed
me. One sermon on the temptation of Christ that he preached
was very striking. Familiar passages seemed to unfold new
meanings under his touch and in the light of his spiritual
experience. God was to him a tremendous reality. Constantly
and in everything he dealt with God. In a very real way
he dealt with Satan too. His conflicts with the evil one
at times were such that he would give himself for days to
fasting and prayer. Even when travelling, I have known him
fast a whole day over some difficult matter that needed clearing
up. That was always his resource — *fast and pray.*"

When Taylor eventually reached Hongtong, he was as
impressed as Stevenson had been. He planned to recognize
Hsi's unusual gifts by setting him apart for special pastoral
responsibilities in the south Shanxi area. Hsi was reluctant
to accept at first but, once he agreed, he gave himself to
fasting and prayer for three days, literally touching no food,
until the ordination service. Taylor invited all the missionaries working in the district to join him in laying hands on
Hsi, and prayed that God would set him apart to watch
over and feed the sheep of God.

Montagu Beauchamp set off with Taylor on the long journey
west to Hanzhong, close to the border with Sichuan. Taylor
rode a mule, and another carried their belongings; Beauchamp preferred to walk. It was so hot that most of the
travelling had to be done at night, and they constantly lost
their way. Sometimes Beauchamp would fall asleep from
exhaustion while walking along, and in the daytime wake
up to find that Taylor had rigged a mosquito net over him
to keep the flies away.

Many times, the tall and athletic Beauchamp walked waist
deep across fast-flowing rivers with Taylor on his shoulders
and Chinese men on either side to weigh them down. At
one river they found a few houses whose residents made a

handsome profit from carrying travellers across.

"The river is impassable today," they told Taylor and Beauchamp. But with curious logic, they added, "For a thousand cash each we will take you across."

"Outrageous!" said Beauchamp and began to wade into the water, which was rising quickly in torrential rain. When the men saw that the foreigners were not to be deterred, they came and helped, glad to be paid a fair price. The river continued to rise quickly and the two missionaries realized that if they had arrived half an hour later they would have been unable to cross.

On the other side of the river was a small village without an inn. Unable to continue in the heavy rain, the travellers could only find a pigsty to shelter in. With no alternative they turned the rightful occupant out, borrowed some benches, took the doors off their hinges for beds and, wrap-ping themselves up in their plaids, got ready to spend the night as comfortably as they could. However before long the pig returned in a huff, charged their makeshift door (which quickly fell in), and settled down contentedly to share her accommodation with the director of a large missionary society and a gentleman who on the death of his father became Sir Montagu Beauchamp.

On one occasion, Beauchamp heard Taylor singing and caught the words, "We thank thee, Lord, for this our food."

"Where on earth is the food?" Beauchamp asked.

"It can't be far away," replied Taylor with a smile. "Our Father knows we are hungry and will send our breakfast soon. But *you* will have to wait and say your grace when it comes, while *I* shall be ready to begin at once!"

Sure enough, a minute or two later they met a man selling ready-cooked rice.

Beauchamp recalled that whenever he woke before dawn to feed the mules, he would see Taylor reading his Bible by the light of a candle. On long journeys Taylor used to pray lying down. Now in his mid-fifties, he found kneeling too exhausting. Sometimes he would go back to sleep again after his quiet time with God.

After a journey which lasted 24 days, they eventually arrived at Hanzhong. Taylor was able to see the medical work which Dr William Wilson had been doing there for four years, and to inspect the school run by a team of six unmarried lady missionaries. Another important task was to discuss a strategy for entering Sichuan, so that William Cassels and other Anglican members of the CIM could establish a district of the Church of England. They spent a day in fasting and prayer — and before the end of the year the first CIM missionaries began to work in Eastern Sichuan.

The last meeting in Hanzhong was held in summer twilight in the courtyard of William Wilson's home. Lamps shone out under the broad eaves of the open Chinese guest-hall. Above was the open sky and a million stars.

"We shall read from Philippians chapter three," Taylor began. As he read the chapter through he seemed to place particular emphasis on verses seven and eight. "'What things were gain to me, those I counted loss for Christ. Yes doubt-less, and I count all things but loss for the excellency of the knowledge of Christ Jesus my Lord: for whom I have suffered the loss of all things, and do count them but dung, that I may win Christ ...'

"What we give up for Christ we gain," Taylor said in his talk, "and what we keep back is our real loss ...

"As I travelled here," he said, "I passed hundreds of towns and cities with, as far as I know, not a single Christian in any of them!"

"We seemed to lose sight of the speaker," Wilson recalled, "and hear only the voice of the Holy Spirit. It was a time of humbling and confession, nearly every one was broken down ... there were we, comfortably settled down, taking for granted perhaps that we had obeyed our Master's command, practically forgetting that Hanzhong was not the world, and that people even in the villages at hand might never hear of Christ unless we set ourselves to go to them."

"DOING IT HANDSOME" 40

There years had elapsed since Hudson Taylor had first circulated his proposals for a China Council. In the middle of November 1886, it met for the first time at Anqing. Taylor, John Stevenson and the superintendents of the provinces aimed to clarify the mission's *Principles and Practice* which had evolved over the years, for the benefit of missionaries and future members. Before they got down to business, they spent a week in prayer and fasting.

The members of the council published their decisions in a *Book of Arrangements*, or "little grey book", which Taylor eventually sent to all the stations of the mission. The book said that the relationship of the China Council to Taylor, as General Director, with regard to affairs in China was the same as the London Council's relationship to him with regard to affairs at home. It set out instructions for probationers, the treasurer, the secretary in China, the superintendents, senior and junior missionaries, and women; it spoke about dress, Chinese customs, avoiding offence to the Chinese, and securing rights from mandarins. It adopted a course of Chinese study prepared by Stevenson and Fred Baller, to be used at the Anqing Training Institute.

Writing in the book about leadership, Taylor said, "The principle of godly rule is a most important one, for it equally affects us all. It is this — the seeking to help, not to lord; to keep from wrong paths and lead into right paths, for the glory of God and the good of those guided, not for the gratification of the ruler. *Such rule always leads the ruler to the Cross*, and saves the ruled at the cost of the ruler ... When the heart is right it loves godly rule, and finds freedom in obedience."

John Stevenson recalled: "We all saw visions at that time. Those were days of heaven upon earth; nothing seemed difficult." And another dramatic development in the history of the CIM also emerged from this first meeting of the China Council. It appears to have originated with Stevenson. Back in September 1886, he had written a letter to Jennie which said: "We are fully expecting at least one hundred fresh labourers to arrive in China in 1887." Taylor seems at first to have taken the view, with other members of the China Council, that Stevenson was being too ambitious. But before leaving Anqing, he led the others in praying for one hundred new missionaries in 1887.

When the council dispersed, Taylor and John Stevenson spent a few days tidying up and finalizing the draft of the *Book of Arrangements.* Pacing up and down, as was his habit, Taylor dictated letters to his secretary. When he repeated words he had written to Jennie, "a hundred new missionaries in 1887", his secretary glanced up with an expression of unbelief. Stevenson never forgot the expression on the man's face, nor what Taylor, who had also noticed it, said next:

"If you showed me a photograph of the whole hundred, taken in China, I couldn't be more sure than I am now."

John Stevenson sent out a note to every member of the CIM, "Will you put down your name to pray for the Hundred?" and cabled London, "Praying for a hundred new missionaries in 1887".

"The accepting and sending out of the Hundred," Taylor

told Jennie, "will require no small amount of work, but the Lord will give strength; and no little wisdom, but the Lord will guide. There is an all-sufficiency in Him, is there not?"

At each meal, Hudson Taylor and friends began to sing the prayer:

Oh send the Hundred workers, Lord,
Those of Thy heart and mind and choice,
To tell Thy love both far and wide —
So we shall praise Thee and rejoice:
And above the rest this note shall swell,
My Jesus hath done all things well.

A veteran Shanghai missionary said to Hudson Taylor, "I am delighted to hear that you are praying for large reinforcements. You will not get a hundred, of course, within the year; but you will get many more than if you did not ask for them."

"Thank you for your interest," Taylor replied. "We have the joy of knowing our prayers are answered now. And I feel sure that, if spared, you will share that joy by welcoming the last of the hundred to China!"

Taylor sailed from Shanghai on January 6, 1887, with ice on the decks, and arrived in London on February 18. Friends of the CIM had heard of the project and invitations for him to speak in many parts of Britain and Ireland poured into Pyrland Road.

For a venture like this, more than prayer would be needed: as so often, prayer and hard work would have to go together, and Taylor took on a heavy share of it. He spent an incredible year travelling around the United Kingdom speaking at meetings and conventions in most large towns and cities; writing hundreds of letters, sometimes thirty or forty in 24 hours; interviewing hundreds of candidates anxious to respond to his invitation to go to China; dealing with opposition from the London Council to the Book of Arrangements; and keeping in touch with Stevenson in China over detailed administrative problems.

"I'm utterly used up," he told Stevenson," and tempted to wish that my turn had come. But He giveth power to the faint."

During the long periods of separation, Hudson and Jennie exchanged frequent notes. "Darling, my heart trembles for you. Do get all the rest you can," she begged. "It will not pay to kill yourself, even to get the Hundred."

"Hundreds are finding blessing through our meetings," he told her. "We are not separated for nothing. Yesterday I caught myself thinking: By this time next week I shall be on my way home. I shall be with my Jennie! You see what it is to have too little to think of!"

Taylor celebrated his 55th birthday on May 21, 1887, and by the 26th the CIM had notched up 21 years since the *Lammermuir* sailed. On the day of the anniversary meetings a thousand pounds was received, one of many large donations towards the expense of sending out the Hundred.

Taylor began his address at the anniversary meetings by recalling the words of a coloured evangelist, "When God does anything, He does it handsome!"

"The Lord is always faithful," he told his audience. "People say, 'Lord, increase our faith'. Did not our Lord rebuke His disciples for that prayer? It is not great faith you need, He said in effect, but faith in a great God. Though your faith were as small as a grain of mustard seed, it would suffice to remove mountains. We need a faith that rests on a great God, and expects Him to keep His own word and to do just as He has promised.

"Now we have been led to pray for a hundred new workers this year. We have the sure word, 'Whatsoever ye shall ask in my name, I will do it, that the Father may be glorified in the Son'. Resting on this promise, it would not have added to our confidence one whit if, when we began to pray in November, my dear brother-in-law, Mr Broomhall, had sent me out a printed list of a hundred accepted candidates. We had been spending some days in fasting and prayer before the thought was suggested to our minds. We began the matter aright, with God, and we are quite sure that we shall end it aright. It is a great joy to know that 31 of the Hundred are already in China, but it is a greater joy to know that more than a hundred of our workers in China are banded together in daily pleading with God to send out the whole Hundred.

"And by the Hundred we mean one of God's 'handsome' hundreds! ... Whether He will give His 'exceeding abundantly' by sending us more than a literal hundred, or whether by stirring up other branches of the Church to send many hundreds, which I should greatly prefer, or by awakening missionary enthusiasm all over the Church and blessing the whole world through it, I don't know. I hope that He will answer prayer in all these ways; but sure I am that God will do it 'handsome' ...

"I do want you, dear friends, to realize this principle of working with God and asking Him for everything. If the work is at the command of God, then we can go to Him in full confidence for workers; and when God gives the workers, we can go to Him for means to supply their needs. We always accept a suitable worker, whether we have funds or not. Then we often say, 'Now, dear friend, your first work will be to join us in praying for money to send you to China.'

"As soon as there is money enough, the time of the year and other circumstances being suitable, the friend goes out. We don't wait until there is a remittance in hand to give him when he gets there. The Lord will provide in the meanwhile, and the money will be wired to China in time to supply his wants ... Let us see to it that we keep God before our eyes; that we walk in His ways, and seek to please and glorify Him in everything, great and small. *Depend upon it, God's work, done in God's way, will never lack God's supplies* ...

"And now, if this principle of taking everything to God and accepting everything from God is a true one — and I think the experience of the China Inland Mission proves that it is — ought we not to bring it to bear more and more in daily life? The Lord's will is that His people should be an unburdened people, fully supplied, strong, healthy and happy ... Shall we not determine to be 'careful for nothing, but in everything by prayer and supplication with thanksgiving' bring those things that would become burdens or anxieties to God in prayer, and live in His perfect peace?

"... I have not known what anxiety is since the Lord taught me that the work is His. My great business in life is to please God. Walking with Him in the light, I never feel a burden."

A friend wrote to Taylor from Ireland: "I have had conversations with three people, all of them Christians, who seem to have received a new thought at your meetings — as if God really *means what He says* when He gives us His promises."

Every day, in the quietness of the early morning, Taylor read his Bible. And later in the day, as he travelled the country, he shared what God had shown him at meeting after meeting, sometimes expounding a passage, a verse or a phrase.

Reporting on a meeting fifteen hundred people attended near Glasgow, Taylor's secretary wrote, "It was a mighty message last night. Many were broken down, to be lifted up by God. After a precious exposition of Zephaniah 3, Mr Taylor spoke very simply and very straight to the heart on 'Trusting God'. He did not finish till close on 9 pm, but you could have heard any ordinary clock tick most of the time."

The response to Taylor's straightforward accounts of what God had done and of the vast needs that remained to be met by totally committed and trusting disciples, was dramatic. At one meeting in Edinburgh, 120 people offered themselves for missionary work abroad. By the middle of October 1887, 89 candidates had been accepted and were preparing to go. By early November Taylor was able to announce that 102 candidates had been accepted for service with the CIM, and that enough money had been given to pay for their passages to China. By the end of the year all 102 had sailed. This figure included two associate missionaries, so that God not only answered the many prayers, but answered them with total precision!

During the year as a whole, six hundred men and women offered themselves for service abroad. The London Council refused to lower its standards, however, and rejected five out of every six candidates.

"You must continue very earnestly in prayer," Taylor told John Stevenson, "and secure the prayers of our friends generally, that God will magnify His Name and adequately sustain the work with funds. Nothing is clearer to me than that obtaining a hundred this year we have obtained a second hundred; to send them out and sustain them will require another ten thousand pounds in additional income, and in times like these it is a tremendous rise from a little over twenty to forty thousand pounds annually. One is so glad that God has Himself asked us the question — 'Is anything too hard for the Lord?' But if we get less prayerful about funds, we shall soon get sorely tried about funds.

"Every day," the letter continued, "I feel more and more thankful to God for giving you to us and for giving you such general acceptance. No human prescience or wisdom is sufficient for your position, but so long as you continue to seek His guidance in every matter, and in the midst of the pressure of work take time to be holy and take time to pray for the workers, the Lord will continue to use and own and bless you."

By January 1888, Taylor was the director of a substantially enlarged mission. In his New Year message, he wrote, "Let us never forget that, if we make no appeal to man, we need very, very definitely to continue our appeal to God. A God-given, God-guided, spiritual impulse is expressed in every donation we receive; and this, which makes our work peculiarly blessed, will always keep us peculiarly dependent upon Him. How can we sufficiently praise Him for this happy position, this necessity of trustfulness?"

Hudson Taylor felt sure there would be a "big Hallelujah" when the last of the Hundred reached China. "It is not more than we expected God to do for us, but it is very blessed; and to see that God does answer, in great things as well as small, the prayers of those who put their trust in Him will strengthen the faith of multitudes."

Among those who welcomed the last of the Hundred was the elderly missionary who had felt so sure the mission's prayers would not be completely answered.

MR MOODY IS OVERRULED 41

November 1887, the month the Hundred was finally made up, also saw the arrival of Henry Frost at Pyrland Road. Just short of thirty years old, Frost came from a successful American family which had helped found Harvard University. A careful study of the Bible had convinced him that the heathen were lost, and could be saved only by faith in Christ. It was therefore the duty of the church to do everything possible to present the gospel to them. Seeing a picture of the Cambridge Seven dressed in Chinese clothes, and reading about the CIM, had inspired him to give his life to China's evangelization. So he had come to England to suggest Hudson Taylor should establish a branch of the CIM in North America. Before their meeting, he wrote outlining his proposal.

Taylor was in Scotland when Henry Frost arrived, and his first experience of life at Pyrland Road was of the daily prayer meeting which, he wrote, "deeply impressed me, its simplicity, earnestness, comprehensiveness and spirituality being beyond anything I had ever known."

Prior to their first interview, Frost built up a mental picture of Taylor as tall and rather portly, with black hair and beard and a full, deep voice. When he was finally shown into Taylor's room, the man who rose from his desk and walked towards him was, as Frost recalled later, "shorter than I expected, and had fair hair, blue eyes and the pleasantest and gentlest of voices."

"Welcome to England, to the mission and to my home," Taylor said, taking Frost's hand in both his. "I am deeply interested in the matter of which you have written and have already prayed much about it."

It seemed to Frost that at that moment he had a revelation "first of a man and then of his God. Never before had I seen one so humbly tender or so divinely noble. From that moment my heart was fully his ... and also, in a new and deeper sense, his Lord's."

The interview lasted an hour.

"Come and see me again this evening," Taylor said. "My brother-in-law, Benjamin Broomhall, will join us for another discussion."

Frost returned to his lodgings with the cheerful impression that Taylor was encouraging him to hope that the mission would be extended to America. But in the afternoon, as he discovered later, Taylor met Broomhall who turned out to be against Frost's proposal.

"American missionary societies will not welcome the transfer of a British organization to American soil," Broomhall argued.

At the evening interview, Frost found Taylor just as friendly as before. They prayed together. But when the conversation began, he gradually realized that something had changed.

"There is a difference," said Taylor at one point, "between planting and transplanting trees. In the one case they are liable to perish, but in the other — as in the planting of an acorn and the growing up of an oak — they are likely to thrive and become so firmly rooted that they will stand the severest storms of wind and rain. It would not be best to accept your suggestion. My answer must be a refusal. We must hope for an uprising in America of a purely American society on the lines of the China Inland Mission, but indigenous in every way."

The decision was apparently final, and Frost said little. Then he remembered that Taylor had spoken of returning to China the following spring.

"Would you be willing to travel to China by way of America, if you were invited to speak at Niagara-on-the-Lake and at Mr Moody's Conference at Northfield?"

"Yes, I think such invitations might be accepted," replied Taylor.

Frost returned to his lodgings "physically and spiritually in the deepest darkness." He had felt sure that his visit to England was according to God's will, and kept asking himself, *How can I ever again be sure of the guidance of God?*

✷ ✷ ✷ ✷ ✷

In the summer of 1888 Hudson Taylor made his first visit to America, travelling with his son Howard, now 25 and a qualified doctor, his personal secretary S F Whitehouse, and Liverpool evangelist Reginald Radcliffe and his wife. The journey took a week, and when the SS *Etruria* tied up at the wharf at New York, Henry Frost was there to meet them.

The conference at Niagara-on-the-Lake was described as a "great gathering of deeply taught Christians." Taylor was only able to speak twice and said very little about China, preferring to concentrate on the theme of the beauty and glory of Christ.

"We were certainly lifted into 'the heavenlies'," Frost said, "and into the very presence of God." He recalled Taylor referring to himself as "the little servant of a great Master".

Hudson Taylor and Howard had to leave the conference before it ended in order to join Moody in Chicago, but speakers Reginald Radcliffe and Robert Wilder continued to emphasize the importance of obeying Christ's command to go into all the world to preach the gospel. Wilder's influence was to lead to the birth of the American Student Volunteer Movement and later the Inter-Varsity Fellowship.

"How much would it take to support a missionary with the CIM for a year?" someone asked Radcliffe.

"Fifty pounds," Radcliffe replied, leaving the American to convert to dollars by multiplying by five, and incidentally underestimating the amount required.

The committee decided to give the whole of the collection (taken in Taylor's absence) to the CIM. It amounted to over five hundred dollars — enough on the Radcliffe reckoning to provide for two missionaries in China for a year. This was handed to Henry Frost with the request:

"Please pass this to Mr Taylor and suggest that it should be used for American workers in connection with the CIM."

Before the conference ended, private spontaneous donations and more collections brought the sum to two thousand dollars. Henry Frost, as the treasurer taking charge of these funds, had bulging pockets.

Frost decided to travel immediately to his father's home in Attica, where Taylor was staying. He wondered how the leader of the CIM would react to the news that a substantial sum had been collected for his mission. He missed his train connection and arrived in Attica at midnight, disappointed that he would have to keep his good news to himself until the morning. But Taylor was at the station to meet him.

"How do you do, dear brother?" said Taylor.

Frost said little until they reached the privacy of Taylor's room.

"Mr Taylor, I have good news for you. The Niagara Conference has put into my hands enough money to support eight missionaries in the China Inland Mission."

Taylor's face fell and he said nothing for a while. Then: "I think we had better pray."

The two men knelt at Taylor's bed and Taylor asked God what it all meant.

They got up and Taylor, still looking solemn, asked:

"Was anything said by the donors of the money about

its being used for North American workers?"

"Yes, it was requested that it should be put to that use."

"This is serious," said Taylor, more to himself than to Frost.

"We parted that night about one o'clock," recorded Frost. "Both of us were happy. But the larger and more mature man was holding peculiar communion with his God, and to him, under such circumstances, the 'secret place' meant solemnity of mind and heart."

Henry Frost and Howard Taylor both painted vivid pictures of Hudson Taylor preaching at meetings chaired by D L Moody. One such occasion was at the YMCA auditorium in Chicago in September 1888. There was Taylor, "small in stature", about to bring a great audience into the presence of God. Behind sat D L Moody, as Henry Frost recalled, "large and upright in his central chair on the platform" with many speakers gathered about him. Taylor stood in silent prayer for a moment, conscious of his total dependence upon God, before leading in audible prayer. And then he spoke "as a little child might speak, as a prophet might speak, as one who sees a vision of a needy land and a dying people might speak." When he finished after an hour, there was what Frost described as "a great sigh from the listening throng" and then a short silence.

Moody stepped forward. "Will the ushers now take up a collection."

Taylor jumped quickly to his feet and spoke quietly to Moody.

"Didn't I make it clear beforehand that the China Inland Mission doesn't take collections?"

"Yes, but we mustn't lose such an opportunity," Moody said, signalling to the ushers to go on. Taylor asked permission to explain his position to the audience.

"I am grateful to you and the Chairman for your generous impulse. However the mission I represent has always refrained from taking collections, in case money that might be given to the older missionary societies should be diverted from its regular channels. It is our desire to help and not hinder the work of the denominational societies, quite properly maintained through such offerings. If anyone wishes over and above their accustomed gifts to have fellowship with the China Inland Mission, they can communicate with us through the mail."

"Well," said Moody, "you are the first man I ever met who refused a good collection!"

No offering was taken. A Christian merchant left the meeting glad that the twenty dollar note he had intended to donate stayed snugly in his wallet. But after a sleepless night and a troublesome conscience he sent off a five hundred dollar cheque to be used in the evangelization of inland China.

✳ ✳ ✳ ✳ ✳

A serious illness which threatened the life of his father kept Frost at home for some weeks while Taylor preached. But this gave him more time to think and pray, and he saw the way things were going. Now that money had been collected for North Americans to work with the CIM, it seemed inevitable that the earlier decision not to establish an American branch would have to be reversed. "I dare not seek to influence you," Frost wrote to Taylor from his Attica home, "yet I ask most earnestly that you will consider the question, Will it not be well to establish a branch here? I have much to say to you upon this, if you are led to listen to it."

"I think we must have an American branch of the mission," Taylor wrote to John Stevenson in China. "Don't be surprised if I should bring reinforcements with me." The decision to think in terms of an international mission was not made without a struggle. "I never felt more timid about anything in my life," he said later. But, having made the decision, he began to appeal powerfully for young Americans to go to China.

"To have had missionaries and no money would be no trouble to me," Taylor told one audience during his visit, "for the Lord is bound to take care of His own: He does not want me to assume His responsibility. But to have money and no missionaries is very serious indeed. And I do not think it will be kind of you dear friends in America to put this burden upon us, and not to send some from among yourselves to use the money. We have the dollars, but where are the people?"

✻ ✻ ✻ ✻ ✻

"I was always watching Taylor in those days out of the corner of my eye," Henry Frost recalled. "To tell the truth, he was in some ways a mystery to me ... It was not that he was unnatural. Indeed, I had never seen anyone so natural as himself. Nor was it that he was so spiritually fantastic. He was the sanest man I ever had to do with. Nevertheless, there was a spiritual quality about him which gave me surprises at every turn and kept me on the lookout for new and strange experiences."

Frost remembered an occasion, while Taylor was staying in the family home in Attica, when they met to plan a series of meetings. Frost was curious to see how a godly man got guidance from the Lord. Taylor sat down beside Frost at his desk.

"Before we begin to plan, don't you think we had better pray?"

Frost agreed. Taylor folded his hands and bent his head.

"Dear Lord, we are little children and it is not in us to direct our own steps. But you, Lord, know everything — will you give us the wisdom we need? In the name of Jesus, Amen."

Then he turned to Frost and asked, "Have you any timetables?"

Timetables! Frost thought. *Timetables! How utterly commonplace! I have been dealing with timetables all my life and have never connected them with getting guidance from on high. But the man of God has actually asked for timetables! When will wonders cease?*

Frost got some timetables out of his desk.

"Do you suppose there is a general map in one of these?" Taylor asked.

Frost found him a general map.

"Now," said Taylor, "here is Attica, and I must start west from Toronto when I leave for China. What lies between?"

The two men worked out an itinerary, date by date and city by city so that Toronto would be reached at the right time; and Henry Frost reckoned he had learned a lesson about guidance. It was first prayer, then common sense, and it was childlike trust all the way through.

❉ ❉ ❉ ❉ ❉

Travelling with Taylor on a train to Montreal, Henry Frost read a critical magazine article headed *Hudson Taylor in Toronto.* Angry about the article's contents, and anxious that Taylor shouldn't read it, he tried to hide it under a pile of papers. But Taylor had heard about the article and picked it up to read.

"Hudson Taylor is rather disappointing," he read. "I ... had in my mind an idea of what (great missionaries) should look like ... He being professedly one of the great missionaries of modern times must be such as they. But he is not ... A stranger would never notice him on the street ... except, perhaps, to say that he is a good-natured looking Englishman. Nor is his voice in the least degree majestic ... He displays little oratorical power ... He elicits little applause ... launches no thunderbolts ... Even our Goforth used to plead more eloquently for China's millions, and apparently with more effect ... It is quite possible that were Mr Taylor, under another name, to preach as a candidate in our Ontario vacancies there are those who would begrudge him his probationer's pay."

Taylor put the magazine down and didn't say anything for a few moments. Then he smiled at Frost.

"This is very just criticism, for it is all true. I have often thought that God made me little in order that He might show what a great God He is."

The two men got into their sleeping berths, Frost above Taylor. Frost lay there in the darkness as the train rattled on towards Montreal, thinking about the remarkable man who lay beneath him. *It is not hard for a little man to try to be great; but it is very hard for a great man to try to be little. Mr Taylor, however, ... has entered into that humility which alone is found in the spirit of the lowly Nazarene.*

✳ ✳ ✳ ✳ ✳

Wherever Taylor now preached, young people, some students, offered themselves as missionaries to China; donations continued to come in. What Henry Frost had described as the "solemn look" on Taylor's face passed away. There was no need for anxiety now that God's will had become so plain. By the middle of September over forty men and women had applied to join the CIM, and eventually crowded farewell meetings were held in Toronto in honour of eight young women and six men who had been judged suitable to travel out to China with Taylor. Invited to speak at one of these meetings, a father told what it meant to part with his daughter. "I have nothing too precious for my Lord Jesus. He has asked for my very best; and I give, with all my heart, my very best for Him." In later years, Taylor often recalled the phrase "nothing too precious for my Lord Jesus" as one of his most treasured memories of that first visit to America.

Between five hundred and a thousand people went to Toronto station to cheer as the train carrying fourteen brave north Americans steamed away. Then the well-wishers walked four abreast back through the streets of the town, singing as they went.

THE PLAIN MEANING
OF CHRIST'S WORDS 42

Hudson Taylor and the first contingent of North Americans bound for China crossed the Rocky Mountains by the Canadian Pacific railway, and sailed west from Vancouver in October 1888. Before they came in sight of China, Taylor received news of the deaths of two CIM members. One was Herbert Norris, head of the Chefoo school, who had been bitten while protecting his boys from a mad dog, and died of hydrophobia. More bad news greeted their arrival at Shanghai: another member of the CIM team had died of typhus, and John Stevenson's daughter, Mary, had lost her sanity on arrival in Shanghai following a shock on the voyage out. For weeks on end, Taylor had Mary and other patients to care for at a time of acute pressure of office work. In the room next to his, Mary raved and tore her clothes and sheets. It took several people to hold her when her mania was at its worst. Maggie M'Kee died of black smallpox at an inland station; William Cooper, hard at work at Anqing, caught double pneumonia but subsequently recovered.

"We are passing through wave after wave of trial," Taylor

wrote. "Each day has its full quota. God seems daily to be saying, 'Can you say, "even so, Father," to *that*.' But He sustains and will sustain the spirit, however much the flesh may fail. Our house has been a hospital; it is now an asylum. All that this means the Lord only knows ... The night and day strain are almost unbearable ... But I know the Lord's ways are all right, and I would not have them otherwise."

On top of all this, some members of the London Council and other friends of the mission in England were disagreeing with what had happened in America. In reply to criticism, Taylor wrote to one member of the Council telling him that he would be glad to have his views on the American question but pointing out that without visiting America it was difficult fully to understand the issue. "I should have been as fearful as you are, if I had not been there ... I purposely made all the arrangements tentative, pending my return to England and having opportunity for full conference about them." He told Jennie, "Satan is simply raging. He sees his kingdom attacked all over the land, and the conflict is awful. But that our Commander is Almighty, I should faint. I think I never knew anything like it, though we have passed through some trying times before."

He had been separted from Jennie for many months now. He wrote: "I feel sometimes, dearie, as if the charm and even power of life were taken out of me by these long absences from you ... Hope deferred makes the heart sick ... but I cannot shake it off. Longing removes the power of thought ... The cross does not get more comfortable, does it? But it bears sweet fruit."

Perhaps the fruit he had in mind was the spiritual life of the mission. He spoke of it as "higher than ever before" and reported conversions to Christ in a number of areas.

Trials hitting the mission, and his own daughter's acute mania, naturally tested John Stevenson: "I never went through such a distressful period; everything seemed crowded into those terrible months. I do not know what we would have done without Mr Taylor; but oh, the look on his face at times! The special day of fasting and prayer was a great help. We never found it to fail. In all our troubles, in all our forward movements, in times of need, whether as to funds or spiritual blessing, we always had recourse to fasting and prayer and with a quick response."

And on Taylor again: "Oh, his was a life worth looking into — searching through and through! Get a man like Mr Taylor, and you could start *any* mission tomorrow. It was most wonderful — his life. I never knew any other so consistent; and I watched him year in and year out, and had exceptional opportunities for doing so. He walked with God; and his life bore the light all through. And he was ready to help in sickness or any trouble. For self-denial and practical consecration, one could not but feel, he stood alone."

Taylor decided that tensions at home were too serious to deal with by letter. He hadn't achieved half he'd intended to on this visit — but Mary Stevenson was recovering, and plans for the new CIM premises in Wusong Road, Shanghai, were complete and with the builder. A mission house, prayer meeting hall, business quarters, and homes for senior mission staff were to be built. Taylor had spent hundreds of hours working on the plans and pretty well knew by heart the measurement of every door and window.

He arrived back in England in May 1889. To his great relief he was able to smooth ruffled feathers in the London Council, at least as far as related to setting up the American branch. By July he was able to report to John Stevenson, "I do not think things have been so cordial for years. In all this there is abundant cause for gratitude and praise." However, tensions between the London and China Councils and complaints about Taylor's leadership style were to rumble on for years.

❈ ❈ ❈ ❈ ❈

Hudson and Jennie celebrated Jennie's 46th birthday on Sunday October 6, 1889, at her father's home in Hastings. On another Sunday by the sea 24 years before, Hudson Taylor had committed his life to God for the evangelization of inland China. Now he reflected on the words of Jesus recorded in Mark 16: 15, "Go ye into all the world, and preach the gospel to every creature". Until that day in Hastings he had never asked himself the question: "What did our Lord *really* mean by *to every creature?*" He'd worked for years carrying the gospel far and wide; he'd developed strategies for reaching inland provinces — but he'd never realized the plain meaning of Christ's words.

"How are we going to treat the Lord Jesus with reference to this command?" he wrote that Sunday. "Shall we definitely drop the title 'Lord' as applied to Him, and take the ground that we are quite willing to recognize Him as our Saviour, so far as the penalty of our sin is concerned, but are not prepared to own ourselves 'bought with a price' or Him as having any claim on our unquestioning obedience? Shall we say that we are our own masters, willing to yield something as His due, who bought us with His blood, provided He does not ask too much? Our lives, our loved ones, our possessions are our own, not His: we will give Him what we think fit, and obey any of His requirements that do not demand too great a sacrifice? To be taken to heaven by Jesus Christ we are more than willing, but we will not have this Man to *reign* over us.

"The heart of every Christian will undoubtedly reject the proposition, so formulated; but have not countless lives in each generation been lived as though it were proper ground to take? How few of the Lord's people have practically recognized the truth that Christ is either *Lord of all*, or is *not Lord at all*! If we can judge God's Word, instead of being judged by that Word; if we can give to God as much or as little as we like, then *we* are lords and He is the indebted one, to be grateful for our dole and obliged by our compliance with His wishes. If, on the other hand, He is Lord, let us treat Him as such."

So Hudson Taylor made his decision. A definite, systematic effort must be made to carry the good news of the gospel to *every* man, woman and child in China. That was Christ's command. It should be obeyed. This was how it could be done: if a thousand evangelists each taught 250 people daily, then in a thousand days — three years — 250 million people would hear the gospel.

He recognized the objections. Some would say it was impossible for one evangelist to reach 250 people a day. But many years earlier he and William Burns had used methods which enabled them to do just that. He well understood that his calculation took no account of the work being done by more than a thousand missionaries already in China; or of the immense work being done by Chinese Christians, which he knew would become increasingly important and effective.

Another objection might be that at the end of Matthew's gospel the command was not just to preach but also to baptize and instruct — "teaching them to observe all things whatsoever I have commanded you." That was why so many missionaries were busy with schools work and in building up Chinese churches. Taylor recognized this and counted it a vital part of the work of the CIM. What he was suggesting was a new initiative in addition to the variety of work already being carried on.

So Taylor prepared for the December edition of *China's Millions* a paper headed "To Every Creature", arising from the insights and vision God had given him at Hastings. His target audience was the whole Christian church, not just the CIM and its supporters. He argued for urgent action on four fronts. First, prayer for one thousand evangelists for China; second, "united, simultaneous action by the whole body" of Christians; third, intelligent cooperation to avoid neglect in one region or duplication in another; fourth, sacrificial giving by churches and individuals in support of their missions.

✳ ✳ ✳ ✳ ✳

In November and December, Taylor visited Sweden and Denmark with his son Howard. He had been invited to try to develop closer ties between the Swedish Mission in China and the CIM. Taylor packed Swedish halls and meeting places, and giving to the work in China was generous. One lady pressed into Taylor's hand a beautiful watch.

"It is for *Herren Jesu*," she said, "*Herren Jesu*, the dear Lord Jesus."

When Queen Sophia invited Taylor for a private audience, one of the ladies in waiting came to his hotel and took him in a royal carriage the five miles to the palace outside Stockholm. The Queen spoke to Taylor about China and asked him to give a Bible reading. Hudson read from 1 Kings 10: 1-13: "And when the queen of Sheba heard of the fame of Solomon concerning the name of the Lord, she came to prove him with hard questions ... Blessed be the Lord thy God, which delighteth in thee, to set thee on the throne of Israel: because the Lord loved Israel for ever ..."

As far as we know, none of the Queen's questions was too hard for Taylor; he showed her the CIM map of China and talked about the work of the mission. Then, after coffee and sandwiches, the Queen shook Taylor's hand warmly and left.

"Everywhere the people were drawn to Mr Taylor," Josef Holmgren, who had invited him to Sweden, recalled. "He showed much love and affection, which also was returned. It was a joy to see how the children gathered round him in the families we visited, although they could not understand what he said. He spoke very friendly to them and patted their heads, telling them some nice stories."

Taylor had been invited to preach the opening sermon at the General Missionary Conference in Shanghai, so in the spring of 1890 he began his eighth visit to China. The journey gave him an opportunity to reflect and pray further about the meaning of Christ's words *To every creature*. The conference would give him an opportunity to take forward his call for the thousand evangelists.

However, another period of separation from Jennie was painful: "Darling," he wrote to her on the journey, "I feel I have been forgetting self-denial in the true sense; hence my unwillingness to be separated from you; and this I fear has brought me under a cloud. In one sense, God and His work have been first; in another, they have not been so as they should. I have not knowingly neglected the work; but I left you unwillingly instead of joyfully ... I do want to be wholehearted in God's service. May He work this in me."

On board the ship he drafted the outlines of his major conference sermon, which would be on the theme, "The heart of Jesus and His sufficiency". Dealing with the feeding of the four thousand (Matthew 15: 29-39), he would say, "I am so glad it was a *great* multitude, so great that the disciples thought it simply impossible to feed them. Yet the multitude were in real need, and the need too was immediate. It must either be met at once or not at all ... Let us notice that in these circumstances the presence of the disciples alone would not have sufficed. They might perhaps have said, 'Poor things!' They might have regretted that they had not more bread with them; but they would have left the multitude hungry. But Jesus was there; and *His presence* secured the carrying out of His compassionate purpose. All were fed, all were filled, all went away satisfied and strengthened; and the disciples were not only reproved and instructed, but were enriched also."

✳ ✳ ✳ ✳ ✳

When Taylor finally addressed the large audience in Shanghai drawn from all the Protestant societies working in China, he spoke for an hour and departed from his prepared address with a passage on the power of the Holy Spirit. This was to be one of his great themes during the closing years of his life.

"If as an organized conference, we were to set ourselves to obey the command of the Lord to the full, we should have such an outpouring of the Holy Spirit, such a Pentecost as the world has not seen since the Holy Spirit was outpoured in Jerusalem. God gives His Spirit *not* to those who desire to be filled always — but He *does* give His Holy Spirit 'to them that *obey* Him'. If as an act of obedience we were to determine that every district, every town, every village, every hamlet in this land should hear the gospel, and that speedily, and were to set about doing it, I believe that the Spirit would come down in such mighty power that we should find supplies springing up we know not how. We should find the fire spreading from missionary to flock, and our native fellow workers and the whole Church of God would be blessed. God gives His Holy Spirit to them that obey Him. Let us see to it that we really apprehend what His command to us is, now in the day of our opportunity — this day of the remarkable openness of the country, when there are so many facilities, when God has put steam and telegraph at the command of His people for the quick carrying out of His purposes ...

"It would only take 25 evangelists to be associated with each society to give us one thousand additional workers."

The conference closed by issuing an appeal for a thousand men within five years for all forms of missionary work in China including teachers and medics. It was a weighty appeal, coming as it did from the leaders of English, American and European societies. Taylor was appointed chairman of the committee set up to report the outcome.

❊ ❊ ❊ ❊ ❊

That April, the CIM opened its substantial new China headquarters in Shanghai. Two hundred turned up at Wusong Road for the occasion, including three good friends from Hudson's earliest years in China: William Muirhead, Joseph

Edkins and John Nevius. They paused at the entrance to
read the inscription, "To the glory of God and the furtherance
of His Kingdom in China." The CIM wasn't mentioned.
A few days later, Archibald Orr Ewing, whose generous giving
had made the new premises a reality, married a member of
the mission in the prayer hall.

✳ ✳ ✳ ✳ ✳

The conviction that Australian Christians ought to be doing
something towards the evangelization of China came inde-
pendently but simultaneously to four Melbourne ministers,
and led to an invitation to Hudson Taylor to visit the British
colony. He arrived in August, as usual attracting large crowds
to meetings at which he spoke.

At a large Presbyterian church in Melbourne, the chairman
introduced Taylor to the audience as "our illustrious friend".

Hudson stood quietly for a second or two with "the light
of God on his face", as it seemed to one present.

"Dear friends," he began, "I am the little servant of an
illustrious Master."

Taylor's host in Melbourne for a fortnight, the Rev H
B Macartney, described himself as having a "particularly
nervous disposition" which in a busy life kept him "in a
tremor all day long". While there was anything to be done,
he said, "nervous agitation possessed me."

"I am in the study," he said to Taylor, "you are in the
big spare room. You are occupied with millions, I with tens.
Your letters are pressingly important, mine of comparatively
little moment. Yet I am worried and distressed, while you
are always calm. Do tell me what makes the difference."

"My dear Macartney," Taylor replied, "the peace you speak
of is in my own case more than a delightful privilege, it
is a necessity. I couldn't possibly get through the work I
have to do without the peace of God 'which passes all
understanding' keeping my heart and mind."

"Here is a man almost sixty years of age," Macartney wrote,

"bearing tremendous burdens, yet absolutely calm and unruffled. Oh, the pile of letters! any one of which might contain news of death, of shortness of funds, of riots or serious trouble. Yet all were opened, read and answered with the same tranquillity — Christ his reason for peace, his power for calm."

Behind the Macartney home in Melbourne was a large area of common ground overgrown with heather and Australian wild flowers. Macartney recalled that, after he had dealt with his correspondence, Taylor would walk out on to the common and stand looking at the colour and beauty around him "with the rapture of a child."

Actually, Macartney cannot have been aware of some of the pain within Taylor's mind. The agony of another long separation from Jennie and the children was almost unbearable. And the news from England was that Hudson's son, Charles Edward, now aged 21 and a student at Cambridge, was "far from God" and a bad influence at home. Even so, Hudson had written to Jennie on the journey to Australia, "Do you think you *could* rightly join me on my return to China, darling?"

In Queensland, Taylor had been invited to stay with the Rev John Southey and his wife in Ipswich, near Brisbane. Southey was 34, an English clergyman with three children who had come to Australia on his doctor's advice following an illness. As Southey waited at the station for Taylor's train, he expected someone of striking appearance to arrive; the actual meeting was a disappointment, as he confided to his wife when he arrived home with their visitor.

"But," he added, "I'm sure he is a good man."

After a short conversation with Hudson, Mrs Southey snatched a confidential word with her husband.

"Look at the light in his face!"

John Southey came to agree about this and reflected on the reason. "So constantly did he look up to God, and so deep was his communion with God, that his very face seemed to have upon it a heavenly light. He had not been many hours in the house before the sense of disappointment gave place to a deep reverence and love, and I realized as never before what the grace of God could do ... In the house he was all that a guest should be, kind, courteous, considerate, gracious. He at once fell into the routine of the household, was punctual at the meal table, studied to give the minimum of trouble, and was swift to notice and to express his thanks for every little service rendered. We could not help noticing the utter lack of self-assertion about him, and his true because unconscious humility."

The appeal for the Thousand from the Shanghai conference had reached the Southeys, and they discussed with Taylor the possibility of responding themselves. Although they gained the impression that he felt their offer was inspired by God, they also noticed that he was careful to put before them in detail the conditions they could expect to find in China. He told them about climate, discomforts, the lack of medical care and the trauma of parting from their children. He thoroughly enjoyed pottering about in their garden and said to Mrs Southey:

"You won't have a garden like this in China!"

John Southey eventually became the CIM's Home Director for Australia and New Zealand.

✻ ✻ ✻ ✻ ✻

Towards the end of November 1890, Taylor sailed for China with the first party of missionaries from Australia and Tasmania to work with the CIM in China — four young men and eight women. Arriving in Shanghai shortly before Christmas, Taylor found the best possible treat awaiting him: Jennie had returned to China after an absence of nine years. Relatives and staff in Pyrland Road had arranged to release her from responsibilities at home. Never again would Hudson and Jennie endure a long separation.

Between January and April 1891, seven parties arrived in Shanghai from Europe, the United States, Canada and Australia — the last including John Southey — adding 78 new missionaries to the CIM's strength. And in February two parties of Scandinavians arrived within a week of each other: fifty members of the Scandinavian Alliance Mission which would be an associate mission of the CIM to work on the same lines. The Scandinavians loved music and singing, and to the accompaniment of their guitars they taught those living and working at Wusong Road a whole repertoire of Swedish hymns. And all these new arrivals formed a part of the coming thousand.

WANTED: THE HOLY SPIRIT'S POWER 43

"Missionaries are the frontline troops of western nations in their designs on China; they use magic powers to corrupt the Chinese; they extract unborn children from their mothers' wombs and scoop out the eyes of the dead to make silver; Jesus debauched the women of Judea and was put to death for violating the king's harem; Christians worship a pig (a play on the Chinese word for "Lord") and refuse to honour heaven, earth, the sun, moon, stars, ancestors, and the sages."

These charges were made in a series of pamphlets issued with the encouragement of an official in Changsha, capital of the anti-foreign province of Hunan. Largely as a result, riots broke out during 1891 all along the Yangzi valley. Even at Shanghai, where the great river meets the sea, the authorities had to contend with looting and violence. A Wesleyan missionary, not a member of the CIM, was murdered while waiting for a Yangzi steamer, as was the European customs official who tried to help him. Roman Catholic missionaries suffered too. But no members of the CIM lost their lives and no CIM station was attacked in a riot, although many were threatened.

Foreign governments sent gunboats to defend their nationals and insisted that the imperial government order provincial authorities to protect the missionaries. Beijing wasn't too keen to do this, but in the face of superior force had little choice but to comply.

"I look on the recent riots as Satan's reply to the Conference appeal for a thousand additional workers," Taylor wrote. "God will have His response, however; and while the enemy is mighty, God alone is almighty." He issued a circular to all his missionaries on how to act in times of danger: "We are continually encouraging our converts to brave persecution and to suffer loss for Christ's sake, and they are apt to think that it is easy for us to speak in this way, seeing that, as far as they can tell, we are well-off and exposed to no danger or loss. When, therefore, we are in danger they will mark our conduct very closely, and judge for themselves how far we really believe that 'Sufficient is His arm alone, and our defence is sure' ... Years of teaching would not impress them as our conduct at such times may do."

During October the rioting subsided, partly due to continuous rain (for which the CIM had been praying) and partly as a result of pressure from Beijing on the provincial authorities.

After five years carrying the heavy burdens of Deputy Director, John Stevenson had been forced to return to Britain for a break, leaving Taylor in sole charge and unable to leave Shanghai. "Even you, dear Mr Howard," Taylor wrote to the Home Director in London, "can scarcely realize what it is to be out here, to know and love our dear workers, to hear of their sorrows and difficulties, their disappointments and their strifes; learning of sickness, needing arrangements for succour if possible; receiving telegrams asking direction in peril, or telling it may be of death; accounts coming in of massacre and arson, and all the untold incidents of our ever varying experience — not to speak of the *ordinary* responsibilities and pecuniary claim of a mission now approaching five hundred in number. There is just one way to avoid being overwhelmed — to bring everything as it arises to our Master; and He does help, and He does not misunderstand."

✳ ✳ ✳ ✳ ✳

The China Council's role in the revision of the *Principles and Practice* and the *Book of Arrangements* had annoyed some members of the London Council.   These tensions lasted well into the 1890s, led to the resignation of nearly thirty missionaries, and caused Taylor to remark, "Satan is certainly very busy".   When Taylor was away from London, he felt that members of the London Council were taking no notice of him or keeping information from him. Benjamin Broomhall's work as an anti-opium campaigner also seemed to be distracting him from his administrative work with the CIM — an accusation which Benjamin said was "cruelly unjust".

Perhaps rivalry between the London Council and the China Council was inevitable.   Taylor intended the China Council to have executive powers, using the regional superintendents' daily experience of practical problems.   However, the London Council saw itself as the chief council of the CIM and other councils as subordinate.   The case for giving maximum power to the London Council was put by William Sharp, who argued that it had to answer to supporters and donors for the CIM's activities in China.   Sharp's words lived up to his surname when he told Taylor, "You have a council nominally to advise you, but it should be recognized as having administrative power.   When it doesn't accord with your views you try to force your council to fall in with your views.   I could wish you were led to let the mission get on by itself while you concentrated on expounding the Scriptures and stirring up the churches." This extreme attitude wasn't shared by others.

To give major power to the London Council would run counter to a fundamental principle on which Taylor had founded the CIM — direction in China. When the London Council intervened on behalf of some missionaries who objected to aspects of the *Book of Arrangements*. Taylor responded that these were "field" not "home" matters.

He and the China Council set out their reasons for insisting that affairs in China should be run in China. Referring to the now international nature of the CIM they argued, "to fuse the whole into one united body of workers is a matter of the utmost moment. Everything tending to keep up a feeling of distinctness and separation is to be avoided ... 'No man can serve two masters.' The introduction of the proposed principle [of London having the last word] would in practice not only lead many to become disaffected, but to feel and say, 'We come from such and such a body; we owe allegiance to them, not to you' ... A task already sufficiently difficult would be made ten times more so."

The London Council responded by insisting that the Christian public wouldn't be happy for Taylor to devolve executive powers to the China Council. He alone must take decisions on dismissals; London must have a proper say in the final version of the *Principles and Practice* and the *Book of Arrangements*; and they wanted the right to make representations to the China Council.

When a letter containing the council's demands arrived in Shanghai in November 1891, Taylor felt that the mission had reached its gravest crisis to date. "You have not funds," he told the council, "to support five hundred missionaries; you cannot protect them against an insurrection or in riot; you cannot come out here and administer the affairs of the mission; we must walk before God." As he took up their points one by one, Jennie felt the strain was too much and that it might kill him.

But the constitutional crisis didn't totally preoccupy him. He was lovingly tending plants he had gathered in the Rocky Mountains, and had glazed the veranda of his room in Wusong Road to suit some plants from an island in the Torres Strait.

Nor did Taylor let constitutional wrangling keep him from

discerning the spiritual needs of the mission. In March 1892 Taylor issued an important circular to every member of the CIM. After reporting recent conversions of sailors, Chinese servants, residents and visitors to Shanghai — more than for several years previously — he wrote: "The supreme want of all missions in the present day is the manifested presence of the Holy Ghost. Hundreds of thousands of tracts and portions of Scripture have been put into circulation; thousands of gospel addresses have been given; tens of thousands of miles have been traversed in missionary journeys but how small has been the issue in the way of definite conversions! We as a mission have much need to humble ourselves before God. There has been a measure of blessing among us and souls have been saved, but where are the ones that chase a thousand, or the two that put ten thousand to flight? Where are the once-thirsty ones, now filled, from whom flow rivers of living water? ...

"Few of us, perhaps, are satisfied with the results of our work, and some may think that if we had more, or more costly machinery we should do better. But oh, I feel that it is *divine power* we want and not machinery! If the tens and hundreds we now reach daily are not being won for Christ, where would be the gain in machinery that would enable us to reach double the number? Should we not do well, rather, to suspend our present operations and give ourselves to humiliation and prayer for nothing less than to be filled with the Spirit, and made channels through which He shall work with resistless power? ...

"Souls are perishing *now* for lack of this power ... God is blessing *now* some who are seeking this blessing from Him in faith. All things are ready, if we are ready. Let us ask Him to search us and remove all that hinders His working by us in larger measure. If any of us have been tempted to murmur, to think or speak unkindly of fellow workers; if light conversation or jesting 'which are not convenient' have been indulged in; if we have allowed less important things to take time and attention that God's direct work should have had; if our Bibles or secret prayer have been neglected, let us confess the evil before God and claim His promised forgiveness, carefully avoiding such occasions of weakness for the future. And having sought the removal of all hindrances and yielded ourselves up in fresh consecration, let us accept *by faith* the filling, and definitely receive the Holy Ghost, to occupy and govern the cleansed temple."

On April 16, 1892, the proceedings of the China Council were suspended. The minutes of the meeting recorded that, "Instead of meeting for conference, the China Council united with the members of the mission in Shanghai in seeking for themselves, the whole mission in China and the Home Councils, the filling of the Holy Spirit."

The council's prayers were answered. "God is working in our midst," Jennie wrote that same month, "emptying and humbling one and another, and filling with the Holy Spirit. We are having frequent meetings full of liberty and power."

✳ ✳ ✳ ✳ ✳

In May 1892, Hudson and Jennie sailed for Canada to get the benefit of Henry Frost's advice and to meet the North American Council. Frost persuaded him to stay on for a complete rest. Once back in Britain, Taylor met first with individual members and then with the full London Council, who began to soften their demands though differences and some hard feelings remained. Some thought that Benjamin might resign and Taylor, wishing to avert a crisis, suggested and organized a day of prayer and fasting.

Constitutional problems were not the only difficulties facing the mission at this time. 1892 was proving a bad year for funds. In 1887, the year of the Hundred, £30,000 had been donated to the CIM; nearly £33,000 in 1888; nearly £49,000 in 1889; nearly £30,000 in 1890; just over £36,000 in 1891. But monthly receipts of little more than £2,000 were the norm during 1892. This drop in income was almost certainly the result of rumours about prolonged wrangling over the running of the mission.

On October 3, 1892, Taylor returned from a trip to Scotland to find that donations in September had been particularly small, and the normal monthly telegram giving details of the month's remittances had not yet been sent to Shanghai. Charles Fishe, now Financial Secretary, was waiting to discuss the situation with Taylor.

"I think we should wait another day before cabling Shanghai," said Taylor. "Meanwhile, we should set aside normal business to wait on God for funds."

"But we cannot add to September's remittances whatever comes in now in answer to prayer," Fishe pointed out. Funds were normally sent only once a month.

The two men agreed to send the telegram listing the small September receipts. At midday, the Pyrland Road staff met to pray specifically about this financial crisis following several months of poor giving.

Late that afternoon a letter arrived at Pyrland Road enclosing a cheque for five hundred pounds, and stating that the money was for "immediate transmission to China".

The autumn meetings of the China Council were in progress when the first telegram with news of September's small donations arrived. Members of the council thanked God for deliverances from past crises and prayed for larger sums to come in. Twenty-four hours later the news of the five hundred pounds arrived; and John Stevenson announced that he had received an additional five hundred pounds from another source. The minutes of the meeting record that "the members of the council rose and sang the Doxology."

✳ ✳ ✳ ✳ ✳

In January 1893, Henry Frost arrived in London from Canada. He played an important role not only in pouring oil on troubled constitutional waters but also in finding solutions to problems. Businessman Walter Sloan was appointed Mission Secretary to take over management of the routine office work in London, with a place on the council, giving General Secretary Broomhall more time for his anti-opium campaign and public relations work. By March the difficulties which had nearly torn the mission apart were solved. It was agreed that the London, China and North American Councils would meet to advise directors and have no executive power. The controversial *Book of Arrangements* would be broken up and used in separate sections to guide each grade of missionary. Henry Frost was appointed Home Director for North America; and John Stevenson was by now widely accepted as Deputy Director.

A FAMILY TREK 44

I n February 1894, Hudson and Jennie left England together
for Hudson's ninth visit to China. They travelled via
America and arrrived in Shanghai in April where Geraldine
Guinness, who had travelled with them, married Hudson's
second son, Howard. The couple were to write a well-loved
biography of Hudson Taylor.

After some weeks in China, Hudson and Jennie began
to talk of returning to England to get involved in furthering
the "Forward Movement", as the follow-up to the appeal
for the Thousand was known. Then problems arose in the
northern provinces, which Taylor decided needed his personal
attention. Although it would mean a three or four month
journey in parts of China where no railways had been built,
Hudson and Jennie set off just as the hottest time of the
year arrived.

Howard and Geraldine returned to Shanghai from their
honeymoon to find his parents gone. Doctor Howard feared
the effect of the journey on his father's health, and the
newly married couple set off in pursuit, finally catching up
with the Taylors senior at Hankou.

"The journey may cost you your life, father," said Howard.

"Yes, and we should not forget 'We *ought* to lay down our lives for the brethren'" (1 John 3:16).

A family party of five left Hankou in May — Hudson and Jennie, Howard and Geraldine, and Joe Coulthard who had served with the CIM in China since 1879 and had married Hudson's daughter Maria two years earlier. Every day, except Sundays, they spent fourteen hours on the road. Howard and Geraldine were impressed with the friendliness and accessibility of the people, and the family-loving Chinese were intrigued with the family relationships — it seemed so natural to them for the five to be travelling together.

"See how they all smile at us!" said Geraldine.

"Perhaps it's because we smile at them," replied Howard.

The newlyweds were not impressed with the inns used for night-time stops — they actually compared them unfavourably with English cowsheds. But they conceded there was something to be said for the wheelbarrows, the classic means of transport in the province of Henan at that time. Built of strong wooden frames, these had one large wheel in the middle, handles at both ends and a bamboo matting roof. Passengers were allowed to pile up food baskets and light baggage in the front, and used their own bedding as cushions. Howard and Geraldine found it a consolation that the wheelbarrows were at least designed "to carry two victims rather than one"! They sat either side of the wheel facing backwards.

"As soon as we were in," Geraldine recorded, "one powerful young barrowman slipped the broad canvas strap across his shoulders, lifted and balanced the barrow — throwing us backward at a sharp incline — and called to the other man in front to pull away. With a creak, a jolt, and a long, strong pull, the cumbrous machine moved slowly forward. The dust began to rise around us from the feet of the men and the wheel track in the sandy road. With a gasp we clung, as for dear life, to the framework of the barrow, rumbling heavily over ruts and stones. Dry and oil-less, the slowly revolving wheel set up a discordant wail; large beads of perspiration stood out upon the forehead of the man scarcely a yard away from us, bending so determinedly to his task; the friendly crowds disappeared in the distance, and our journey was begun."

After ten days, the party arrived at the busy market town of Zhoujiakou in northern Henan. Here, at Coulthard's station, seventy members of a flourishing Chinese church greeted the tired travellers warmly. Among them ex-Mandarin Chen, dressed in a pale silk gown, bowed to Hudson Taylor.

"But for you, Venerable Sir, we should never have known the love of Jesus."

Chen handed Taylor a large sheet of red paper on which he had written this delightful note:

I bathe my hands and reverently greet —

The Venerable Mr Taylor, who from the beginning raised up the CIM with its worthy leaders, elders and pastors.

You, sir, constantly travelling between China and the foreign lands, have suffered much weariness and many labours ... And in our midst you have shown forth the seals of your apostleship — 2 Corinthians 12:11 (last clause) and 12 (first and second clauses). It is the glorious, redeeming grace of the Saviour that has blessed us, but it has been, sir, through your own coming amongst us and leading us in the true way; otherwise we had not been able to find the gate whereby to enter the right path ...

God grant you, our aged Teacher, to be spared to await the coming of our Lord, when Jesus Christ shall become King of kings and Lord of lords (Revelation 18:14). We are assured, sir, that you will certainly hold high office in the Millennial Kingdom, and reign with Jesus Christ a thousand years; also that at the close of the Millennium you will closely follow Jesus when He ascends up to heaven.

Among our own household, and indeed throughout the little church in and around Zhoujiakou, there is no one who does not esteem you highly.

Respectfully wishing peace,

The very unworthy member,

Chen named Pearly Wave

I bow my head and respectfully salute.

"I am unworthy to invite the Venerable Chief Pastor to my mean abode," said Chen.   Instead he took charge of preparing and cooking a Chinese feast which he sent to the whole Taylor family to eat at Coulthard's home. The meal, prepared meats of the type used in ancestral worship, arrived in six enormous basins. When Chen heard that Taylor had to avoid pepper, he himself prepared some special food for the party to take with them when they continued their journey. These beautifully packed Chinese takeaways were delivered under cover of another delightful note.

Honourable and Most Reverend Mr Taylor:
Chen of the Pearly Wave bows his head.
I write this respectfully to present to you some travellers' provisions — minced meat boiled in oil, spiced apricot kernels, and pickled water melon. Be pleased graciously to receive these at my hands. Of the spiced meats, one kind without cayenne pepper is for the special use of the aged Teacher, the other with capsicum is for the consumption of Mr Coulthard and your second princely son. I write this note on purpose to wish you peace.

First day of the Midsummer moon.

Armed with Chen's generous provisions, the party set off on the next stage of the long journey, travelling for some weeks by mule-drawn carts. A long period of heavy rain had turned the roads into quagmires. The rivers, fed by mountain streams, had risen to well above their normal depth, in places turning the fords into rushing torrents of water. At one stage the party approached a deep ford and were about to cross when, to the annoyance of the carters, another cart drove down the bank and entered the river ahead of them. This was seen as a great insult by the Chinese, being quite contrary to the convention that you never overtook unless invited to do so.

"But it will give us a chance to see what sort of crossing they make of it," someone observed prophetically.

Missionary party and carters watched as the mules waded out deeper and deeper, managing to keep their footing until at the middle of the river they paused on a sandbank for a rest. Then the spectators on the river bank watched in horror as mules, cart and passengers slithered down into the main course of the river. The water rose and began to pour into the cart. The Taylor party carters shouted from the bank:

"*Bu-cheng, bu-cheng*! It's all up! It's all up!"

The current caught the cart and it began to roll over and over. The helpless onlookers saw first the cartwheels above the water, and then the battered covering. The mules disappeared from view altogether, and there seemed no hope for the passengers. At last the cart came to rest at a bend on the opposite bank. Incredibly, the Chinese carters and passengers were dragged out alive. The Taylor party didn't attempt to follow suit, and instead took a long and winding route to a ferry which carried mules, carts and travellers safely across the river.

✳ ✳ ✳ ✳ ✳

Weeks later, towards evening, the party approached Xian. Looking west across the plain from a distance of ten miles they could make out its turreted wall, gates and towers silhouetted against a red sky. The city was the capital of a vast plain with 22 governing cities, 60 market towns, and countless villages spread over 12,000 square miles of central

Shaanxi. In eight years, a team of CIM pioneers led by Thomas Botham had overcome violent opposition and opened many stations in the area. The Scandinavian fifty had arrived as the pioneers' work was bearing fruit, and armed with their guitars they had even managed to establish a work in the notoriously anti-foreign capital.

The purpose of Taylor's epic journey was to thrash out arrangements for the Scandinavian associates to work in harmony with Botham and the original pioneers.

George Easton and the Scandinavian Hendriksen, in Chinese dress and big straw hats, welcomed the Taylor party and escorted them into the city. Each home in which the members of the party stayed had a well supplying clean, cool water.

"After our long thirsty journey," Taylor said to the young Scandinavians at a celebration of the Lord's Supper, "what refreshment we have found in the cool, delicious water springing up in your own dwellings, always within reach! We have never thirsted since coming to Xian. And the Lord Jesus gives me a well, a spring of living water deep down in my heart — His presence there at all times. What do we do with our wells? We go to them and draw. Drinking we do not thirst. So, having Jesus, drinking of the spring He gives, we need never thirst again."

The Scandinavian associates had been criticized because, as a German newspaper in Shanghai reported, "twenty unmarried unprotected females" were in danger without male missionaries to help them. "Can the Chinese fathom their good intentions — without the current of suspicion running in another direction?" Taylor agreed guidelines governing the behaviour of the women missionaries, and, in the case of Scandinavian single women, waived the CIM's rule forbidding marriage until after two years service in China. He arranged to reserve for the Scandinavians a large area of the Xian plain, including the capital, for evangelism and church planting; Hendriksen would be recognized as senior missionary associate working with Thomas Botham.

Moving north-east into southern Shanxi towards the end
of July, Hudson and Jennie accepted an invitation to stay
for a few days with Pastor and Mrs Hsi.   The Hsis conducted the Taylor family through a series of courtyards to
an open space where a meal had been prepared.   A dozen
or more masts supported a brown awning roof, and beyond
a suite of rooms had been prepared.   Lamps were lit on
the tables; fresh straw mats covered the floors; new bamboo
curtains and coloured hangings adorned the doors and windows; and the Hsis had put new white felt rugs on the beds.
They had spread the tables with red covers with a square
of rich green silk neatly in the centre.   Shiny brass basins
stood on little stands with clean white towels and new cakes
of the very best Pears' soap!

The pastor and his wife stood beaming.

"It's nothing.   It is altogether unworthy.   Gladly would
we have arranged far better for our Venerable Chief Pastor
and his family."

During the stay, the pastor waited on his guests at table
helped by a team of assistants.   Every time Taylor thanked
him, he would reply:

"What, sir, have you suffered and endured that we might
have the gospel!   This is my joy and privilege.   How could
I do less?"

❋ ❋ ❋ ❋ ❋

That June of 1894, Chinese and Japanese troops had both
landed in Korea, and while the Taylors were enjoying Pastor
Hsi's hospitality war was declared between the two countries.   By the time Taylor arrived back in Shanghai, things
were going badly for China. Fearing that the Chinese might
vent their anger against the enemy towards foreigners in
general, Taylor decided that he was needed in China, and
abandoned plans for an early return to England.

CONQUERING PREJUDICE 45

The war between China and Japan erupted after many years of intrigue and rivalry between the two countries over the control of Korea, which the Chinese had dominated since the seventeenth century.

When the Japanese attacked the port of Weihai, about two hundred severely wounded Chinese soldiers dragged themselves the forty miles along the coast through deep snow to Chefoo. They arrived with clothes saturated in blood. One man walked all the way with his kneecaps shattered, and another with a bullet through his lung. Others had crawled on their hands and knees and arrived with frostbitten feet. Some died on the way.

In Chefoo Arthur Douthwaite, a surgeon with twenty years experience in China, had built up a CIM hospital which attracted over twenty thousand outpatients a year and performed hundreds of operations. He hurriedly called in a team of untrained missionaries to help him carry out emergency operations. They removed seven bullets from one man. The CIM took in 163 men altogether and cared for them, bringing the love of Christ to them at a time of intense need and breaking down prejudice against missionaries over a wide area.

At the end of the war a Chinese General came to the Chefoo hospital, accompanied by a brass band and a unit of soldiers. He erected a gold-embossed inscription expressing the thanks of the Chinese army. When he heard that stone was needed to build a new school at Chefoo he arranged for it to be provided from an army quarry and transported by soldiers.

For centuries, the Chinese had regarded the Japanese with contempt. It therefore came as a bitter blow to their national pride when the enemy inflicted a decisive defeat on them. The treaty of Shimonoseki, which brought the war to an end in April 1895, forced the Chinese to acknowledge the independence of Korea and pay a large indemnity to Japan. Taiwan was among territories ceded to Japan.

The end of the war also marked the end of the five-year period set by the Shanghai Conference in the appeal for the thousand missionaries. As chairman of the committee set up to monitor results, Taylor was able to report that 1,153 new workers had been added to the missionary strength in China during the period. While acknowledging this magnificent answer to prayer, Taylor pointed out that only 480 of them were men. And as many would be working in coastal provinces, the task of preaching the gospel "to every creature" in China remained to be carried out.

"An important crisis in China's history has been reached," he wrote on behalf of the committee. "The war just terminated does not leave her where she was. It will inevitably lead to a still wider opening of the empire and to many new developments. If the church of Christ does not enter the opening doors, others will, and they may become closed against her ... Time is passing. If a thousand men were needed five years ago, they are much more needed now ..."

The CIM now had 621 members, settled in 122 main stations, ninety of which were in formerly unoccupied inland provinces. On his 63rd birthday, May 21, 1895, Taylor issued a circular inviting every CIM member to join him in praying for many more Spirit-filled missionaries for China.

Knowing his strength to be declining, Taylor planned to consolidate an organizational structure which would enable the right people to direct the CIM without the man who had launched it being at the helm. He made William Cooper Assistant Deputy Director in China. Aged 34, and with twelve years experience in China, Cooper would deal with all administrative correspondence except that addressed to either Stevenson or Taylor and marked "Private". Powerfully built, he had strong convictions and an independent turn of mind, though he expressed himself with courtesy, almost diffidence.

"I don't like to oppose you so often," he said to Taylor on one occasion in the early days of the China Council. "I think I had better resign."

"No, indeed!" replied Taylor. "I *value* such opposition: it saves me from many a mistake."

Since May 1886, James Broumton had been treasurer and statistician for the mission. "Everything had to be balanced up to the cent," he observed. "Mr Taylor was very particular about the details."

With the opening of the Wusong Road premises, Broumton joined the Shanghai headquarters staff and devoted himself to accounts and statistics for another eleven years, earning high praise from Taylor. Charles Fishe also moved to Shanghai after seventeen years experience as a missionary and administrator. Stevenson, Cooper, Fishe and Broumton now formed a Standing Council of Advice when the rest of the China Council were dispersed in the provinces.

❅ ❅ ❅ ❅ ❅

Since 1886 William Cassels, one of the Cambridge Seven, had been developing the mission's work in Sichuan. At the Saturday missionary meeting of the 1895 Keswick Convention, the Chairman announced that Cassels would be consecrated Bishop of West China. The CMS would guarantee his stipend and he would come on to their roll of missionaries while "fully retaining his position in the CIM". Cassels was consecrated in London on October 18, 1895. "I cannot but think," Taylor commented, "that it will be for the advantage of China. Mr Cassels's department is surpassed by nothing in the mission for spirituality or success."

✳ ✳ ✳ ✳ ✳

In May 1896, Hudson and Jennie set off on the return journey to England. Stevenson was temporarily in England, but Taylor was confident that they could leave the direction of affairs in China to William Cooper.

For some years, the demands of running the mission in England had outgrown available space in Pyrland Road. Back in May 1893, the London Council had considered detailed plans for new headquarters premises at a site in Newington Green, a stone's throw from Pyrland Road. Offices, a meeting hall, thirty bedrooms and public rooms had been built and a home for missionary candidates was opened.

When Hudson and Jennie arrived back in London in the summer of 1896, after an absence of well over two years, the new building was already in use. The couple deliberately kept secret the time of their London train, although it was well known at Newington Green that they were on the way.

The Saturday evening prayer meeting was crowded when Hudson and Jennie arrived at Newington Green by cab. As they walked towards the open door of the meeting hall, they were intrigued to see the narrow three-storey building with additional rooms in its gabled roof. The plans Hudson had studied so thoroughly in 1893 had become a reality. Carved in stone above the open door, they read the words HAVE FAITH IN GOD.[1] Inside they sat quietly at the back of the prayer meeting — and after the final "Amen" delighted

---

[1] The inscription can still be seen on the building, which is now used by the Evangelical Alliance as a students' hostel.

friends and supporters crowded around the couple to exchange greetings. Hudson and Jennie now made their home in Newington Green.

Benjamin Broomhall had retired while the Taylors were in China, although he and Amelia still lived in 2 Pyrland Road; Walter Sloan succeeded Benjamin as secretary.[2] "My aim," Taylor recorded at this time, "is to get every part of the work into such a condition that it can be carried on without me, and with this in view I visit different branches of it in turn." He spoke at a busy series of meetings and conventions in many parts of England. One of his great themes was still the "Forward Movement" — the call to preach the gospel *to every creature*.

✳ ✳ ✳ ✳ ✳

In the spring of 1897 Hudson Taylor visited Germany and encountered some hostility to the CIM. The leaders of the Lutheran State Church didn't approve of the mission's interdenominational basis, and others were sceptical about the notion of fundraising by faith. Many leading ministers and missionary society secretaries gathered in the Berlin drawing room of the Baroness von Dungern — all eager to assess the 65-year-old Taylor, but not all in sympathetic mood.

"The stranger who stood in our midst," the Baroness recorded, "was not of an imposing appearance, and his fair curly hair made him look younger than he really was."

"You are the son of a Methodist preacher," the first questioner began, "and have been connected with Baptists. You have recently accepted a number of highly educated young men who are members of the Established Church. How are they able to work with Methodists, Baptists and so on?"

"In our chief aims," Taylor replied, "we are all one in

---

[2]All the Pyrland Road houses still stand with the original numbering, and Number 6 has an inscription recording Hudson Taylor's use of the building for the work of the CIM.

Christ. Furthermore, China is large enough for the missionaries to be distributed over the various provinces in such a way that each denomination is able to retain its particular order of church government. Only recently we have been glad to welcome an English bishop, a member of the CIM, to Western China so that our workers from the Established Church are not lacking the care of a spiritual head and guide. The great work of the mission field, which is a call to us all, overrides theological differences, and our motto remains, 'All one in Christ Jesus.'"

"Such a mixture of church and sectarians would be impossible with us," whispered the Director of the Gossner Mission.

"It is remarkable," Taylor continued, "how the Lord Himself has chosen His instruments, so that even the most insignificant, in His hand, are able to be 'to the praise of His glory'. Surely this is as it is in creation: there are strong and beautiful oak trees, but there are also little flowers of the meadow; and both the oak and the flower have been placed there by His hand. I myself, for instance, am not specially gifted, and am shy by nature, but my gracious and merciful God and Father inclined Himself to me, and I who was weak in faith He strengthened while I was still young. He taught me in my helplessness to rest on Him, and to pray about little things in which another might have felt able to help himself ...

"He knew the desire of my heart, and simply trusting like a child, I brought all to Him in prayer. Thus I experienced, quite early, how He is willing to help and strengthen and to fulfil the desire of those who fear Him. And so in later years, when I prayed the money came."

"Will you tell us," someone asked, "whether it is true that after you had moved a large audience by putting the need of missionary work in their hearts, and someone rose to make a collection, you went so far as to hinder it?"

"I have done so more than once," Taylor replied. "It is not our way to take collections, because we desire to turn aside no gifts from other societies. We receive freewill offerings, but without putting pressure upon people. After such a meeting they can easily find an opportunity, if they wish, to send their gifts — which so far has been done freely."

"We have heard," said a Lutheran clergyman, "that in that way some quite large sums are sent in. But *we* aim at training our congregations to systematic giving."

"That's a very important matter," Taylor replied. "However, one is led so, while another is led otherwise. Each must act according to his light. As I said before, for my weakness' sake the Lord has acknowledged my way of working and praying, but I am far from advising anyone to copy me. You do well to train individuals, to train the whole church to systematic giving ..."

For over an hour the questions came, until the Baroness von Dungern intervened.

"Mr Taylor has promised to be present at another meeting this evening and I think we ought to spare his strength. He has been standing at his own request, while all this time we've been sitting comfortably around him."

"Just then," the Baroness recorded later, "a sunbeam touched his face, so full of joy and peace, bringing a brightness as from above — and I could only think of Stephen, who saw heaven opened and Jesus at the right hand of God."

"We must all take shame before this man," someone whispered.

"Yes," said the Director of the Gossner Mission, "you are quite right! We will not trouble our friend any further." He stood up, walked across the room, put his arm around Taylor's neck and kissed him.

"How beautifully," the Baroness concluded, "this heavenly-minded man was able, in the humility of his heart, to conquer all the hidden prejudice against him and his work!"

✳ ✳ ✳ ✳ ✳

Back home that summer, funds for the general purposes of the mission were low. Taylor prayed and worked, taking on a heavy load of meetings which eventually damaged his health. A severe bout of neuralgia and headaches forced him to accept his doctor's advice.

"Take a complete rest. Leave the running of the mission to others for several months."

So Hudson and Jennie travelled to Davos in Switzerland. The best tonic, over and above the healthy effect of the mountain air, was news of an answer to their prayers. J T Morton, a London wholesaler and merchant, had given ten thousand pounds to the mission's general fund.

Within a few days of making this generous donation Morton died. On their return to England, Hudson and Jennie learned the contents of Morton's will. He had left the CIM a quarter of his estate, a share which would amount to at least one hundred thousand pounds! The legacy was to be used for evangelistic and educational work, and would be paid in instalments of ten or twelve thousand pounds a year for ten years.

This gift represented a major transformation of the CIM's financial position, especially bearing in mind the value of money at that time and the purchasing power of the pound sterling in China. We should multiply the amount by fifty to appreciate its equivalent value today.

Taylor saw that the donation could prove a mixed blessing. It might reduce the mission's sense of dependence on God, and cause difficulties at the end of the period when new initiatives financed on the strength of the money would have to continue. He had no doubt that the gift was from God in answer to prayer, but it would be useless unless it went hand in hand with an increase in spiritual power, faith and prayer. He linked it in his mind with the prayers he had been bringing to God for eight years — that Christians from all over the world would support taking the good news of Jesus *to every creature* in China.

Hudson and Jennie sailed via America for China in November 1897, planning to do all they could to add impetus to evangelistic efforts in every province of the Empire.

"WHAT COSTS LITTLE IS WORTH LITTLE" 46

A fter China's war with Japan, the major European countries had begun a series of aggressive moves against a weakened and demoralized China which threatened to make the Empire more subject to the West. They demanded that some ports be leased to them, that large sections of the country be recognized as their spheres of influence, and that concessions for railways be granted to foreign firms.

These hostile moves had fuelled anti-foreign feeling in China. Some Chinese wanted to attack foreigners everywhere and if possible drive them from China. Others argued that it would be more sensible for the nation to adopt western ways. So reform movements with support in official and educated circles advocated some quite revolutionary changes. However, loss of confidence in the imperial government grew as more Chinese realized the extent of the nation's defeat at the hands of Japan, and the way it was being humiliated by western powers. Secret societies thrived. In 1895 riots broke out in Sichuan. Mercifully no CIM lives were lost, partly due to protection given by local mandarins, though mission property was damaged.

On August 1, 1895, in the coastal province of Fujian, the Rev Robert Stewart with his wife and child and eight other CMS missionaries were murdered by members of a secret society. Hudson Taylor, and many like him, realized then that a new era had dawned. For some reason God had withdrawn the hand that had protected missionaries and their families from violent death in China.

In the summer of 1898, however, the forces in China working for reform found a champion in the young Emperor. Guang Xu had read radical literature, including works not only of Chinese writers but also of Timothy Richard. He instituted what later became known as the Hundred Days of reform: from June to September edict after edict modified civil service and military examinations, established schools and a university to study new western learning, and encouraged Chinese railway building.

The reforms generated stiff opposition, and reactionary elements looked to the powerful personality of the Express Dowager for support. In September she took charge of the government, keeping Guang Xu imprisoned in a portion of his own palace although permitting him to retain the title of Emperor. She arrested and executed many of the reformers, and reversed many of the reforming edicts.

Local riots and uprisings now occurred frequently. Hudson Taylor wrote of the political situation that there seemed "little hope of averting a complete collapse". The Empress's actions encouraged feeling against foreigners throughout the country; and as most westerners in the inland provinces were missionaries, hostilities were particularly directed against them.

Taylor was grateful to God for the remarkable fact that for 32 years, since the arrival of the *Lammermuir* party in 1866, not one single CIM life had been lost through violence, accident or in travelling. Property had been damaged; missionaries, including Taylor, had been injured at times, but lives had always been spared. His son and daughter-in-law believed that "there had grown up in Mr Taylor's mind a restful confidence in God that He *would* thus protect His servants in the mission, especially defenceless women, working alone in their stations, at a distance often from the nearest missionaries."

✻ ✻ ✻ ✻ ✻

For some months after arriving in Shanghai for his tenth visit to China, Taylor was virtually confined to his room with another bout of illness. On the outward journey he had visited Dr A T Pierson, the American Bible teacher, author and hymn writer, who had himself subsequently suffered a serious illness. "Ah, how much pains the Lord takes to empty us and to show us He can do without us!" Taylor wrote to Pierson from Shanghai in April. However during this period he took the opportunity to hold discussions with over two hundred members of the mission.

By November 1898, Hudson was well enough to set off with Jennie for Chongqing, where the first CIM mission station in Sichuan had opened in 1877, for a conference of West China missionaries. The journey took them hundreds of miles up the Yangzi, first by steamer and then by more primitive boats negotiating mid-winter rapids.

About halfway, at Hankou, they heard the tragic news of the death of Australian William Fleming — the first CIM martyr. Down in the south-west province of Guizhou, Fleming had been murdered together with his friend and assistant Pan Shoushan, a convert from the Black Miao tribe. "How sad the tidings!" Taylor wrote to John Stevenson. "Blessed for the martyrs but sad for us, for China, for their friends. And not only sad, but ominous! It seems to show that God is about to test us with a new *kind* of trial: surely we need to gird on afresh 'the whole armour of God'. Doubtless it means fuller blessing, but through deeper suffering. May we all lean hard on the Strong for strength ... and in some way or other the work be deepened and extended, not hindered, by these trials." These were sadly prophetic words.

The conference gave Taylor a chance to meet and hold discussions with Bishop Cassels and other leaders of the CIM's work in Sichuan. But he had to abandon plans to visit other western mission stations, partly due to an outbreak of rioting in the area but also because the 66-year-old Taylor became very ill with bronchitis and seemed likely to die. Jennie nursed him night and day, holding on to God in faith that he would recover. Then, in the quietness of another room, she knelt to pray.

"Lord, we can do nothing! Do what you will. Undertake for us."

Hudson knew nothing of Jennie's prayer, but when she returned to his room he looked up.

"I feel better, dear," he whispered.

From that moment he began to regain his strength.

Although Taylor's health improved during the return journey to Shanghai, the couple decided to spend the early summer of 1899 at the CIM's coastal health station at Chefoo. This gave them a chance to get to know the staff and pupils of the three flourishing schools. They enjoyed watching the children's games. On Foundation Day a boat race was followed by cricket and tennis matches, an address from Taylor and, on a warm evening, what was described as a "social" in the quadrangle. Jennie remembered the lights from the music room shining out on to the quad and blending with the moonlight as one of the teachers, "a beautiful musician", serenaded them.

Hudson spent long hours that summer praying for the Forward Movement. But between prayers, he and Jennie took time off to draw up plans for a quiet home for themselves. Hudson had bought a plot of land high on a hill two days by steamer from Shanghai. Here they hoped to build a house where they could get away from the busy demands of the Shanghai headquarters. Its great delight would be an upstairs veranda on three sides, with a glorious view of wooded hills stretching down to the plain two thousand feet below.

Despite his illnesses, Taylor attended all but one of the

eight meetings of the China Council held between January 1898 and September 1899. Then he and Jennie, together with Howard and Geraldine, sailed out of Shanghai bound for America. After a detour to fulfil speaking engagements in Australia and New Zealand, they sailed across the Pacific to California and travelled by train to New York.

✳ ✳ ✳ ✳ ✳

Three thousand five hundred people filled every seat in the vast Carnegie Hall, New York, for the Ecumenical Missionary Conference in April 1900. Large overflow meetings allowed the public to join the nearly 1,900 official delegates from over a hundred missionary societies. The President of the United States and the Governor of New York attended to welcome the participants.

The subject of Hudson Taylor's address had been billed as "The source of power for foreign missionary work". Now a month away from his 68th birthday, he sat on the platform with the most distinguished men in the missionary world. As he waited to speak he looked out into the great auditorium with its two tiers of boxes and three circular galleries. He stepped forward, characteristically stood a moment in silent prayer, then he raised his head and smiled briefly.

"Power belongeth unto God," he began.

Henry Frost never forgot the occasion. "As he begins to speak, his voice takes on a kindly, compassionate quality. A hush which can be felt falls on the vast audience. Old and experienced leaders in missionary service, seated on the platform, lean forward to catch the quiet words."

Taylor continued his address: "... We have tried to do, many of us, as much good as we felt we could easily do, or conveniently do, but there is a wonderful power when the love of God in the heart raises us to this point that we are ready to suffer, and with Paul we desire to know Him in the power of His resurrection (which implies the death of self), and the fellowship of His sufferings, being made conformable to His death. It is ever true that what costs little is worth little ..."

Frost recalled: "The people in the body of the house are deeply moved. And all through the audience, hearts are opened to the Lord, spirits become eager to be and to do what God desires, and resolutions are formed to give and go." Over thirty years later, Frost still met men and women who told him that Hudson Taylor's address that morning radically changed their lives.

From New York, Taylor went on in May to speak at a series of meetings in Boston with Dr A T Pierson, now fit again after his illness. At one of these Taylor seemed to lose his train of thought, and began to repeat two sentences over and over again:

"You may trust the Lord too little, but you can never trust Him too much. 'If we believe not, yet He abideth faithful; He cannot deny Himself.'"

Pierson came to the rescue and took over the meeting, later recording his reflections on the incident. "There was something pathetic and poetic in the very fact that this repetition was the first visible sign of his breakdown, for was it not this very sentiment and this very quotation, that he had kept repeating to himself, and to all his fellow workers during all the years of his missionary work? A blessed sentence to break down upon, which had been the buttress of his whole life of consecrated endeavour."

Taylor's doctor son, Howard, described the illness which followed as a "rather serious breakdown"; and his later biographer A J Broomhall says that the "breakdown was physical exhaustion sapping his memory and mental ability". The American visit had to be cut short, and Hudson and Jennie arrived back in London in June 1900.

Taylor was too ill to take meetings or even to write a letter; Jennie arranged for them to travel to Davos in Switzerland, where she could help him begin a slow convalescence.

❋ ❋ ❋ ❋ ❋

Since Hudson and Jennie had left China, in September 1899, the political situation had deteriorated. The country's defeat by Japan, the seizure of ports by European powers, the beginning of railway construction by foreigners, fear that the Empire would be partitioned by European powers, bitter feeling against some missionaries, and outbreaks of famine all contributed to a growing sense of unrest. The hostility to missionaries was stirred up, as so often, by rumours about cruel and immoral practices and disturbance of cherished customs.

The Empress Dowager ordered local militia units to stand ready to defend the country; because these units practised gymnastic exercises they became known as "Boxers". The units began to adopt the slogan *mie yang*, "Destroy the foreigner"; they were joined by undisciplined mobs, became associated with secret societies, and indulged in charms and occult practices which they believed would protect them from enemy weapons.

By the end of 1899, Boxer bands began to persecute Christians with little discouragement from provincial authorities. On the last day of the year an English missionary from the Society for the Propagation of the Gospel in Foreign Parts was murdered. The British authorities protested vigorously and succeeded in having several men punished. In June 1900 the Empress Dowager, ignoring more moderate counsel from some advisers and against the wishes of her son the Emperor, issued an edict ordering foreigners to be killed throughout the Empire. Thus China pitted herself against the rest of the world.

"COUNTED WORTHY OF A MARTYR'S CROWN" 47

Although the Boxer uprising of 1900 was as much anti-foreign as anti-Christian, missionaries and Chinese converts to Christ became the chief sufferers. Missionaries were more widely scattered outside the ports than other foreigners; and the Boxers dubbed Chinese Christians "secondary devils", believing them to be traitors against their country and its culture.

Violence was much worse in the north-east than in many other parts. This was partly because many Chinese officials tried to protect foreigners, realizing how foolish it was for their country to take on the western world. In fact moderate officials managed to alter the words of the imperial order from "whenever you meet a foreigner you must slay him" to "you must protect him" in the telegrams sent to many provinces.

Roman Catholics suffered severely in the uprising. In the Beijing area between fifteen and twenty thousand Catholics lost their lives; the graves of Ricci and other seventeenth and eighteenth century missionaries were desecrated. In Shanxi about two thousand Catholic Christians were killed, including two bishops and a number of priests.

Gansu province, by contrast, was reported peaceful. Although the authorities ordered the missionaries to return to Europe, they remained at their posts. In Yunnan, down in the far south-west, a traveller found a European priest in September 1900 who hadn't heard of the Boxer outbreak. When told that the consul had ordered all French citizens to leave the area, he refused to go, saying he couldn't abandon his flock until he had heard from his bishop.

Protestants had been in North China, where the upheaval was most severe, for only forty years. So they had a smaller number of converts to face persecution. However, while fewer Protestant than Roman Catholic Chinese Christians were killed, more Protestant missionaries lost their lives.

As the danger in the Beijing area rose to a peak, Protestant missionaries and some of their converts gathered with many other members of the foreign community in the official residence of the British Minister. About seven hundred Protestants were beseiged there for nearly eight weeks, assisted by a few hundred foreign troops who had been in Beijing before communications with the coast were cut. Finally a strong force organized by western countries and Japan managed to reach Beijing from Tianjin and capture the city. Only a few of those who had been under seige died.

However, many Chinese Christians were killed in the rest of Zhili, as the province around Beijing was then called. The worst massacre was at Baoding, where on the last day of June and the first of July fifteen missionaries from the CIM and two American missions were murdered. Some of the spectators were deeply impressed by the calm way the martyrs met their deaths.

In Shanxi, the worst outrage occurred in the governor's *yamen* at Taiyuan, where 34 Protestant missionaries and twelve Roman Catholics were beheaded, watched by the Governor. At Xiaoyi, CIM missionaries Emily Whitchurch and Edith Searell were killed while kneeling in prayer; at Fenzhou in August seven members of the American Board Mission and three members of the CIM were killed.

Away from the north-east, the most severe persecution was in Zhejiang, south of Shanghai. Here the telegram ordering the extermination of foreigners seems to have come through unaltered. After hesitating, the governor published it, although he soon withdrew it. But at Qu Xian a mob killed the magistrate for striving to protect foreigners, and went on to massacre eleven members of the CIM.

In other provinces, no Protestant missionaries died. Most of them seem to have taken the consuls' advice and made their way to the treaty ports. Many churches and chapels were destroyed and Chinese Christians roughly handled, but comparatively little blood was shed.

Altogether in China, over 130 Protestant missionaries and over fifty of their children died. The CIM lost 58 missionaries and 21 children. The total number of Chinese Protestants killed may have approached two thousand.

✳ ✳ ✳ ✳ ✳

Some attempt was made at first to keep the full story of the Boxer massacres from a very weak Hudson Taylor, convalescing in Davos. But it was inevitable that he eventually learned the tragic news contained in a succession of telegrams from China. Still in the state of mental and physical exhaustion which had broken him down in America, he said, "I cannot read; I cannot think; I cannot even pray; but I can trust."

Jennie sent a letter to China in July, part of which read: "Day and night our thoughts are with you all. My dear husband says 'I would do all I could to help them: and our heavenly Father, who has the power, *will* do for each one according to His wisdom and love'." When some of the worst news arrived in the middle of August, Taylor was so weak that he could hardly cross the room unaided; his pulse rate fell to only forty per minute.

By October, however, he was well enough to study more

details of the events in China. Geraldine Taylor joined him one morning; outside snow had fallen on the mountains. Taylor had been reading about events in South Shanxi where Pastor Hsi had worked until his death in 1896. Tearfully, he told Geraldine of letters he had just read from Emily Whitchurch and Edith Searell, written the day before they were killed.

"Oh, think what it must have been," he said, "to exchange that murderous mob for the rapture of *His* presence, *His* bosom, *His* smile!"

He paused, trying to control his voice. "They do not regret it now," he continued. "'A crown that fadeth not away. They shall walk with me in white, for they are worthy'". His mind had gone to the Book of Revelation (3:4).

Taylor went on to speak of a group of CIM refugees who had managed to escape from the most dangerous areas and assemble in Shanghai; he said he wanted to travel out to join them.

"I might not be able to do much, but I feel they love me. If they could tell me their sorrows and I could only weep with them, it might be a comfort to some."

"There is no one in the world who could give such sympathy as you could, Father. But you cannot make the journey now."

William Cooper, Assistant Deputy Director, was one of those who fell victim to Boxer murderers. It was therefore some consolation to Taylor that the burden of directing the CIM on the spot, and of seeking to comfort the bereaved, need not be borne by Deputy Director John Stevenson alone. Dixon Hoste, one of the Cambridge Seven, had come east from Henan to Shanghai for the summer and was on hand to assist Stevenson at a time when the pressure might have been more than he could bear. Taylor had been convinced for some time that Hoste was the man God wanted to succeed him. So in August 1900, believing that his own death couldn't be far away, Taylor sent a telegram to Shanghai appointing Hoste Acting General Director of the mission.

✳ ✳ ✳ ✳ ✳

When it was all over, western countries agreed that the Chinese government should pay missionary societies and Chinese Christians a total of four hundred and fifty million taels (nearly seventy million pounds) in compensation. At first Hudson Taylor believed that it would be right to refuse compensation for loss of life, but to accept it for mission premises and property. Later after the London and China Councils discussed it, the CIM decided not to claim anything nor accept any compensation even if it was offered. They wanted to show the Chinese "the meekness and gentleness of Christ." This became the firm policy of the CIM, which had suffered more than any other society. Individuals, however, could accept compensation for personal losses if they wished. Some criticized the decision, but the British Foreign Office approved of it and the British Minister in Beijing sent a private gift of £100 to the CIM and expressed his admiration and sympathy.

Few other Protestant missionary societies followed the CIM's line; most came to favour reimbursement for destroyed property. Bishop Stephen Neill has commented, "later history suggests that the greater wisdom was that granted to Hudson Taylor". Neill also noted that the first instalment of compensation paid to the United States was returned to build up a fund for the education of Chinese, and that the payment of subsequent instalments was remitted.

✳ ✳ ✳ ✳ ✳

The heroism and steadfastness shown by both Roman Catholic and Protestant missionaries in China during the Boxer uprising can hardly be praised too highly. Not one missionary attempted to recant, or wavered in the face of death. And none of the letters written by CIM members at this time reveal any bitterness against the men of violence, or any thought of revenge.

The majority of Chinese converts also remained true to their faith when a simple act of compromise could have saved their lives. Some non-Christian Chinese officials also, at risk of imperial displeasure and sometimes at the cost of their lives, protected foreigners in their areas and helped others to escape.

"I have been writing to some relatives of those we have lost, " Taylor said towards the end of 1900, "to comfort them in their sorrow, and to my surprise they forgot their own bereavement in sympathizing with me." In fact three hundred members of the mission wrote to him from Shanghai expressing sympathy at the news of his illness. He replied in December 1900:

"As we have read over your signatures one by one we have thanked God for sparing you to us and to China. The sad circumstances through which we have all suffered have been permitted by God for His glory and our good, and when He has tried us and our native brethren He will doubtless reopen the work at present closed, under more favourable circumstances than before.

"We thank God for the grace given to those who have suffered. It is a wonderful honour He has put upon us as a mission to be trusted with so great a trial, and to have among us so many counted worthy of a martyr's crown. Some who have been spared have perhaps suffered more than some of those taken, and our Lord will not forget. How much it has meant to us to be so far from you in the hour of trial we cannot express, but the throne of grace has been as near to us here as it would have been in China ...

"When the resumption of our work in the interior becomes possible we may find circumstances changed, but the principles we have proved, being founded on His own unchanging Word, will be applicable as ever. May we all individually learn the lessons God would teach, and be prepared by His Spirit for any further service to which He may call us while waiting for the coming of our Lord."

THE ROAD TO HEAVEN 48

By the summer of 1901, Hudson Taylor had regained enough strength to make a trip west to the Chamonix Valley at the foot of Mont Blanc. Unfortunately, a slip on some pine-needles while walking in the woods brought on a recurrence of his old spinal trouble, and for several months he was once again confined to his room. He recovered sufficiently to return to England for a few months and enter into the life of the mission at Newington Green.

Shortly before his seventieth birthday, in May 1902, he returned to Switzerland where he and Jennie settled on the northern edge of Lake Geneva. In the little village of Chevalleyres, set amid meadows and orchards two miles north of Vevey, they rented a sitting room and bedroom with a balcony and veranda facing the rising sun. Their rent included meals served in their rooms. On their daily walks they quickly made a circle of friends, from the Count and Countess at the medieval chateau at nearby Blonay to the local small-holders and chalet dwellers. It wasn't long before Chevalleyres became what Hudson's son and daughter-in-law described as "a CIM centre up among the mountains".

Robert Wilder, the American student leader, came to stay for six months. "It was not so much what your father *said* but what he *was* that proved a blessing to me," he told Howard and Geraldine. "Your father bore about with him the fragrance of Jesus Christ. His strong faith, quietness, and constant industry even in his weakness touched me deeply ... To see a man who had been so active compelled to live a retired life, unable to pray more than fifteen minutes at a time, and yet remaining bright, even joyous, greatly impressed me. I remember his saying, 'If God can afford to lay me aside from active service, surely I should not object.' Not one single complaint or murmur did we ever hear from his lips. He was always cheerful — rejoicing in the flowers by day and studying the stars at night."

Hudson and Jennie, who had reluctantly spent long periods of their married life separately, relished these unbroken days when they could enjoy each other's company. "They were lovers still," recalled Howard and Geraldine of these days when the frail couple enjoyed rail and steamer excursions together, and slowly toiled arm in arm far up mountain paths to some favourite spot with a glorious view across the lake and the Alps. Taylor had time to take up again his hobby of photography, and spent long hours developing his photographs and studying flowers gathered with all the enthusiasm his father had encouraged 65 years earlier.

Since the breakdown of his health in America, he had been able to concentrate only on easy reading, correspondence and the book which had been his daily companion all his life. He read the Bible through for the fortieth time in forty years, enjoying new insights gleaned by comparing the renderings in French versions.

Though he had made Dixon Hoste Acting General Director of the mission, he retained the title of General Director and received regular reports from Hoste and Stevenson. But when Hoste arrived in Switzerland in November 1902, Taylor handed over to him the full Directorship of the mission, knowing that this appointment was approved of by the other directors and councils. "I am thankful that you have been led to select, perhaps, the most prayerful man among us," said Archibald Orr Ewing.

* * * * *

In July 1903, Taylor discovered that Jennie, now sixty, had an internal tumour. Her mother had died of cancer and, fearing the worst, Hudson sent off a telegram to his son. Howard and Geraldine travelled to Chevalleyres and called in an internationally famous cancer specialist who examined Jennie under chloroform.

"It's cancer," the eminent doctor told Howard. "But I'm afraid the disease is so far advanced that an operation wouldn't be useful."

Neither Hudson nor Jennie asked to hear the detailed results of the examination and presumably concluded that, as an operation wasn't necessary, the growth must be a simple tumour. As they didn't ask, neither was ever told the truth. But who can say what Hudson suspected?

The couple spent the winter in Lausanne within easy reach of a skilful doctor and the English church. With the coming of spring 1904, Jennie grew weaker and they returned to Chevalleyres where they rejoiced to hear news of increasing numbers of conversions in China. Jennie, now very thin, and a still weak Hudson were glad to sit quietly together on the veranda watching the birds in the cherry blossom above a carpet of narcissi and forget-me-nots.

Howard arrived in Chevalleyres in June, followed a few days later by Jennie's daughter Amy, now 28. After the end of June Jennie was too weak to dress, but with the French windows open on to the veranda she could enjoy both the view and fresh air.

"I couldn't be better cared for or happier," she told a friend. "I'm nearly home — what will it be to be there! The Lord is taking me slowly and gently."

And in a note to Geraldine, "You'll know the comfort

that dear Howard is, and Amy and dear father — all so loving and ready to spoil me in everything. So tenderly the Lord is dealing with us! There seems nothing to wish for, only to praise."

In the evening of July 29, Jennie found it difficult to breathe. Hudson was at her bedside.

"No pain, no pain," she kept saying.

Before the next day dawned, she whispered to Hudson, "Ask Him to take me quickly."

He hesitated, and then, "Dear Father, free her waiting spirit."

Five minutes later, the prayer was answered.

✳ ✳ ✳ ✳ ✳

They buried Jennie in the shadow of the church at La Chiesaz with its grey old tower clad in crimson creepers. From time to time Hudson, clutching flowers for Jennie's grave, would walk down past Blonay Castle to the church and sit beneath a cedar tree looking, sometimes through his tears, to the lake and the mountains.

In the weeks following Jennie's death, he took comfort from a French text hanging on the sitting-room wall:

Celui qui a fait les promesses est fidele

"Faithful is He who made the promises."

✳ ✳ ✳ ✳ ✳

As spring approached in 1905 Taylor felt fit enough to make another visit to China, his eleventh. Howard and Geraldine went with him, via America, and they landed in Shanghai on April 17. They spent Easter in Yangzhou, where Hudson and Maria had survived the great riot 37 years earlier.

At Zhenjiang, Taylor walked to the cemetery by the river where Maria and four of his children were buried.

He spoke to a group of young missionaries about to set off for inland stations: "It's a great privilege to meet you here. I have met many here in days gone by. My dear wife died by me here. In spirit our loved ones may be nearer to us than we think; and He is near, nearer than we think. The Lord Jesus will never leave nor forsake us. Count on Him; enjoy Him; abide in him. Do, dear friends, be true to Him and to His Word. He will never disappoint you."

At Hankou, on April 29, 1905, three remarkable China veterans met at the home of Dr Griffith John, the LMS missionary — and someone had the sense to take a photograph. All three sported fine beards and wore thick overcoats. Dr William Martin, 78, the American Presbyterian and Doctor of Divinity, sat on the left beside a potted palm; he had come out to China 55 years earlier. Dr Griffith John, 73, who also had experience of China going back half a century, stood in the middle while Taylor, the baby at only 72, sat in a basket chair on the right. Griffith John, with plenty of Welsh fervour, and Hudson Taylor sang hymns together.

Taylor then travelled with his son and daughter-in-law north into Henan by train, covering in a few hours a journey which had taken two weeks by wheelbarrow only eleven years before. The party visited seven CIM stations in Henan at one of which, on Taylor's 73rd birthday, the Chinese Christians presented him with a scarlet satin banner with the words *O man greatly beloved* inscribed on it. They returned to Hankou on May 26, the 39th anniversary of the sailing of the *Lammermuir*.

On Monday May 29, Taylor set off by steamer with Howard and Geraldine, Dr Whitfield Guinness and Miss af Sandeberg (whose family had entertained Taylor in Sweden) for Changsha, the capital of Hunan, which he had never before visited. Hunan had traditionally been China's most anti-foreign province, and only eight or nine years previously, there had not been a single Protestant missionary settled in the province. Now well over a hundred worked there from thirteen societies in partnership with Chinese Christians.

Steaming south-west across the Donting lakes and up the Xiang River, the party found themselves the only foreigners aboard a brand new boat. The weather was hot and they took full advantage of the fresh breezes on deck, none more so than Whitfield Guinness and Miss Sandeberg who announced their engagement a few days later.

At Changsha, Taylor climbed to the second floor of the pavilion on the highest point of the city wall, and enjoyed the view of Hunan's hills, the Xiang River valley and the city below. They visited the site which the governor of Changsha had offered to the CIM for a hospital.

On Saturday June 3, Changsha's missionaries from six societies attended a reception at the CIM mission house, so that they could meet the man whose society now numbered over eight hundred missionaries. The sitting room opened on to a lawn, surrounded by trees and flowers, where tea was served. Hudson Taylor appeared dressed in a suit of Shandong silk and mingled with his guests for over an hour. Dr Frank Keller noticed the expression of pure joy on Taylor's face.

When the last guest had left, Howard persuaded his father to go upstairs for a rest and Dr Barrie, one of the CIM missionaries living in the house, went with him. They talked for a while and then Taylor got up and fetched two fans, handing one to Barrie.

"Oh, why didn't you let me bring them?" asked Barrie.

"I wanted to get *you* one," Taylor replied.

Their conversation turned to the subject of prayer.

"It's a great privilege to bring *everything* to God in prayer," said Barrie. "But I sometimes hesitate and feel that some things are really too small to pray about."

"I don't know about that. There's nothing small, and there's nothing great: only God is great, and we should trust Him fully."

Later, while Taylor took supper in his room, Geraldine stood alone on the roof platform above the house watching the shimmering lights of the city now that darkness had fallen. Then she went down into her father-in-law's room.

Hudson Taylor was in bed beside a chair on which a lamp was burning. He was apparently reading a pile of letters. Geraldine adjusted his pillow and sat on a chair beside him. He said nothing, so she began to talk about the pictures in the *Missionary Review* magazine, which was open on the bed. Taylor suddenly turned his head and gasped. Seeing that he was unconscious, Geraldine ran to the door.

"Howard! Dr Keller! Do come quickly!"

Dr Keller arrived first — just in time to see Hudson Taylor slump on to his pillow. His breathing stopped; his expression changed; and China's friend looked, as it seemed to Geraldine, like a child quietly sleeping.

✵ ✵ ✵ ✵ ✵

A young Chinese evangelist and his eighteen-year-old bride had been reading Taylor's *Retrospect*, newly translated into Chinese, and decided they wanted to meet the author. At the CIM house in Changsha, they were told the sad news but allowed to join one of the small groups who gathered at the bedside.

"Do you think that I might touch his hand?" the evangelist asked.

He held Taylor's hand in his.

"Dear and venerable pastor," he said. "We truly love you. We have come today to see you. We longed to look into your face. We too are your little children. You opened for us the road to heaven. You loved and prayed for us long years. We came today to look upon your face. You look so happy, so peaceful! You are smiling. Your face is quiet and pleased. You cannot speak to us tonight. We do not want to bring you back: but we will follow you. We shall come to you. You will welcome us by and by."

They carried the coffin — the best the Chinese Christians who insisted on buying it could find — down to a ship moored at the Xiang River. The captain flew his flag at half-mast as they sailed north-east to join the mighty Yangzi.

At every river station flowers and wreaths were carried on board, so that when John Stevenson met the boat at Zhenjiang the coffin lay hidden beneath a mass of colour. Dixon Hoste conducted the funeral and committed the body to the ground beside Maria and four of their children.

In 1988, Dr Jim Taylor, Hudson's great grandson, discovered the monument stones preserved in the former British Consulate in Zhenjiang, now a museum. The inscription was intact: "Sacred to the memory of the Rev J Hudson Taylor, the revered founder of the China Inland Mission, born May 21, 1832, died June 3, 1905. A man in Christ."

EPILOGUE

James Hudson Taylor III
General Director, Overseas Missionary Fellowship

E ighty-five years have passed since Hudson Taylor died, deep in the heart of China. And 125 years since he founded the China Inland Mission. *J Hudson Taylor: A Man In Christ* is thus well timed to mark the anniversary. My great-grandfather passed on to the mission his passion for taking the good news of salvation through Christ Jesus to everyone in China. And his principles, unchanged, continue to characterize that mission: depend on God's faithfulness; identify with the people you go to — those whom no one else is reaching with the gospel; teach the believers and train their leaders.

After his death, "China's spiritual need and claims" continued to challenge deeply dedicated young people from the West. They knew the cost of loving Jesus. Borden of Yale responded to the call of Muslim work in northwest China, but died in Egypt on the way. At about the same time J O Fraser[1], musician and engineer, was prayerfully laying the foundation for phenomenal church growth among the Lisu tribesmen on the southwestern borders of China. The young couple John and Betty Stam fell as martyrs at the start of Mao's Long March, in 1934 — a grim prelude to the testing by fire that the whole church in China would itself experience during the collectivization of agriculture, the Great Leap Forward and Cultural Revolution (1956–76).

The Chinese church itself experienced amazing growth and exciting new developments. From 100,000 in 1900 its membership rose to seven times as many (over 700,000) in 1950. Strong Chinese leaders such as John Sung, Wang Mingdao, David Yang, Watchman Nee and Andrew Gih emerged. Work was launched among students, and indigenous mission movements sprang up. The Japanese invasion of China and World War II uprooted many missionaries, and the CIM headquarters had to move temporarily

[1]See his biography *Mountain Rain* (OMF Books)

from Shanghai to Chongqing, far up the Yangzi River. The entire Chefoo school was marched off to concentration camp. Our teachers led us as we sang:

God is our refuge and strength,
A very present help in trouble.
Therefore will not we fear .....
The Lord of hosts is with us,
The God of Jacob is our refuge. (Psalm 46:1,7)

Separated from parents for more than five years, we learned that God can be trusted.

But the greatest testing was yet to come. In the late forties the Communist armies swept triumphantly southward. As Phyllis Thompson has so poignantly described in her book *China: The Reluctant Exodus*, between 1949 and 1952 every member of the mission was forced to leave China. Cast upon God for guidance as Hudson Taylor had been on Brighton Beach 86 years earlier, leaders of the China Inland Mission met in Bournemouth, England. Once again in obedience and faith a momentous decision was made.

All available missionaries were redeployed and new workers recruited as the mission pressed forward into the rest of East Asia. From its new headquarters in Singapore, the goals became Japan, Taiwan, Hong Kong, the Philippines, Thailand, Malaysia, Singapore, and Indonesia. Later Vietnam, Laos, Cambodia, and Korea were added. For some countries the time was short, the harvest urgent.

With the door to China firmly closed, and many of these countries regarding anything labelled "China" with grave suspicion, the time-honoured name China Inland Mission gave place to Overseas Missionary Fellowship (OMF).

The new vision was for the speediest possible evangelization of East Asia's millions — a church in every community and thereby the gospel to every creature. Where the church already existed, the mission found openings for partnership. In other countries the task was pioneer evangelism and church planting.

The approach was two-pronged. Asia's burgeoning cities with their concentration of civil servants, students, and blue collar workers were of strategic importance; at the same time neglected areas and hidden tribal groups, the unreached "inlands" of East Asia, needed to be occupied. Languages were reduced to writing, and the Bible translated. In each field basic theological education and the publication and distribution of Christian literature were given high priority. The mission made its major medical thrust in rural Thailand, with three hospitals and a leprosy control programme. Here, too, it later became deeply involved in working among refugees. Community development programmes were launched in the Philippines, alcoholic rehabilitation in Japan, and work among prostitutes in Taipei and Bangkok.

In 1965, OMF celebrated its centennial and prepared for a new century. The Fellowship recognized with joy that a mature church was emerging in many countries of East Asia. It longed to become a new instrument for mission in true partnership with the churches. Councils were formed in several East Asian countries where the vision of sending their own missionaries to other lands was bright and growing. Today there are eight such national Home Councils. A beautiful fraternal link was also forged with the Indian Evangelical Mission which has sent several missionaries to serve with OMF in Thailand.

The Overseas Missionary Fellowship is steadily evolving into a fellowship of Christians from East and West serving shoulder to shoulder in response to God's sovereign call. This biblical partnership is still at an early stage, but the possibilities under God are also limitless.

Hudson Taylor's passion was to share Christ with China, and for 85 years the CIM pursued that vision with singleness of purpose. When the Lord of the harvest saw fit to uproot the mission in the early 1950s, the vision expanded to embrace all of East Asia. Now as AD 2000 approaches He is calling OMF to broaden its horizons yet again, to take the Good News to East Asians wherever they may be. Many thousands far from home are accessible, who may return as Christians to their homelands. While more and more countries are restricting missionaries' freedom of entry, "professional" skills are still welcomed. This too calls for a creative response.

Meanwhile OMF is still deeply committed to the Chinese people. We can never forget that we came into existence as the China Inland Mission. Ever since our "reluctant exodus" we have called the church worldwide to prayer for our brothers and sisters in China, and to share in proclaiming the gospel and nurturing millions of new believers through radio broadcasts and the provision of Bibles and Christian literature. God is at work in China today in a remarkable way.[2] The Fellowship has no desire to re-establish itself there in the form it used to have. But we long to learn from our brothers and sisters in China, to serve the Chinese church, and to cooperate with them in Christ's matchless service in any way they may wish. Hundreds of millions in China, including many minority people groups, are still without Christ.

Eighty-five more years of experiencing God's faithfulness have been added to Hudson Taylor's remarkable testimony. Through revolution, world war, and times as turbulent as any he faced, the mission has continued to be sustained by God's presence and to continually experience His power, provision and protection. God does not change.

The lessons in discipleship highlighted in *J Hudson Taylor: A Man In Christ* are not limited to a man or the organization he founded. They are abiding principles that can be learned and lived by any Christian, whether student or home-maker, employer or employee. The key is to act on them.

September 1989
Singapore

---

[2]See *God Reigns in China* by Leslie Lyall, and *China — The Church's Long March* by David Adeney.

ACKNOWLEDGEMENTS

I want to thank Dr Jim Broomhall for giving time to talk to me about Hudson Taylor and answering many queries by letter and telephone; he also kindly made available to me the typescript of Books Six and Seven of his *Hudson Taylor and China's Open Century* prior to their publication. Dr Broomhall went through my completed draft of this book correcting mistakes and suggesting improvements. Readers who want to follow up aspects of the Hudson Taylor story will almost certainly find them dealt with in Jim's irreplaceable series.

I am grateful to Sheila Groves for working through large sections of my draft and I am sure greatly improving the final result — though the shortcomings which remain are of course my responsibility.

OMF staff in Sevenoaks quickly and efficiently answered my requests for items of source material; Edyth Banks and the team at OMF Books in Singapore have been of immense help editorially; Billy Graham kindly took time out of his incredibly busy life to read my manuscript and write the Foreword; Edward England sustained me throughout with his characteristic words of encouragement; and my own family — Sheila, Timothy and Joseph — preserved my sanity. My thanks to you all.

I trust that the book which has emerged will make some contribution to our understanding of the man who thought of himself as the little servant of a great Master.

Roger Steer

PRINCIPAL SOURCES USED

Anderson J N D (ed), *The World's Religions* Inter-Varsity Fellowship 1950
Baedeker K, *Switzerland* Baedeker 1907
Broomhall A J, *Hudson Taylor and China's Open Century* Hodder & Stoughton
    and the Overseas Missionary Fellowship Books 1 to 7 1981–1990
    (parts of final book consulted in typescript)
Broomhall M, *Hudson Taylor: The Man who believed God* CIM 1929
Broomhall M (ed), *Hudson Taylor's Legacy: Daily Readings* CIM 1931
Cambridge History of China Volume 10 Cambridge University Press 1979
Latourette K S, *A History of Christian Missions in China* SPCK 1929
Latourette K S, *A History of the Expansion of Christianity* Volumes 1 and 6,
    Eyre & Spottiswood 1938
Latourette K S, *The Chinese: Their History and Culture* Macmillan 1942
Lyall L T, *God reigns in China* Hodder and Stoughton and the Overseas Missionary
    Fellowship 1985
Lyall L T, *New Spring in China?* Hodder and Stoughton and the Overseas Missionary
    Fellowship 1979
    Occasional Papers of the China Inland Mission Volumes I to VI, CIM 1872
Neill S, *A History of Christian Missions* Penguin Books 1964
Palmer A W, *A Dictionary of Modern History 1789–1945* Penguin Books 1962
Parker E H, *China and Religion* Murray 1905
Pollock J C, *Hudson Taylor and Maria* Hodder and Stoughton 1966 edn
Steer R J, *George Muller: Delighted in God* Hodder and Stoughton 1975
Stock E, *The History of the Church Missionary Society* Volumes I to III 1899–1916
Taylor Dr and Mrs Howard, *"By Faith"* Henry W Frost and the China Inland
    Mission CIM 1938
Taylor Dr and Mrs Howard, *Hudson Taylor in Early Years: The Growth of a Soul* CIM
    and RTS 1911
Taylor Dr and Mrs Howard, *Hudson Taylor and the China Inland Mission:*
    The Growth of a Work of God CIM and RTS 1918
Taylor J Hudson, *After Thirty Years, Three Decades of the China Inland Mission* CIM 1895
Taylor J Hudson, *China's Spiritual Need and Claims* Morgan & Scott 1887
Taylor J Hudson, *Retrospect* Overseas Missionary Fellowship 1974 edn.